Steven Bilakovics

# Democracy without Politics

**HARVARD UNIVERSITY PRESS**

Cambridge, Massachusetts, and London, England   2012

*Library of Congress Cataloging-in-Publication Data*

Bilakovics, Steven, 1974–
  Democracy without politics / Steven Bilakovics.
    p. cm.
  Includes bibliographical references and index.
  ISBN 978-0-674-05822-4 (alk. paper)
1. Democracy—Philosophy—History. 2. Democracy—History. I. Title.
JC421.B52 2012
321.8—dc23    2011026679

*For Timery and Jason*

# Contents

*That which we can find words for is something already*
*dead in our hearts; there is always a kind of contempt in*
*the act of speaking.*
  —Nietzsche, *Twilight of the Idols*


*To understand the specificity of the present situation, one*
*ought to reconstitute its genesis, so that we understand*
*that our democracy seeks to institute a political and thus*
*human order that is free of all "incorporation" . . . , a*
*political and human order that is purely "spiritual." This*
*idea conflicts with appearances: doesn't our society give a*
*large place to the body and hardly any place to the soul?*
*In reality, our society is the one in Western history that*
*most systematically reduces the role of the body.*
  —Pierre Manent, *A World beyond Politics?*


*It could be said that people are losing the "will" to act*
*socially, or that they are losing the "desire." These words*
*as pure psychological states mislead because they do not*
*explain how a whole society could lose its will together, or*
*change its desires. They further mislead in suggesting a*
*therapeutic solution, to shake people out of this self-*
*absorption—as if the environment which has eroded their*
*social will and transformed their desire might suddenly*
*welcome changed individuals with open arms.*
  —Richard Sennett, *The Fall of Public Man*

# Introduction

## *Democracy as Self-Subverting*

> Every government harbors within itself a natural flaw that
> seems inextricably intertwined with the very principle of its
> existence
>
> —Tocqueville, *Democracy in America*

### *Playing Politics*

"Politics" has probably always been something of a dirty word. In America today it seems exclusively and irretrievably so. Polling data over the past half century has made clear the American people's increasing "dissatisfaction" with their politics and "distrust" of their government. Perhaps the most striking trend in more than three decades of the General Social Survey, for example, is the deterioration of "confidence" in political institutions and processes (even as opinions on a wide array of other issues have remained remarkably static).[1] When one considers this trend in conjunction with the long-term decline in political participation, from voting rates on out, a general contempt of contemporary politics is hard to deny; as the belief that America is "on the wrong track" grows more pronounced, the available practices of politics are rejected as a means to make things better. Indeed, beyond a failure to provide solutions, the condition of our politics is cited as a large part of the problem—as the very evidence that America is on the wrong track.[2]

More revealing even than the statistical representation of Americans' low opinion of politics is the rhetorical culture within which today's politics takes shape. Listening to the language that citizens, politicians, and journalists use to persuade one another, we begin to understand the particular mode of Americans' contempt of politics; beyond the fact that Americans hate politics, an analysis of our political rhetoric helps us

1

diagnose precisely how and why Americans hate politics. Consider what the following phrases—and their pervasiveness—tell us about the specific character of Americans' attitudes and beliefs regarding politics. We hear political debate shot through with the bad-faith accusation of "playing politics."[3] Elections, those most pivotal of liberal democratic moments, now comprise the "silly season," during which people say the most preposterous things to gain the least competitive advantage.[4] And outside the electoral moment, "politics as usual" is cast as inane, at once a childish game divorced from reality and a fraud wherein opportunistic maneuvers are (barely) disguised as reasoned arguments.[5] The alternative intentions of "playing politics"—of speaking in a political context—can only be to manipulate or to pander. Similarly, it seems unimaginable not only that political partisanship and disagreement can be anything but "petty" and "bickering" but also that political moderation and compromise represent anything but an unprincipled lack of "core conviction."[6] The alternatives are the calculated obstructionism of "playing the blame game" and the calculated expediency of "flip-flopping."[7] And even as the majority of Americans apparently consider it self-evident that their elected representatives are in the pockets of "special interests," the chronic complaint is that these degenerate characters "don't get anything done." The alternatives are corruption and gridlock.[8] Surveying this no-way-out rhetorical landscape, we might well conclude that politics, far from a means of addressing collective problems and purposes or a mode of exercising our freedom, has become something of a stage for us at our worst. Today, "political" and "cynical" seem to be synonymous.

Articulated in such language, contemporary political disenchantment apparently follows from something other than rational apathy and goes beyond the sense that political actors and institutions are usually corrupt. Rather, the practice of politics seems to be perceived as *absurd*—as a sphere of human activity devoid of meaning and so undeserving of respect. "Politics" is a game, both constituted and removed from reality by its idiosyncratic set of rules. It can be played more or less fairly, to be sure, and it can be more or less dramatic and entertaining, but ultimately politics is something that is played. And like any game, it seems bizarre, pointless, and sort of silly to the outside observer, even (or especially) when played for the highest of stakes.

The conceptual metaphor of politics-as-game frames a strikingly consistent rhetorical strategy of persuasion, evident in the examples above.[9] One begins by invoking crisis or warlike conditions or by asserting some truth obvious to plain common sense or by asserting the obviousness of crisis. In any case, it's made clear that we need not meetings and talk and disputation but decisive and immediate action (the telling assumptions being that speech and action are incompatible species and that to "get something done" we must set aside or rise above words: "Stop Talking; Start Doing," as one recent advertising campaign puts it; "Rhetoric or Real?" as a common CNN sidebar asks).[10] In this sense, persuasion within the rhetorical culture of "playing politics" takes effect as an attack upon rhetoric—in a sort of performative contradiction, words are used to reject the need or efficacy of words.[11] Moreover, insofar as the politics of democracy is premised upon the possibility of replacing force with persuasion—insofar as argument serves as the very medium of democratic politics—the rhetoric of "playing politics" takes effect as an antipolitical rhetoric. To be sure, politics may proceed in economic terms, in which language is used to signal self-interest and argument is reduced to bargaining. But how absurd will this type of politics appear in times of pervasive and persistent crisis? When persuasion by means of giving reasons for one's political position is taken as either a "fiddling" waste of time in the face of emergency (when persuasion must give way to the force of necessity) or as just the public mask of private self-interest (when service to the public good is a dire necessity), we are left with a politics of negotiation in times of necessity—drastic times met by trifling and petty measures. Reduced to this, the democratic mode of politics cannot but seem out of place, incongruous with experience and detached from pressing reality.[12]

Today's political alienation is thus much more intractable than if apathy or corruption were solely at its root. An apathetic people can always be "awakened," and a corrupt system can always be reformed (especially, it is often presumed, in times of crisis). But what is to be done when democratic politics is experienced as nonsense—as quite literally a theater of the absurd, the play where nothing happens? What is to be done when the practice of politics becomes transparently vacuous and farcical—reduced to deploying trite slogans and repetitive gibberish ("talking points") to move demographic pieces into position at key places on the board ("battleground states") so as to put a mark in the win column for the red or the blue team, with the consequence of nothing much changing? What is to be done when what was once considered the most human of activities becomes a "horse race"? Our options, it seems, are to step back and lampoon this political burlesque, with its ludicrous caricatures and clichés, or to suspend thought and reflection and throw ourselves in as fan(atic)s.

How have we ended up with such a dead-end political vocabulary? How can we work our way out when words spoken in the context of politics are just assumed to be "spin"—when language is assumed to conceal rather than convey meaning? How can we reform our politics when such uncritical cynicism undermines reflection, argument, and action? What is to be done when, as one recent account puts it, the world of politics appears an "unfit place for human habitation"?[13] One conclusion seems warranted already: political reformation (assuming these terms are not mutually exclusive) must come from outside democratic politics.[14]

*Why Is Democratic Politics So Unpopular?*
*Market Structures and Liberal Systems*

Given the long-term nature of the phenomenon, Americans' growing distaste for politics cannot be explained exclusively in terms of recent events (Vietnam, Watergate), prevailing conditions associated with the perceived performance of government (booming or busting economy, crime rates), or contemporary transformations (the post–cold war phase of globalization, the rise of the news media of consolidated ownership and multiplied venues).[15] As important as these factors surely are in altering the style and substance of—along with even our perceptual modes of access to—today's political campaigns, for instance, our analysis of political disaffection, to be of sufficient scope, must consider more sustained conditions, relatively long-standing aspects of the American political system and American society, and even broader trends of which America is a part.

Theorizations of this sort typically revolve around the characterization of ours as a liberal democratic political system embedded in a "market society." The reasoning here generally follows one of two paths. First, in our modern, middle-class, commercial republic, people are otherwise occupied by matters both noble and base and so are "rationally ignorant" of and uninterested in a complex political process that daily effects them little; the consumer-citizen chooses to spend finite resources elsewhere.[16] In turn, the ordinary running of government is intentionally (and perhaps fortunately) entrusted to institutional mechanisms, elected representatives, and technocratic "experts." Second, consumed by the need to make a living and with their political power institutionally channeled into the merely symbolic act of voting in occasional elections, citizens are reduced to spectators of a distant and byzantine political system dominated by organized "special interests" and oligarchic "elites." Moreover, in our age of globalizing corporate capitalism, politics becomes just economics by other means; money is power, and in our pay-to-play political system, the people's putative authority amounts to sound without fury. "Democracy" has been co-opted and reduced to an empty rhetoric, used by those in power to keep those out of power docile. In the first line of reasoning described here, the reigning popular sovereign happily abdicates direct rule, if not ultimate authority; in the second, a citizenry longing for more significant political power is institutionally and materially locked out of political space.[17]

Neither of these familiar views is wholly convincing, though. The first (wherein the liberal democratic political system makes possible the semipublic governance of an apolitical populace) predicts political apathy but not the contempt so widely and vocally expressed today. While surely rationally disengaged from politics, the majority describes itself less as apolitical than as antipolitical. How can we account for the widespread lack of respect for all things political that accompanies our lack of interest?

The second view (wherein the liberal democratic political system obstructs more direct and robust democratic participation) makes perfect sense of this contempt. But it apparently misrepresents the expressed desires of the majority of Americans. Recent research calls into question the extent to which people want or would affirm their own increased participation in democratic politics. Combining national survey data with an analysis of what people (reconstructed into "focus groups") actually said, the important work of John Hibbing and Elizabeth Theiss-Morse finds, "The last thing people want is to be more involved in political decision making: They do not want to make political decisions themselves; they do not want to provide much input to those who are assigned to make these decisions; and they would rather not know all the details of the decision-making process."[18] Why is this? Hibbing and Theiss-Morse argue that our aversion to taking part in the politics of democracy is not primarily a response to the particular defects, inequities, or ugliness of our political system. It is not, for example, the perception that politics is dominated by special interests and self-serving politicians that sours us on the whole endeavor. Indeed, they find that citizens are motivated to participate in politics to the extent that they are largely by fear of "being played for a sucker" by those in power.[19] Along deeply Tocquevillian lines, as we shall see, people appear willing, even eager, to embrace political powerlessness, but resent any abuse (or perhaps even sign) of privilege—in this case, those in power taking advantage of their privileged position to take advantage of us.[20] And it is this prospect that compels citizens to intervene in the political process.

Even as people assume selfishness in their elected officials and corruption in their governing institutions, though, they apparently don't want to "return power to the people." The people are not exactly populists; they seek "to weaken the power of institutions but not strengthen the power of ordinary people."[21] The authors identify three primary reasons why people turn down political power. First, people say they have neither the time nor the interest and don't want the burdens of responsibility. Second, in their political roles and capacities, people apparently have no more faith in each other, or even in themselves, than in their elected representatives. We don't trust politicians, but neither do we trust ourselves as citizens. Hibbing and Theiss-Morse write, "People overwhelmingly admit that they and the American people generally are largely uninformed about political matters. They also have reservations about the trustworthiness of the American people, with half of the people not trusting their fellow citizens."[22] Finally, people demonstrate an abiding aversion to the very stuff of democratic politics—to addressing common issues, goals, and conflicts by means of arguing together. Two primary explanations are offered. First, the majority believes that Americans are basically unified rather than factious, thinking that "Americans generally agree on overall societal goals" and that "the common good is not debatable."[23] The common good is a matter of common sense, and so disagreement does not seem reasonable. Conflict becomes a sign that there is something very wrong with us and our government; insofar as politics is a stage for conflict, it displays us at our worst. Second, and similarly, people think that arguing both should be unnecessary and actually is inefficacious. The majority considers arguing to be "a complete waste of time" and just "bickering" and "pointless conflict."[24] Perhaps not surprisingly, the public overwhelmingly supported (by 86 percent) the proposition "Elected officials should stop talking and take action."[25] As useless as it is ugly, the politics of argument is as such rejected; the good citizen of democracy participates, we might say, as conscientious objector.

Weighing against the notion that political cynicism is rooted in the American people's experience of being institutionally and materially locked out of a distant political system, Hibbing and Theiss-Morse conclude, "People do not like politics even in the best circumstances; in other words, they simply do not like the process of openly arriving at a decision in the face of diverse opinions. They do not like politics when they view it from afar and they certainly do not like politics when they participate in it themselves." Simply, Americans "yearn for 'the end of politics.' " This leads people, the authors write, to a dilemma: "People want to turn political matters over to somebody else because they do not want to be involved themselves, but they do not want to turn decision making over to someone who is likely to act in a selfish, rather than other-regarding, manner." The perceived way out of this dilemma is to place power in the hands of virtue. Today, the relevant virtues are formulated as empathetic selflessness and problem-solving competence. Above the world of self-interested partisanship, people seek in a representative not so much an official responsive to their policy preferences as a part Burkean disinterested trustee of the common good and part Clintonian feeler of their pain. At the same time, given the desire for quiet decisiveness in decision making, people tend to favor government (administration) by "business leaders" and "nonelected, independent experts"—politics reduced to a business or a science, wherein things get done efficiently and progress toward shared goals is measurable.[26]

Hibbing and Theiss-Morse dub this the politics of "stealth democracy"—"government by autopilot" that renders the processes of politics at once trustworthy and unseen (like a stealth bomber, power operating from on high).[27] In the people's ideal form of democratic politics, decisions are made "efficiently, objectively, and without commotion or disagreement" while decision makers display the personable selflessness of empathy and/or the impersonal selflessness of impartiality.[28] To introduce an idea we shall return to in considering Claude Lefort's theory of democracy, what we want on this account is the providential power of nobody—power that is effective but evidently unheld. A human agent might be thought to approximate this combination of efficacy and selflessness: the Cincinnatus figure who rises above the paradox of republican politics, wherein the pursuit of power demonstrates an absence of the very virtues that qualify one to hold power. An institutional agency might be thought to approximate this combination: the military, today's last bastion of power in the hands of (martial) virtue; the Supreme Court, with its impersonal body of impartial experts (as opposed to the "activist judges" of a "politicized" Court). Perhaps this helps explain why the military receives a great and growing vote of confidence from the American people even as confidence in most every other institution crumbles and why the least democratic branch of the American government is by far the most popular.[29] And the very realization of this combination would be the seating of power in some perfectly virtuous (empathetic and impartial, efficient and effective) superhuman agency.

Expressing an almost equally low regard for direct democratic participation and popular power as for liberal democratic institutions and procedures, Americans' aversion to politics runs deep, below the liberal political system, to the practice of democratic politics as such.[30] This picture is complicated, of course, by the possibility that we have been in some way programmed or seduced into such beliefs and so into political powerlessness. To simplify for the time being, the common course of this argument holds that we have been led or manipulated or subconsciously reconstructed to imagine human association as at bottom a market and human beings as at bottom bourgeois. In turn, we buy into "purchasing power" and the need satisfaction of "consumerism" as the essence of freedom, reject equality as incompatible with individual opportunity and collective prosperity, embrace governance according to hierarchical business models and "market forces" as necessary and proper in a world of competition and complexity, accept decision making as the work of a technocracy, and so on. Today, the argument extends, the market order is taken as no less than natural: given, spontaneous, inescapable, even coded into our biology. Moreover, market orders are taken as Natural: endowed as our faith with a sort of religious moral significance.[31] Consequently, politics (along with everything else) is perceived as an essentially economic activity, preconceived in terms of competitive self-interest and judged by the logic of efficiency. On both counts, a robustly democratic politics is reflexively dismissed by the people themselves as unrealistic. Citizens believe themselves lacking not only the time and expertise but also the requisite public-spiritedness to manage democratic politics. Prejudiced against our own political possibilities and capacities, we come to hold that in the modern world we simply cannot afford the luxury of democracy.[32]

There is much to recommend this interpretation. That "education policy" is most always and without dissent framed by the necessity of "not falling behind in global competition" stands as only one (if perhaps the most dispiriting) example of our tendency to appraise the human world in economic terms.[33] Yet, the notion of market society as Platonic cave is not wholly convincing. The very fact that "market society," "consumer culture," and so on are invoked almost exclusively to condemn them, never to affirm them as legitimate or aspirational, undermines the analysis of capitalism as effectively "totalizing."[34] Far from being indoctrinated into an unquestioned capitalist consciousness, people constantly question and regret the costs of capitalism. Every word of praise for the efficiency, prosperity, and freedom following from the unplanned and unregulated open market is accompanied by scorn for "a culture of fast-food homogenization," hierarchical corporatism ("Big Oil," "Big Tobacco"), the Almighty Dollar, "affluenza," self-indulgent luxury, conspicuous consumption, the rich getting richer, ubiquitous advertising, selling out, Hollywood vanity, inauthenticity, shallowness, and greed.[35] If Americans are materialistic consumers, it would seem that they are self-loathing materialistic consumers. Indeed, American culture seems largely composed of the criticism of what that culture is perceived to be.

The widespread view that we exist blindly invested in the one-dimensional shadows of consumer culture undermines itself: were we fully socialized into the cave, we would not know it, much less be prone to decry it. More than any reality the concept represents, I shall suggest, "market society" captures our imagination to such an extent today for two main reasons. First, various ingredients of open-market economics are easily translated into goods that we do passionately affirm. Second, as a reductive exaggeration of elements of society that are prevalent, the notion of a "consumer society" preys upon our insecurities as precisely the type of corruption of human association we fear possible, likely, even inevitable. Indeed, the fear of a creeping, tempting, infecting, colonizing bourgeois ethos is constitutive of our social form; it is how we imagine dehumanization.

A robust interpretation of American society would thus recognize, for instance, that we *transform* consumerism by representing it in terms of self-expressive freedom and personal empowerment even as we dread the descent of modern life into a homogenized and stultifying consumer culture, devoid of anything lofty and challenging, populated by herds of last men or cheerful robots. Similarly, we *elevate* greed by making the effort to philosophize it as good (the spur to individual striving, and so to collective prosperity and human progress) even as we anxiously await the dissolution of society into a base and degrading greediness. We love opportunity and hate opportunism. Any plausible interpretation of our social form must account for this dualism and so must look toward the multidimensionality of the wider frame of reference by which we judge the market elements of our society.[36]

### The Antipolitics of Democratic Openness: Cynicism and Idealism

In response to the shortcomings of the views outlined above, my argument proceeds in two parts. First, insofar as one can make general claims about a "society," "culture," "zeitgeist," or "age," ours is rendered more fully intelligible as a democratic society rather than as a market society. Second, a society so constituted fosters the particular manner of contempt for politics so widespread today, the reflexive cynicism that we might juxtapose to reflective skepticism and a vigilant distrust of those in power.[37] Building upon the works of Alexis de Tocqueville, I argue that the democratic "social state" tends to be taken by its inhabitants as natural and even as a quasi-sanctified, providential order of human association—and that both the liberal democratic form of government and the direct democratic practice of politics are devalued within democratic society. There is an *antipolitical prejudice* inscribed in the democratic way of imagining, understanding, and evaluating the world.

My analysis of the sources and modes of contemporary political cynicism focuses on what we might call "democratic openness."[38] Modern democratic society, I shall argue, is in large part principled upon openness—that is, upon the type of freedom that comes to the fore in the context of democratic equality. This is the freedom that takes center stage with the democratic revolution's destruction of hierarchy as the ordering principle of nature, society, and self. It is the freedom of open-ended, revolutionary possibility—of what Tocqueville captures in the paradox of "indefinite perfectibility."

As I elaborate below, by its very nature the principle of openness is as expansive in its legitimacy as it is impossible to put into form and practice. More accurately, the authority of openness as our standard of judgment of goodness, truth, and beauty is premised precisely upon its being irreducible to particularity—to its being made manifest in the here and now of the conventional world. The result is a regime that takes shape via schism between the world we imagine possible, even inevitable, and the world we experience as real, even inescapable. Framed by the freedom of openness, by the impossible promise of possibility without limits, democratic society harbors a tendency toward idealism as extreme as its concomitant tendency toward cynicism.

How does this democratic *duality* of idealism and cynicism manifest itself? Most obviously, in times of openness all barriers to progress—to the opening of society and self—are taken as contingent and arbitrary. As such, their persistence is experienced as equal parts inexplicable, inescapable, and intolerable. For instance, we demand of ourselves the beautiful impossibility of judging others solely upon their abstract moral and spiritual qualities rather than upon physical appearance or social status, and we assess our lingering closed-mindedness severely, as indicative of something deeply wrong with the present—a sad sign of "just the way the world works."[39] As Tocqueville explains, progress toward an ideal might well be experienced as regression when met by the promise of open-ended perfectibility, and unchecked revolutionary ambition might easily turn into unchecked resignation to reality's intransigence. A second manifestation of the cynicism/idealism duality follows in that the very condition that enables us to envision indefinite perfectibility also enables us to foresee indefinite imperfectibility. There are two directions to the boundless potentiality of an open world. For instance, the impending transcendence of fettering materiality and the impending decadence of unfettered materialism—autonomy and licentiousness—seem equally possible. Finally, and perhaps most significantly, this duality manifests itself in that any attempt to represent, establish, or institute the essentially indefinite principle of openness can only be met with a sort of buyer's remorse of spent potential, defining and thereby diminishing the authority of openness. The spirit of democracy, as has often been observed, is in the dreaming, as something neither actual nor necessarily apart but rather "always to come." Idealization in times of openness lies not in achieved perfection but in the concept of perfectibility rendered indefinite, not in end or form realized but in open-endedness and transformation as such—in revolution's promise of an always *imminent transcendence*. Just as the purity of religious faith is thought preserved by its transcending conventionality, temporality, materiality, particularity, and the partisan striving for power (whether of church or state), democracy's principle maintains its universal authority by remaining uninvolved with the ways and means of worldly orders and powers. At the same time, democratic faith does not differentiate between this world and the next. Democracy's aspirational norm of openness cannot be represented in conventional form—including those of democracy itself—but nor can it be deferred as a world apart from the here and now. Present as unrealizable possibility, democracy's aspiration remains as sublime as its ordinary practices appear absurd. Relative to the sublime freedom of openness, the experience of freedom that follows from the political practice of democracy—the "political freedom" Tocqueville cherishes perhaps above all—seems mundane and even oxymoronic.

Recognizing this unmediable conjunction of norm and form, and in turn the co-operation of idealism and cynicism, we can account for a second mode of antipolitical rhetoric inscribed in democratic society. The first mode degrades politics to the status of an absurd game and to petty economics. This is the rhetoric of "playing politics" described above. The second mode elevates politics to the status of revolutionary transcendence, whether toward the past or the future, or both. This is the rhetoric of "It's morning again in America" and "We have the power to begin the world over again."[40] In his "Reclaiming the American Dream" election-night acceptance speech, Barack Obama offers an exemplary iteration: "If there is anyone out there who still doubts America is a place where *all things are possible,* who still wonders if the *dream of our founders* is alive in our time, who still questions the power of our democracy—tonight is your answer."[41] Framed by the characteristic idealism of democratic openness—of limitless possibility and the dream of renewal—we are likely at once uplifted, tempted to dismiss such rhetoric (and perhaps rhetoric as such) as just so much fanciful talk, and moved to view the conventional practice of politics as by comparison just so much meaningless power playing.

Many have recognized, of course, that there is a great gulf between the respect granted our democratic ideals and that which is denied our democratic institutions, and that the promissory language of democracy so far outstrips its actual practices that we may well grow disillusioned and reject democracy altogether. As I have begun to detail, my work aims at diagnosing why and how this situation takes shape. What is it about democracy as a principle of human organization that has enabled it to achieve the status of unquestioned ideal? How is this status maintained despite the fact that democracy's promises are unkept—indeed, palpably unkeepable? Why do we not lose faith when our faith is not rewarded? Or better, why does our faith seem to deepen right along with our disappointment?[42] I argue that the democratic principle has achieved its status not despite but because it is utterly unrealistic and yet seems an utterly natural—free, informal, authentic—basis of human organization, requiring for its realization only the revolutionary dissolution of present reality's obstructing artificiality. In turn, the democratic ideal manifests not in opposition to cynicism but precisely as the cynical contempt of the conventional world. Our growing cynicism is not evidence of ideals unmet but of our ideals in effect. Contempt of the here and now is rendered intelligible not as disappointment but as the affirmation of our faith in democracy.[43]

I suggest, then, that today's often-remarked-upon simultaneous triumph of democratic principles and absence of democratic political practices is no coincidence. A recent UNESCO report, for example, strikingly declares that "basic democratic principles" constitute no less than "a fundamental source of common values that can be described as the common heritage of humankind."[44] Even with such universality accorded democracy, with its status as a sort of moral Esperanto that even its enemies must invoke, not only is popular disdain for political representatives and institutions increasing, but also basic participation in questioning and deciding things in common seems almost nowhere to be found. Everywhere preached but nowhere practiced, democracy is apparently experiencing the best of times and the worst of times. I argue that these two phenomena are intrinsically intertwined. Democracy is not in crisis despite the fact that democratic principles are hegemonic but precisely because democratic principles are hegemonic. By virtue of openness, the democratic principle enjoys a historically unprecedented monopoly of legitimacy even while fostering widespread cynicism regarding the conventional practices of democracy. This schism of principle and practice is constitutive of the modern democratic regime. There is, in turn, a Pyrrhic quality to what Tocqueville terms the "rising empire" of democracy.[45]

*The Market Element of Democratic Society*

To explicate the notion of "democratic society" put forward in the first line of my thesis, I argue (incorporating the terminology, if not the sense of rupture, of Bruce Ackerman's schema of American political development) that we live in a democratic third republic, analogous to the laissez-faire second republic. Where market competition was once massively affirmed as both a fact of the world in which we live and the principle of a free and rightly ordered society, democratic openness stands today as a similarly unquestionable fact/value. Openness is taken as natural (as we experience it in time, the world is intrinsically contingent, in flux and free flowing, uncertain and unpredictable, subject to revolutionary changes, mysterious and open-ended) and normative (society ought to be similarly free of settled absolutes, open to question and change, vitalized by opportunity and mobility, inclusive and pluralistic, inhabited by open minds and open hearts). Where the contract once served as a general metaphor for social integration amid competition, today communication serves such a function amid openness. Rights are thus conceptualized around, not the freedom of contract, but rather the freedom of self-expression (with its component parts of privacy and recognition). Progress is understood as moving toward democratic "humanity" (an all-inclusive diversity of free and equal individuals) rather than toward bourgeois "civilization." And the elision of fact and value under the umbrella of openness fosters the belief that democracy will bloom spontaneously the world over, once obstructions of whatever sort are removed. Consider in this context the familiar phrase "democratic spring," with its attendant assumptions and associations.

While free-market capitalism is still at times affirmed as natural and normative, I argue that it is so affirmed only insofar as it can be portrayed as an aspect of democratic openness. The "free enterprise system" trades on its share of revolutionary dynamism introduced into the world as democratic. Looking at the content of advertising, beyond the fact of its pervasiveness, it's apparent that consumerism is itself "branded" and sold in terms of democratic populism.[46] Any "ethos of consumer infantilization," as Benjamin R. Barber puts it, is less a product of "global marketers . . . explicitly infantilizing adults" (as if people were just raw material to be manipulated) than of the norm of uninhibited openness, expressed in terms of youthful vitality and childlike spontaneity.[47] And if many have more faith in "market forces" (or in the basically Malthusian economics of Darwinian biology) than in democratic institutions and practices, it is because these market constructs seem more in accord with an open world and an open society, unencumbered by arbitrary conventional forms. Along these lines, the full picture of the love-hate relationship with capitalism (and globalization) in democratic society becomes intelligible.

*Nature, Convention, and the Passion for Revolution*

Developing the second line of my argument, I show how the ongoing democratization of society, for all its good and beauty, goes hand in hand with the depoliticization of society. As democratic openness is taken as both the defining attribute of our modern condition and the central principle of proper social arrangements and relationships, the political element of human association is devalued. Framed by the democratic duality of cynicism and idealism, the belief takes shape that we are at once incapable of and better off without the practice of politics. Recall Aristotle's famous claim that "the man who is isolated, who is unable to share in the benefits of political association, or has no need to share because he is already self-sufficient, is no part of the city, and must therefore be either a beast or a god."[48] I argue that within democratic society we consider ourselves both unable to participate in *and* in need of nothing from political association. Democratic man does not consider himself a political animal—a citizen who is capable of and who is in need of persuading and being persuaded in turn.

The key here is that the democratic revolution in the principle of authority subverts not only hierarchical conventions but whatsoever is perceived as conventional—in politics and also in the family, religion, economics, law, morality, and so forth. After the revolutionary dissolution of hierarchy, the social order is no longer thought to potentially instantiate the natural order (natural law made manifest in positive law, for example, or divinity incorporated through the body of the king). The conventional world is "denatured." Further, the world of human contrivance is taken as the very antithesis of untouched nature, as its negation or suppression (Aristotelian habituation is re-presented as Freudian repression, for example). Nature and convention henceforth appear mutually exclusive and without possible mediation. At the same time, though, nature's self-evidence—successively iterated in terms of equality, competition, and openness—remains the standard of judgment for social arrangements and relationships. The truth and goodness of nature are hardly more questioned after the democratic revolution than before (notice the reflexive appeal today of the "all-natural," "organic," "green," and the like). But "natural" comes to mean "spontaneous," "authentic," "raw," "primal," "pristine," and so forth. In its openness, nature—conceived in terms of its vital energy rather than as a harmonious order, in the language of power rather than of peace, and of purity rather than of purpose—is precisely that which cannot be domesticated and embodied in conventional form. Nature is disenchanted but romanticized; conventionality is, as such, debased.[49]

The democratic revolution consequently launches a self-radicalizing quest for what we might call a *social state of nature*—civilization without the discontents, human association unfettered by conventional artifice, expression deeper than words permit, intimate relationships beyond the need for mediating institutions, the immediate experience of the events of the world. Most everything meaningful (whether good, true, or beautiful) is thought hidden or distant, before or after our time, above or below the surface of the present world. The revolution in turn gives birth to a constitutive passion for revolution, for the overturn of conventional norms and forms in the liberating event of opening. This passion takes shape in terms of originalism (the present-transcending, revolutionary return to fundamentals, untouched conscience, archaic traditions and principles) and originality (the present-transcending, revolutionary re-invention or innovation unto a brand-new and novel future)—purity and freshness.

In the context of this social state of openness, the master value of freedom comes to mean being "undomesticated." More specifically, as we shall see, freedom amounts to *mastery* or *escape*—power over others, or a power-free privacy in which one is either by oneself or in intimate union with others. The former is the limitless independence of auto-cratic control, the latter the liberation from all limits and even a this-worldly transcendence of material power and necessity. These are what Tocqueville describes as the freedoms of the savage, as opposed to the artfully staged freedom of democratic political association. And it is the worth of such political freedom—wherein power is both moderated and made effective in association with equal others—that freedom-as-openness undermines and overwhelms. Along these lines, Tocqueville identifies the common source of both the restless activity and the flight into passive isolation so characteristic of democratic peoples.

The upshot of the longing for a social state of nature vis-à-vis the utterly artificial politics of liberal democracy is clear. The contempt for main-stream, scripted and staged, suit-and-tie, teleprompter politics itself be-comes mainstream.[50] Appraised within the context of natural openness/conventional closure, a political system so heavily reliant upon represen-tations, institutional mechanisms, and procedural routines can only seem an absurd obstacle to "plain common sense" and "just getting things done." Where democracy housed in constitutional form might once have been regarded as an elevated form of democracy, it is now considered even by many of its advocates less fully democratic, defensible only inso-far as regrettably necessary.[51] And judged by the norms of informality and intimacy—by "who would I rather have a beer with?"—politicians playing politics within the system can only seem fake and ridiculous, especially when they try to act authentic.[52]

John Edwards, former U.S. senator from North Carolina and candidate for the 2008 Democratic presidential nomination, expressed this manner of contempt for mainstream politics exactly: "My own view is the next president of the United States, or certainly the one after, is likely to be the single candidate who doesn't sound like a politician. I want to tell you on a personal level, I'm trying every way I know how not to [sound like a politician]. . . . The problem is that we're so trained and so conditioned over a long period of time that being normal and real and authentic requires you to shed that conditioning."[53] Speech that seems scripted is as such devalued, on the basis of its scriptedness. Demonstrating informality and intimacy via personal confession is to be the technique of the successful (anti)politician. In a similar vein, "political correctness"—the self-censoring politeness we are forced to cover up with in public, as opposed to the self-expressive and brutal (primitive) honesty of "just telling it like it is"—is the shameful hallmark of our trained and conditioned (domesticated) present. The reflexive suspicion of such hypocrisy passes for wisdom.

Fueled in part by an aversion to the overt phoniness of the liberal political game, proponents of a more radical democracy suggest that "democracy" should be understood not as a political system or form of government but as the disruptive resistance to domination. Genuine democratic freedom and equality are not about collective self-rule, with its need for stable institutions and settled procedures. Rather, democracy is the unruly action that challenges authority of every sort, even of "the people." Protest, not self-government, is the heart of democracy, which beats insofar as every decision and closure is subject to open-ended questioning and "transgression." Sheldon Wolin, today's leading theorist of radical democracy, thus argues that a vital politics of popular protestant power both can only be and ought to be limited to punctuated moments in time. Authentic democracy is at once regrettably and ideally "fugitive,"—epic and episodic.[54] Fugitive democratic association can only be fleeting, given the economic realities the demos faces; the demos' activating sense of common cause is produced by the oppression of an enemy (usually impersonal and structural, in Wolin's account); and genuine democratic action, when it does occur, induces a rupture with the inequities and constraints of routine material reality. The fugitive democratic event, in short, is largely synonymous with revolution.

Attempting to preserve the transgressive, transcendent spirit of the democratic "mode of being" from the rationalizing imperatives of the material realm (where democracy is "domesticated" and "managed" by constitutional formalization and economic systematization), Wolin proposes "accepting the familiar charges that democracy is . . . inclined toward anarchy" and "rational disorganization."[55]

Fugitive democracy is, then, the ideal politics of democratic openness, of revolutionary openings and the renewal of democratic fundamentals. It is also self-subverting. Democracy as significant protest and resistance to domination requires sustained civic organization, one presumes, but such organization would seem to signify the loss of democratic openness. Once a political *movement* to disrupt authority is perceived as a political *organization*, once it seems more systematic than spontaneous, everyday rather than eruptive, it ceases to be authentically radical. The democratic authority of the grassroots uprising turns into the political power of the special interest group. The requirements of political action's effectiveness and sustainability seem inseparable from a sense of devitalization and freedom's domestication.[56] What begins as a theorization of participatory power against systemic power ends in retreat from politics and into righteous powerlessness—a democracy too good for politics. Striving for unconstrained power, the demos turns to fugitive escape. In this sense, the radical democratic practice of politics is no less undermined by the commitment to democratic openness than are liberal democratic formulations.

*Arguing Together: Political Power and Political Freedom*

Offering a distinct theory of robust (if not radical) democracy, I argue that the everyday practice of democratic politics—what Wolin himself at times seems to pursue, though increasingly laments as impossible—still has a place in the modern world. It requires, however, thinking outside the boundaries of the norm of openness, beyond the consequent tendency to formulate associative action as enabled by and limited to extraordinary moments of heroic struggle. The idea of democratic politics should be able to accommodate the common action of ordinary people. As for what counts as "the practice of democratic politics," I take an ecumenical view. Voting, deliberative decision making both in and out of

structured institutional settings, protest in the streets, interest group organization, and community organization: all of these and more are
practices wherein people might meet as citizens, think publicly, argue
together about common problems and purposes, and exercise the authority thereby generated (whether within or against the established
system). Now, this legitimate power can obviously be employed to more
or less legitimate ends. Popular power is only one element of a healthy
democratic regime, but it is of primary concern to me here. As Tocqueville came to recognize, the central threats to the flourishing of modern
democratic society follow not from a tyrannically overactive majority
but from an apolitical or antipolitical citizenry.

Following Tocqueville, I take public association, argument, and action—
the production and use of democratic political power—as a necessary
means to the experience of a more than symbolic, if less than transcendent, freedom. This intermediate freedom manifests as acting in the
world with equal others rather than as the dream of standing over or being apart from others. It is an effective but limited freedom—effective
because limited. As Tocqueville writes, the practice of democratic politics teaches the art of freedom by enabling us to envision being "independent without arrogance and obedient without baseness."[57] One of
my central aims in what follows is to identify ways in which we might
give political form to freedom in democratic society.

*Fundamentalism, Globalization, and Democratic Modernity*

Much of my project constitutes a sympathetic critique of so-called postmodern, post-structuralist, and agonistic theorizations of radical democracy, such as appear variously in the works of Wolin, William
Connolly, Chantal Mouffe, and Wendy Brown, among others. I view
many aspects of the engaged political action described by these writers
as both possible and essential to our social well-being today. However, I
question the diagnosis they offer for the causes of the infirmity of, and
in turn their civic and institutional prescriptions for, the political practice of democracy.

Wendy Brown, for instance, argues that the central threats to democracy in America are the rationalities she stylizes as neoconservative fundamentalism and neoliberal globalization. Today, the citizen "produced"

within these frameworks for understanding and evaluating the world embraces moralistic intolerance, the supposedly unerring imperatives of the global market, and even the synthesis of self-righteous Christianity and self-righteous capitalism, largely to the end of projecting undemocratic state power at home and abroad. The political sphere has been organized in accord with these religious and economic models—the church and the business corporation—as citizens not only concede but actually affirm "de-democratization." Democratic politics and culture are "hollowed out" by the viral incursion of prophetic and profit motives, and public decision making is ceded to pious adherence to the mystical inerrancy of Bible and Market.[58]

Diagnosing the condition of our democratic politics requires, I suggest, reversing the explanatory arrow here to ask the overlooked Tocquevillian question of how our democratic political regime, with its characteristic principle of authority, shapes a common ethos regarding politics, economics, and religion. I argue that the evangelical, expansive rationalities of fundamentalism and globalization actually draw strength from the democratic way of life within which they are embedded. Far from being outside threats to democracy, they are in part expressions of the idea of democratic openness—of the quest for the pre/postconventional, a world before or beyond political, economic, and religious forms. These logics of extremism—of extreme materialism or extreme spiritualism, as it were—proceed from the same passion for revolutionary rupture that lies at the heart of democratic modernity. The radicalization of democracy, in other words, goes hand in hand with the radicalization of religion and economics.

It is ultimately in this sense that democracy is self-subverting: the democratic way of life, principled upon the freedom-in-equality of openness as against hierarchical paternalism and absolutism, is both a precondition of and a threat to the political practice of democracy. The types of human association affirmed as meaningful within the democratic social state of openness are those that seem natural, informal and intimate, given and spontaneous, a state wherein membership is born into. These are the associations of the preconventional family (the tribe, community, nation, culture), or of postconventional humanity (the global village, global market, universal rights community, World Wide Web). The types of freedom affirmed are those of control and of being uncontrolled, whether this requires being by oneself or in intimate union with others. Such norms simply cannot find expression in democratic political association, argument, and action. The product, I argue, is not Brown's "undemocratic citizen, . . . who loves and wants neither freedom nor equality, even of a liberal sort," but rather the antipolitical citizen, who loves and wants freedom and equality of a characteristically democratic sort.[59]

*Plan of the Book*

Four chapters follow. Building upon Tocqueville's interpretation of democratic society, the first chapter takes up democratic education or character formation in the broadest sense, exploring how living in a democratic regime shapes what we experience as meaningful—whether good, beautiful, or true. Tocqueville identifies a series of contradictions within the democratic character: those in democracy are at once the most materialistic and the most spiritualistic; the most practical and abstract minded; the most restless and docile; the most prideful and the neediest. I show that for Tocqueville neither side of these extremes is more characteristic of the democratic way of life. Nor are democratic flights of spiritualism, for instance, simply an epiphenomenal reaction to the excesses of a more essential materialism. Rather, the character of democratic society follows from the simultaneous tendency toward co-constitutive extremes. The democratic revolution, Tocqueville explains, destroys the vast disparities of aristocratic society: the commanding heights of nobility and the depths of servitude dissolve into one vast middle class. Hierarchy collapses into equality. But this very collapse of hierarchy into equality produces new polar oppositions around which democratic society takes shape.

Tocqueville exposes the most significant example of this when he writes of the new norms of elevation and degradation embedded in democratic modernity. With leveling equality comes a stultifying sense of neediness and insignificance, of being lost and adrift in the great gray sea of mass mediocrity. Deprived of examples of aristocratic pride and grandeur, and with the withering of great passions and lofty purposes that accompanies bourgeois materialism and individualism, the inhabitants of democracy fear no less than sinking below the level of humanity. But with the presence of equality comes the absence of hierarchy and hierarchical absolutes, and in this absence arises the thought of freedom-as-openness. The idealizing imagination seizes upon the prospect of being without limits, of infinite revolutionary possibility. Unbound and audacious, democratic peoples dream of no less than rising above the level of humanity. Where the aristocrat commanded, the democrat creates; where the aristocrat stood atop, the democrat rises above. In his individualism, for instance, the "common man" of democracy will demand of himself a sovereign independence and self-sufficiency that is entirely uncommon—indeed, historically unprecedented. And in his materialism, he will gamble all and abandon material well-being for a reckless love of risk and the opportunity for indefinite future gain. In one stroke, then, the democratic revolution in the principle of authority stultifies and liberates, introducing radical new notions of perfectibility and imperfectibility into human association.

In the second chapter, also building upon Tocqueville, I turn to the norms of freedom (mastery and escape) and human association (the family and humanity) inscribed in democratic society. In Tocqueville's account, freedom in aristocratic times meant having a *place* of one's own to stand in public, and so to be seen, heard, and honored. In democratic times freedom means having the *space* to move about restlessly and take to the open road, as it were, or simply having enough power so that one need not move or compromise or depend upon others. Association in aristocratic times was principled upon the political right of command and so upon the social place or station into which one was born. Democratic association too is born into (at least insofar as it is experienced as meaningful), but it is principled upon the egalitarian ties of familial and human resemblance. Along these lines, Tocqueville sums the movement from aristocracy to democracy as the shift from political to natural bonds. The former were put into practice as intricate, formal codes of manners and etiquette demarcating one's due obligations up and down the social chain. The latter coalesce around the simple, relaxed norms of informality and intimacy that span social space. The public posture of the aristocrat is deemed too demanding, absurdly rigorous, cold, and superficial. It is replaced by the more demanding hope of being at home with others, as if by oneself even when with others. In aristocracy even the family was a sort of political entity; in democracy even political associations aspire to the naturalness of the family.

I go on to suggest that all that falls short of this ideal of unmediated intimacy tends to be perceived cynically, as power relations driven by competitive self-interest and strategic calculation (providentially restrained a few degrees short of actual violence by this same self-interested calculation). Competition and intimacy—with their respective currencies of power and love—constitute the poles of democratic society. The market and the family are thought the primary models of human association. As much romantics as we are realists, today's advice holds that we follow our hearts and follow the money. As a mode of human association, politics is conceived of as the blood sport of realpolitik—regrettably necessary and inevitably corrupt—insofar as it conforms to the model of market competition. Insofar as politics aspires to the model of familial intimacy, it will be conceived of as utterly natural and meaningful, rendering the everyday practice of politics alien and absurd by comparison.

In the third chapter, I critique Claude Lefort's theory of democratic society and the democratic revolution. Lefort, a leading interpreter of Tocqueville, wonderfully illuminates the source of the idea of democratic openness in the democratic revolution. The revolution is the original phenomenon of opening, which Lefort describes as "the dissolution of the markers of certainty."[60] The revolutionary beheading of the king constitutes the symbolic demise of the *present father figure*—the visible and audible embodiment of hierarchy—and of the social form organized by the presence of paternal authority. With the disappearance from the scene of the body of the king—the focal intersection of the divine and the mundane—every claim to authority is opened to contestation; opinion unseats command.

Along these lines, Lefort rightly rejects Tocqueville's prediction that democracy's original revolutionary desire for freedom might eventually dissipate under the equality of conditions, inverting to socialism's tutelary despotism (I argue that Tocqueville's own analysis does not warrant his prediction). Democratic equality and democratic freedom are inextricable, two sides of the same coin, born into the world at the same revolutionary moment. Lefort's interpretation helps us to see, moreover, that the rarity of great revolutions in democratic times anticipated by Tocqueville follows not from the waning of the passion for revolutionary openings but rather from the belief that politics is an inadequate vehicle for our transformative aspirations (Tocqueville's conclusion is largely correct, but for the wrong reasons). The passion for revolution isn't lost; it is sublimated into restlessness—into a love affair with technological innovation and the dynamic qualities of science and capitalism (information/digital/genetic/green revolutions); an infatuation with the historical "event" of "turning-point" or "game-changing" crisis; the idea of remaking the world ("democratization" by military or economic, if not political, means); the advertising of every new product as something that forever alters the way we see and do things. In democracy, most every day is depicted as the day everything changed, a revolutionary beginning or departure to new worlds.

At the same time, Lefort's work implicitly confirms Tocqueville's prediction that we will come to see democratic society, precisely in its openness, as natural—providentially given and inevitable. In Lefort's writings, a self-subverting quality of openness becomes apparent: the fact/value of openness itself comes to stand as unquestioned orthodoxy and ontology. In one sense, as many followers of Lefort highlight, the democratic revolution opens the conventional order to interrogation, as no remaining presence can unproblematically represent it in the name of the divine. In another sense, the conventions of the emergent democratic regime come to seem as much inscribed in modern nature—that is, in the revolutionary openness, the inescapable but unpredictable flow of historical time— as aristocratic conventions seemed inscribed in the immutable hierarchy of Nature. In society as in nature, democratic openness is decreed by the unruly rule of history—not as the end of History, but by history's endlessness. Democratization is as natural as change.

In the final chapter, I take up Wolin's theory of democracy as "fugitive"—radically transgressive but fleeting—moments in history. This is the revolutionary practice of politics most in accord with the revolutionary dissolution of the markers of certainty. Another prominent interpreter of Tocqueville, Wolin is led by his commitment to democratic openness to what I describe as an emergency power or executive (as opposed to a legislative) notion of democracy. Here, the unity and energy required for genuine democratic action can only be a short-lived response to crisis. Political association coheres not via argument but only in opposition to collective oppression and suffering—the transient solidarity of a community of victims. Popular power is catalyzed by the experience of popular powerlessness. Yet, precisely because it is so limited in time, democratic action can always claim an unlimited potential for radically creative beginnings and disruptive endings. It does not operate in the world long enough to be economized, constitutionalized, rationalized, systematized, or organized. Such a politics of the extraordinary is never compromised or domesticated, maintaining its youthful integrity and vitality by virtue of its evanescence.

I argue that the extreme idealism and cynicism at the core of Wolin's theory leaves little room for the routine practice of democratic politics. Fugitive democracy is exceptional—an exception to ordinary rules (whether political, economic, or legal) and of exceptionally pure (even otherworldly) quality. All that falls short of this ideal is categorized as co-opted and inauthentic "managed democracy." Voting, for instance, seems more a betrayal than an integral element of democracy. Participation in the extant political system renders one complicit in the production and projection of antidemocratic state power. For Wolin, there is the heroic demos, the manipulated-into-collaboration electorate, and nothing in between.

I conclude by suggesting that there is a certain sort of silence inherent in democratic society. Democracy is duly celebrated as the social form that, in its egalitarianism, allows nearly unlimited freedom of expression and breaks down most every barrier to communication. But what sort of expression is experienced as meaningful within the democratic regime? Which avenues of communication become predominant, and which are left unused?

As I have begun to detail, democratic society is largely principled upon the freedom of openness—the freedom that becomes intelligible only after the revolutionary collapse of hierarchy and advent of equality. This freedom takes shape as the fight for power over, and the flight from, others and the world. In the company of equals, we compete in the antipaternalistic free market, and we relax within the fatherless family of our intimate community.

For all of their polar differences, what competition and communion share as modes of human association is that they have no need of words as liaisons between participants. More specifically, these relationships take shape below or above the level of language deployed in argument, persuasion, and judgment. In the market's civil struggle for power and competitive advantage, arguments might be useful as a strategy for success via sales-pitch manipulation and the masking of our interests (or they might be a useless waste of time in a world where "money talks"). Within the self-regulating system of market "forces" and "mechanisms," judgment is reduced to rational calculation, and we respond to "incentives" rather than persuasion. At the other end of the spectrum, in the realm of familial communion, arguments signify only the sad distance between us and our aspiration to union unfettered by the need for mediation—argument reduced to "bickering" and interpreted as the first sign on the road to divorce.[61] Arguing means we are not "at one with," and the exercise of judgment means we cannot relax and be "at home with." We might express (confess) our inner authentic selves so as to be recognized (to "let someone in"), but ultimately, to be experienced as meaningful, the connection must be deeper than any public presentation allows. It must be rooted in the reflex of compassion toward those like us, in our biological or national blood bond, or in the "chemistry" between us.

Whether we believe ourselves stuck in a world wholly determined by the economics of power (wherein the distinction between force and persuasion either collapses or is deemed absolute) or poised to enter into a world free of power and external authority (wherein persuasion and judgment have no standing), argument as a mode of expression and communication is devalued. The only things that seem impossible in a world of infinite possibility are good-faith arguments and rightful persuasion. Insofar as arguing about how we can and ought to live together is the activity par excellence of the citizen, citizenship is subverted by the extremes of democratic society. The democratic way of life does not ultimately tend toward dissociation, fragmentation, or "atomistic individualism" (quite the opposite, in many ways), but it does dissolve the political element of human association. Absent politics, the coordination of how we are to live together is left to other forces, whether sub- or superhumanistic.

# CHAPTER 1

# "More than Kings
yet Less than Men"

## Tocqueville on the New Extremes
of Democratic Society

> Equality drives men forward and at the same time holds them
> back, spurs them on yet keeps them tethered to the earth.
>
> —Tocqueville, *Democracy in America*

## I. The Dualism of Democratic Society

*Democracy in America Today?*

Not yet two hundred years ago, Alexis de Tocqueville described the
"great social revolution" of democracy as "irresistible" and "already so
powerful that it cannot be stopped." Throughout the Christian world
democracy had "destroyed feudalism and vanquished kings"; in America the empire of democracy held "no less sway over civil society than
over government." The advance of democracy, as Tocqueville famously
put it, seemed no less than a "providential fact": "It is universal, durable,
and daily proves itself to be beyond the reach of man's powers."[1]

Today many argue that if anything is inevitable, it is the decline and
loss of democracy. Sheldon Wolin, perhaps most notably, stands Tocqueville on his head, writing that we are currently witness to "the steady
transformation of America into an anti-democratic society"—it is "evolv-
ing from a more to a less democratic polity and from a less to a more authoritarian society."[2] If there is an irresistible social revolution, it is one
of dedemocratization; democracy appears already so powerless that it
cannot be resuscitated. In this inversion, democracy is the new ancien
régime.[3]

In what is perhaps the mainstream of current academic and public discourse, these extreme positions are actually conjoined around a principle/practice distinction. In principle, democracy is indeed triumphant; in practice, democracy is in severe crisis, with the "warning signs of exhaustion, cynicism, opportunism, and despair."[4] "Few would seem to dispute," we hear, "that democracy is the best form of government seen from the standpoint of principle," yet "the exercise of democracy in the old-established democracies can hardly be judged as inspiring."[5] Democracy is "the sole surviving source of political legitimacy," yet "most Americans have lost faith in their democracy."[6] Even Wolin concurs that one of "the most striking facts about the political world of the third millennium is the near-universal acclaim accorded democracy," with its status as a "transhistorical and universal value."[7]

We are left with the question of why even the most basic practices of democratic political association and action have grown so scarce in a time when democracy has achieved a normative empire historically unprecedented in its global monopoly of legitimacy. A gap between our ideals and reality hardly requires explanation, but we might wonder why the political practice of democracy has waned seemingly in proportion to the waxing of democratic principles. How can we account for this opposite movement?

The mystery is compounded when we consider that even as we expect ever less *of* democracy, we apparently expect ever more *from* democracy. Most every good—freedom and equality, justice and human rights, peace and prosperity, deliberative reason and ethical self-development— is today considered in some way the product of (or simply synonymous with) democracy. Democratization seems the path to a perfected self, society, and world, a sort of secular salvation. Yet, as theorizations have moved away from "minimalist democracy" over the past half century and toward more participatory, deliberative, and radical formulations, the widespread impression is that we are not even living up to the low standards of minimalism.[8] Expectations have continued up as even voting rates have continued down. Has reality ever fallen so far from ideal? Everywhere preached but nowhere practiced, democracy has taken on the characteristics of a utopia.

In what follows, I argue that the simultaneous triumph of democratic principles and tragedy of democratic political practices is no coincidence.

Democracy is not in crisis despite the fact that democratic principles are hegemonic but precisely because democratic principles are hegemonic.

The diagnosis of this Pyrrhic quality of democracy is, I suggest, at the center of Tocqueville's work. While Tocqueville is far from positing Wolin's retrogressive movement toward an *antidemocratic* society, he does foresee and fear the *antipolitical* inclinations of democratic society. In his terms, as the "mores" of our "social state" become more fully democratic, our politics becomes less so. This, as we shall see, is largely because the inhabitants of democratic society are disposed to devalue the political practice of democracy and to harbor a sort of contempt for themselves in their political roles and capacities. Along these lines, we can address at least one aspect of the antidemocratic movement Wolin envisions. He asks why, despite the fact that "all of the elements for radical protest appear to be present," there "has been no general mobilization of outrage," only "astonishing passivity."[9] Following Tocqueville's analysis, we understand that the sphere of politics is no longer considered a vehicle for meaningful mobilization, and so we are left with a politically passive, immobile outrage.

My argument unfolds in four steps (the first in this chapter, the remaining three in the following chapter). First, I explore the apparently contradictory characteristics Tocqueville finds within the democratic social state.[10] Those living in democracy are at once the most materialistic and the most spiritualistic, the most practical and abstract minded, the most restless and docile, the most prideful and the neediest, and so on. I show that for Tocqueville neither extreme is more essentially characteristic of the democratic way of life. Rather, the essential character of democratic society lies in its tendency toward unmediated extremes. Most significantly, after the democratic revolution, we imagine the radical degradation, and the equally radical elevation, of self and society. As Tocqueville puts it, democratic man fears sinking below the level of humanity even as he dreams of rising above the level of humanity. Democratic degradation takes shape in the atmosphere of stultifying middle-class mediocrity, in the inescapable awareness of one's own insignificance and neediness, and in the loss of great passions and lofty purposes that accompanies isolation and felt powerlessness. The democratic individual ends up in the terrible position of being self-centered without cause for self-respect. At the core this experience looms the thought that the domestication of the human being has become a real—even immanent—possibility. Democratic elevation takes shape around the idea of freedom-as-openness, of liberation from worldly limits in the condition of indefinite perfectibility and infinite revolutionary/creative possibility. The dichotomy of base and noble that gave aristocratic society its normative dimensionality translates into the democratic dimensionality of domestication/openness. Fear of collapsing into the petty need for material comfort and pleasure, for instance, is accompanied by the grand aspiration to ensure the victory of the democratic idea in the world. The great paradox of democracy, as we shall see, is that both sides of this dualism are inscribed in the modern political/social principle of equality—in what we might divide out as the postrevolutionary *presence of equality* and *absence of hierarchy*.[11]

Along these lines I argue that modern society cannot be reduced, or degraded, to the ubiquitous contemporary formulation of "market society." In Tocqueville's terms, the social state that takes shape in the wake of the democratic revolution is part "commercial society" but also part "literary society." Inhabitants of the modern democratic regime understand and evaluate themselves as businesspeople in the world, as it were, but also as artists of the world. They exhibit their unchecked "realism" by representing their actions solely in terms of the necessities of competition and compulsive consumption, and their unconstrained "idealism" by thinking it possible to transcend materiality and rewrite themselves and the world. The promise of self-transformation accompanies the felt pervasiveness of fixed banality; the celebration of self-expression is as widespread as the explanatory invocation of self-interest.

For Tocqueville, democracy's literary aspect is largely a relic of its revolutionary birth in France. Over time the audacious passion for revolutionary rupture and re-creation is bound to give way to the timid desire for material well-being and then potentially to a society-wide collapse into the arms of a quasi-paternalistic "tutelary power." At times fatalistically, Tocqueville foresees a tragic narrative arc of democratic society, from revolutionary adolescence through bourgeois middle age to geriatric socialism. The early impulse to freedom succumbs to a fully realized and wholly base egalitarianism. I depart from this view to suggest that democratic society stands in permanent tension between the passion for equality and the passion for revolutionary openness—which is to say, between equality and the notion of freedom inscribed in equality. Indeed, I argue that Tocqueville's own analysis of democracy does not warrant his prediction that the potentially degrading belief in and experience of equality might eventually undermine freedom. Equality and the freedom born of the dissolution of hierarchical absolutes are coconstitutive of democratic society. If the former makes great revolutions rare, as Tocqueville famously predicts, the latter constantly spurs the idealizing imagination's embrace of revolution. I go on to argue that by depriving revolution of politics as its venue, democracy is less likely to make revolution rare than to relocate revolution to the spheres of science, art, and economics or to render revolution a private and personal matter. The passion for revolution is sublimated into the notions of innovation and reinvention, into the norms of creativity and audacious heroism, into the search for the experience of life's transformative events and the rupture onto original nature. If we in modern democratic society need constant comfort and pleasure, so too do we demand constant drama and excitement.

In the second step of my argument, I show that two extreme notions of freedom, accompanied by an extreme notion of freedom's loss, are embedded in our democratic social state. As openness, freedom's meaning coalesces around the poles of mastery and escape. With the collapse of aristocratic command and the consequent unleashing of competition, democratic individuals feel compelled to seek the freedom afforded by power over others. At the same time, these same individuals hope for a power-free zone possible only in isolation or in uninhibited communion with others. The loss of freedom is imagined as similarly total, as domestication, wherein democratic peoples internalize and cling to their enslavement.

Third, I follow Tocqueville in arguing that the democratic principle of equality not only undermines hierarchical conventions but also, in its concomitant principle of openness, "cannot fail to destroy what is purely conventional."[12] In the spheres of the family, religion, economics, and so forth, the democratic revolution gives birth to the quest for a pre/post-conventional social state of nature. Here, the alienating artifice of conventional norms and forms have been rendered unnecessary via the liberating event of opening. As Tocqueville argues, the modes of human association affirmed as meaningful and legitimate within this social state of nature are those of the preconventional, primitive family (community, culture, tribe, and so on) and of postconventional, global humanity (represented as a "global village," a world market, the World Wide Web, a human rights community, and so forth). Certain ideas, I go on to suggest, take hold of the imagination in this context: spiritualism free of religious form, materialism free to run its course in the open market, expression/communication free of words.

Finally, I argue that there is an antipolitical prejudice inscribed in this democratic social state. "Spiritual but not religious" has its cognate, we might say, in "democratic but not political." After the democratic revolution, we come to believe in a world before and beyond politics—at least the politics of addressing common purposes and problems by means of arguing together. The sublime idea of an open way of life cannot find expression in democratic political action and association and can only take flight outside of the confining forms of political institutions and organizations (whether liberal or radical, representative or participatory). From a different angle: in relation to the expansive idea of freedom-as-openness, "political freedom" seems oxymoronic.

Uncovering the new extremes of elevation and degradation native to equality, Tocqueville helps us see how those who live in accordance with the democratic principle might imagine themselves to be as free as they are powerless, at once "more than kings yet less than men."[13] Recall in this context Aristotle's reasoning that "the man who is isolated, who is unable to share in the benefits of political association, or has no need to share because he is already self-sufficient, is no part of the city, and must therefore be either a beast or a god."[14] Much of what I put forward here amounts to the proposition that democratic man does not consider himself a political animal. He is foreign to Aristotle's taxonomy, and indeed unique in history, in thinking himself simultaneously incapable of participating in and above politics—both beast and god.[15]

*Democracy as a Social State*

In Tocqueville's notoriously expansive usage, "democracy" is more the principle of a way of life than merely a form of politics. Living in democracy, the way we understand and evaluate the world, how we think and feel about ourselves and others, what we believe and what we desire, all become somehow characteristically democratic. Taking up democratic education or character formation in the most capacious sense, Tocqueville explores how living within a democratic regime orients what we find meaningful—whether good, true, or beautiful.[16] It is hardly an exaggeration to say that, for Tocqueville, the democratic revolution alters the human condition: democracy becomes the ordering, animating Faith of modern man. Indeed, the revolution carries within it the new human type of "democratic man," bringing to the fore previously subordinate elements and even producing wholly new ideas and beliefs, passions and interests.[17] As our most basic source of authority, democracy becomes our most basic source of self.

All of this is not to say, however, that the concept of democracy isn't fundamentally political for Tocqueville. Even as democracy expands beyond the sphere of politics, Tocqueville asks us to recognize that this revolution could only have begun within the political. While he often writes about the spread of civilization and enlightenment, he interprets modernity as originally and essentially democratic. The pivot of human history is a revolution in the principle of authority—in the way by which power comes to be represented as legitimate authority.[18] At the core of this transformation, the aristocratic right of command is supplanted by the right of equal individuals to consent, contract, and choose (the successive iterations—the radicalization—of equality as the principle of authority). Even in the relationships of ruler and ruled or rich and poor, we hold that, regarding what is most fundamental about the two parties, they are equal. Both equally work for wages, if not for equal wages. Inequality persists, hierarchy does not.

And it is this *political* transformation, this shift in the principle of legitimate human association, that utterly reshapes modern existence. As we shall see, perhaps the most basic conceit of Tocqueville's work is that this transformation in the norms of human relations reorients our beliefs concerning what is real and necessary, what is possible and ideal, and even our perception of time and space. The idea of a democratically integrated society colonizes and reorders every sphere of life, including the life of the mind. And within this social form are generated characteristically democratic modes of politics and economics, religion and morality, the arts and sciences, and public and private life.

For Tocqueville, then, the democratization of authority is the interpretive key to modern existence. To perceive such an interpretive key, Tocqueville suggests, one must recognize those instances when, in effect, fact and value are taken to coincide by the inhabitants of that social state. In democratic times, for example, "men do not hold on to equality solely because it is dear to them; they also cling to it because they believe that it must always endure." And "all consider society a body in progress and mankind a changing tableau in which nothing *is* or *should be* fixed forever." The sense that change is given and inevitable reinforces and is reinforced by the affirmation of social mobility, restless activity, and novelty. The collapse of belief in a stable hierarchy in nature and society signifies a shift in self-evidence; henceforth, equality and impermanence are presupposed as natural and embraced as good. This convergence lends a powerful but unnoticed gravity to the principle of a social state, instilling a "natural inclination" in the "minds and hearts" of its people—"to arrive there it suffices that they not hold themselves back."[19]

To gain interpretive access to a social state, Tocqueville therefore seeks out the silence, conspicuous only from a comparative perspective, surrounding those points where "is" and "ought" overlap in a sort of second nature.[20] For instance: "The French were not just friends of monarchy; they could not imagine the possibility of putting anything else in its place. They accepted it as one accepts the course of the sun and the succession of the seasons. They were neither advocates nor adversaries of royal power. This is how the republic exists in America: without combat, without opposition, without proof, by a tacit accord, a sort of *consensus universalis.*" One of course "meets with exceptions" to the normal state of affairs generated by the principle of a social state—with what would seem unnatural aberrations—but "not with a contrary principle."[21]

From his time to our own, Tocqueville has been criticized for attempting to interpret all aspects of life from the single starting point of democracy. Given the complexity and diversity of modern society, how well does it serve us to think about it in terms of an ideal type of "democratic society" or to theorize the democratic regime as the carrier of modernity? Does it make sense to speak of anything as Tocqueville speaks of equality, as the "dominant fact to which all other facts are related" and the "principle of action that dominates all others"?[22]

Despite such questions, it seems today less that the passion for generalization has subsided than that the starting point has changed. In particular, the notions of "market society" and "consumer culture" are put forth in strikingly analogous terms to those of Tocqueville's democratic social state. "Market society," we hear, "is no longer simply a metaphor, or an analytical concept. It is a living reality. As society becomes a market the values and operative norms of the market become salient to society as well. That is why consumption, the driving force of the market, has assumed a special significance in the contemporary world. . . . It has become existential, the veritable badge of identity. As we consume so we are. Our economic identity as consumers is increasingly overriding our civic and even our human identity."[23] Here, the idea of a society ordered, integrated, and animated by market principles colonizes every sphere of life, carrying with it the new human type of consumer.

Wolin again provides a perfect contrast to Tocqueville, arguing that we live not in a democratic social state but in an "economic polity."[24] Wolin's claim is not merely that power resides with wealth today, although plutocracy is surely one element of the economic polity. Rather, taken as the "ontological principle . . . underlying reality" and "the 'real' constitution of society," economy, not democracy, functions as the "first principle of a comprehensive scheme of social hermeneutics" and "an interpretive category of virtually universal application." Wolin continues, "It is used to understand personal life and public life, to make judgments about them, and to define the nature of their problems. It supplies categories of analysis and decision by which public policies are formulated, and it is applied to cultural domains such as education, the arts, and scientific research."[25] In our economic polity, "market forces" supplant the equality of conditions as the dominant fact/principle of action. Consequently, we are not just friends of the market; we accept its movements as one accepts the succession of the seasons and we cannot imagine the possibility of putting anything else in its place.

As we shall see, Tocqueville shares many of these characterizations and critiques of modern society as market society—the society of bourgeois consciousness wherein, for instance, the self and its "interests" are habitually represented in economic terms. But he is not so reductive in his analysis; market society is just one aspect of modern society. Insofar as we can generalize about such things, modern society is rendered more fully intelligible as originally and essentially democratic, founded in the collapse of hierarchy and in the equalization of conditions. Insofar as we can issue abstractions about existential badges of identity and ontological principles underlying reality, we get further by beginning with the democratic political principle of human association.

With this reorientation and broadening of our interpretative view, we are able to see that notions like free-market competition and consumption are affirmed, often silently, but only to the extent that they conform to and express democratic norms.[26] Our belief in competition, even with its consequent inequalities of winner and loser, is warranted and conditioned by our belief in equality. At least insofar as it is meaningful, competition can only be an interaction between equals. Indeed, society-wide competition is inconceivable outside the context of society-wide equality; competition makes sense only between equals, absent the right of command and heritable status. And while consumerism is surely one part of the democratic whole, an equally significant part is the contempt for commodification and the petty bourgeois preoccupation with material comfort and pleasure. In this sense, the critique of totalizing market capitalism advanced by Wolin and others is best understood as internal to, and indeed constitutive of, modern democratic society. In Tocqueville's terms, within the democratic social state we evaluate our "commercial" norms from a "literary" perspective, and our "literary" norms from a "commercial" perspective.[27]

*On Sex Objects and Soul Mates*

In the summer of 2004, Major League Baseball and Columbia pictures announced a $3.6 million deal to place logos for the movie *Spider-Man 2* on the bases of fifteen stadiums for a weekend. The subsequent public outcry was fierce and extensive. Ralph Nader called the deal "a greedy new low" and "beyond grotesque." U.S. Rep. George Nethercutt, a Washington Republican, sent a letter to the league, arguing that the game should "remain pure" and that "Little Leaguers deserve to see their heroes slide into bases, not ads." Former baseball commissioner Fay Vincent spoke out, saying "I guess it's inevitable, but it's sad. . . . I'm a romanticist. I think the bases should be protected from this." Apparently it wasn't inevitable, however, as one day later the league announced it would not run the ads, relenting to polling wherein close to 80 percent agreed that baseball was "selling out."[28]

Can we infer anything about our "culture" or "age" from this course of events? Does it signal that we live in a consumer culture where everything is for sale or in an age of outrage over everything being for sale? Does it mean that sports is a bottom-line business just like everything else or that athletic competition is understood and valued as a world apart from market competition? One need only look to the film "industry" itself, where artistic expression and bourgeois profit seeking cohabitate, to see this tension played out on a daily basis. Everyone cynically recognizes that movies like *Spider-Man 2* are made to make money, and yet the heroes of these blockbusters (and the actors who portray them) invariable scorn such philistinism. And it's the most romantic love stories that make the most money.[29]

Of course everyone knows sex sells too. While prostitution might be the oldest profession, pornography is the growth industry of the information age. By 2006, pornography generated more money than Microsoft, Apple, Google, Yahoo!, EarthLink, eBay, and Amazon.com combined, and U.S. pornography revenue exceeded the combined revenues of ABC, CBS, and NBC.[30] As with the baseball controversy, though, we should notice a contrary trend toward the opposite end of the cultural spectrum. A 2001 Gallup Poll commissioned by the National Marriage Project at Rutgers University reported, "Ninety-four percent of single men and women, ages twenty to twenty-nine agree with the statement that 'when you marry, you want your spouse to be your soul mate, first and foremost.' Eighty-eight percent believe that there is one person 'out there' who is specially destined to be their soul mate." The report speculates, "In a secular society, where sex has lost its connection to marriage and also its sense of mystery, young people may be attracted to the soul mate ideal because it endows intimate relationships with a higher spiritual—though not explicitly religious—significance." Here, as the antithesis of pornographic objectification and commodification, the "ideal of friendship in marriage . . . has been notched up to a more demanding ideal. People now expect their marriages to be a spiritualized union of souls."[31]

Taking these two trends together, it appears that our juvenile puerility is matched only by our youthful romanticism. The contrary extremes of sex degraded to the purely material and love elevated to the purely spiritual have simultaneously commandeered the mainstream. We seem at once utterly superficial and utterly scornful of superficiality. For all of their obvious differences, though, there are basic similarities between these "soul mate" and "sex object" types of relations. In a common enough formulation, your soul mate is "someone who completes you" and "accepts you no matter what"; soul mates "have two minds, hearts and souls that operate as one." In transcendent intimacy, just as in the total lack of intimacy between sex objects, your partner is "someone for whom you would not have to make major compromises."[32] In either case—whether in spiritual union or in the sex-object marketplace—one remains as free as if alone. And operating as one, in communion beyond the need of formal mediation, soul mates have no more need of words than do sex objects. Both modes of association are unspoken, articulated by means either above or below conversation.

I suggest in what follows that Tocqueville identifies a tendency toward just these borderline extremes in the way we think about the possible and proper modes of freedom and human relations within the democratic social state. Unlike most formulations, though (as in the discussion above, in which the soul mate ideal is merely a secondary reaction to the more fundamental sex objectification of secular society), Tocqueville theorizes transcendent spiritualism and reductive materialism as equal aspects of democratic society—as opposite expressions of the same idea of democratic openness.

## II. Democratic Degradation: Equality, Mediocrity, Domestication

*Mediocrity and the Loss of Passion*

It seems problematic from the outset to interpret Tocqueville as positing a new dimensionality—a new polar opposition between the extremes of human elevation and degradation—as constitutive of postrevolutionary society. Tocqueville himself writes that of all the various traits of democracy he surveys, "the one that seems to [him] most general and most striking" is that nearly "all extremes are being softened and blunted": "Almost anything that stands out is being wiped out and replaced by something average—neither as high nor as low, neither as brilliant nor as obscure as what the world once knew." In a process Tocqueville describes as the exchange of aristocracy's beautiful nobility for the sublime justice of democratic equality, great disparities of authority, honor, wealth, and enlightenment are leveled. In democratic society, he concludes, "we should not expect to encounter the extremes of degradation and grandeur" that define aristocratic society.[33]

Yet the fear of a new sort of degradation, democratic in origin and as bottomless as any found in previous times, is a constant in Tocqueville's writings, from his earliest private letters to his notes for the unfinished second volume of *The Old Regime*. In democratic times we run no less a risk than of man "sinking gradually beneath the level of humanity."[34] I argue that, for Tocqueville, a new notion of degradation arises precisely with the softening and blunting of aristocratic extremes into democratic mediocrity. Paradoxically, a world without great disparities of authority, honor, wealth, and education itself harbors the experience of dehumanization. In aristocracy, the presence of nobility and serfdom simultaneously blurred the lines between man and God and between man and animal; in democracy, these lines are no less blurred even as nobility and serfdom dissolve into one vast middle class.

The inhabitants of democracy have long been represented as tending toward the subhuman and animalistic. Rejecting the principle of hierarchy, democratic peoples end up governed by their base bodily appetites and impulses rather than by the essentially human faculty of reason—they are literally ruled by their lower parts, by gut and groin, rather than by their heads. Tocqueville follows this characterization to some extent, particularly in *Democracy I*. Over time, though, he came to think of democratic dehumanization primarily in terms of the devitalization rather than the disorderliness of soul and city. The collapse of hierarchy degrades less through the subversion of order than through the sapping of energy, in stagnation rather than corruption. The basic danger of equality is not anarchy or licentiousness but the enervation of passions and convictions.[35] For Tocqueville, democratic equality deprives the heart more so than the head its place in human things. Thus, for instance, the bloodless passivity of the majority came to replace the chaotic tyranny of the majority as his central preoccupation. In terms of living in democratic times, he concludes, "I am far less afraid of audacity of desire than of mediocrity."[36]

Tocqueville offers a number of well-known connections between equality and this loss of vitality. On a purely contingent level, the ongoing violent upheavals of the democratic revolution inevitably generate *fatigue*. More significantly, a life of equality—lived without the settled hierarchical orders of aristocracy and so without the possibility of commanding or being commanded—is inevitably one of *uncertainty*, and so of potential paralysis. On a still deeper level, in the *neediness* of their materialism and the felt *insignificance* of their individualism, the new men of democracy will tend to imagine themselves as both soft and small, as subject to all kinds of powerful necessities and as powerless to cope.

There is another equally important connection between equality and docility, though, which is often overlooked. With the collapse of the principle of fixed hierarchy, Tocqueville reasons, the idea of striving enters the imagination and becomes widespread even as people lose sight of any manifest model toward which to strive. In the great gray mass of democracy, people are mobile but directionless because they are without example of greatness. The aristocracy had acquired during their "long, uncontested experience of greatness, a certain pride of heart, a natural confidence in its strength, a habit of being respected," Tocqueville writes, and the show of noble bearing "increased the virility of the other classes by its example."[37] Conspicuous inequalities of honor and authority were to the benefit of the least well off. With the fall of the closed aristocratic order comes the loss of such public displays of grandeur. People are no longer held back, but neither can they so clearly conceive of human elevation; they are no longer deprived of respect, but neither can they habitually envision being respected. A new sense of possibility and openness is born into the world with the demise of immutable hierarchy, but with the collapse of the principle of hierarchy, all that is exceptional and extraordinary—all that stirs the human heart—dissolves into banality. In one stroke the democratic revolution liberates and stultifies the modern imagination.

In a formulation he returns to time and again, Tocqueville writes that the "true nightmare of our period is in not perceiving before oneself anything either to love or to hate, but only to despise."[38] Suffocated by mediocrity, the "spark and grandeur of ambition" fades while "human passions subside and diminish."[39] Democratic man believes in nothing save the individual self-interest that engulfs him, and he hopes for nothing except the material gain he sees everyone pursuing.[40] Ultimately, the same egalitarian man who cannot tolerate subordination to others comes to harbor "such contempt for himself that he thinks the only pleasures he is made to savor are vulgar ones": "He voluntarily limits himself to mediocre desires and never dares to reach for anything high."[41] The collapse of aristocracy is internalized, and even in himself he sees nothing to love or hate, but only despise.

### From Revolutionary Excess to Conservative Defect

For Tocqueville, the condition of pervasive mediocrity harbors an intrinsically democratic type of dehumanization. In a world of mediocrity, we find it difficult to conceive of the kind of goals and to experience the kind of emotions that we would respect as worthy of humanity. In this sense, middle-class equality can be as dispiriting as the deprivations of the serf were debilitating. In the absence of commanding passions, just as in the presence of entrenched barriers, Tocqueville fears that the human race might "stop progressing and narrow its horizons."[42]

Tocqueville typically formulates his contempt for the "little democratic and bourgeois pot of soup" within which he lives as a fall from the epic heroism of those who produced the democratic revolution in France—the "men of '89"—to the inconsequential hedonism of the revolution's epigones.[43] Dumbly "entranced by a contemptible love of present pleasures," endlessly "hastening after petty and vulgar pleasures with which they fill their souls," the inhabitants of democracy have "raised themselves to sovereign power only to gratify trivial and coarse appetites more easily."[44] Indeed, democratic peoples have apparently liberated themselves from paternal authority of every sort, not on the way to Kantian maturity, but so as to indulge a sort of perpetual childishness. Yet this juvenile quality comes with none of the enthusiasm, vigor, and bold idealism of youth. For Tocqueville, aristocratic ambitions no less than aristocratic properties seem democratically partitioned into innumerable small holdings. In equality, the grand and often unruly loves of the few divide into the countless small wants of the many.[45] Mediocre even in his desires, passionless even in his hedonism, democratic man conceives of pleasure seeking only as the mundane pursuit of material well-being. He is too softened and dulled even to properly debauch himself—too decent to be really decadent. Having reduced living well to living easily, he "scarcely imagines" flourishing as anything more than "meeting the body's every need and attending to life's little comforts."[46] His uninspired indulgences take the form not of wild and squandering abandon but of the securing of every little convenience of domestic life. Even the wealthy fall short of aristocratic excess: "They gratify a host of small desires and avoid unruly grand passions. Thus they lapse into limpness rather than debauchery."[47] With the "prevalence of the bourgeois classes . . . over the aristocratic classes," postrevolutionary society thus ends up "more pacific" and "less proud," "calmer and duller, more tranquil and less heroic."[48]

And in this bourgeois limpness, democratic peoples actually grow dependent upon pleasure, ease, and comfort. They love little and hate little but feel themselves to need much. Even as their desires become increasingly petty, they are experienced as increasingly pressing; these individuals want only material well-being and believe themselves unable to do without such well-being. Consequently, Tocqueville predicts that democratic peoples will be in a sense conservative and virtuous, but for all the wrong reasons and in all the wrong ways. In their "spineless passion" for material well-being, in the "need to obtain it at any price," they will cling to any order that promises security, tranquility, and prosperity.[49] They will sacrifice everything for material well-being and will not sacrifice material well-being for anything. And this timid disposition interlaces with temperate virtues just as easily as it does with trivial vices. The "love of one's family, good morals, respect for religious belief, and even the lukewarm and regular practice of the established religion" combine with bourgeois materialism to render men incapable of great good as well as great evil—promoting honesty but forbidding heroism, limiting depravity but not baseness, and leading to orderliness out of enervation.[50] "I reproach equality," Tocqueville concludes, "not for leading men into the pursuit of forbidden pleasures but for absorbing them entirely in the search for permitted ones."[51] In their needy and respectable materialism, the children of the democratic revolution end up too well behaved—moderate to excess.

*From Aristocratic Pride to Democratic Domestication*

At the outset of *Democracy in America,* Tocqueville famously claimed that the work had been composed "in the grip of a kind of religious terror occasioned in the soul of the author by the sight of the irresistible revolution, which . . . continues to advance amid the ruins it has created."[52] By the second volume of *Democracy,* however, the source of his terror ceased to be the radicalization of the revolutionary disturbance: "Standing as I do in the midst of ruins, dare I say that what I fear most for generations to come is not revolution?"[53] Rather, he came to fear a society that would be without disturbance of any sort, peaceful out of lethargy and felt infirmity.[54] He foresees future generations abdicating the democratic place of power, confining themselves "ever more narrowly within the sphere of petty domestic interests" and there becoming "all but invulnerable to those great and powerful public emotions that roil nations but also develop and renew them."[55]

In Tocqueville's account, what we come to lack—despite our prosperity and enlightenment and political sovereignty—is the aristocrat's proud disposition. In one of the great ironies of history, the democratic revolution liberates people from the constraints and inequalities of the aristocratic order even as it undermines the aristocratic conception of the capacity, potency, and agency of man. After the revolution, we are free but believe ourselves powerless. We are no longer duty bound to commands from on high but respect ourselves so little as to believe that we are subject to even our basest impulses and instincts.

We might say that the tragic story of democracy Tocqueville presents runs from the "fall from the heights of limitless pride of 1789" to the equally limitless humility he saw spreading around him.[56] Pride is the virtue par excellence of aristocracy but also of the men who made the democratic revolution in France. In this sense, they were hybrids of aristocracy and democracy—quasi-aristocratic actors striving for democratic ends, uniting the disposition of nobility with the passion for liberty and a just equality. The epic event they produced was necessarily short and unnecessarily terrible, but it was also a moment of "incomparable beauty" and "admirable élan"—"of generosity, of enthusiasm, of virility, and of greatness."[57] It is true, Tocqueville writes, that the men of '89 displayed the aristocrat's erroneous excess of "confidence in the power that man exercises over himself and in that of peoples over their own destiny," but this was a "noble error."[58] The men who "made the Revolution . . . believed in themselves" and in "the power of man": "They readily became impassioned for his glory, they had faith in his virtue. They put in their own strength the prideful confidence that often leads to error but without which a people is capable of nothing but servitude."[59] Those who came after the revolutionary intersection of aristocracy and democracy tended toward the opposite extreme, which is no less an error but much less noble. "After having believed ourselves capable of transforming ourselves," Tocqueville regrets, "we believe ourselves incapable of reforming ourselves; after having had an excessive pride, we have fallen into a humility no less excessive; we believed ourselves capable of everything, today we believe ourselves capable of nothing."[60]

And it is from this crisis of confidence that democratic peoples might allow themselves to decline into a type of degradation historically unprecedented in its character and extent. In aristocratic times, Tocqueville argues, degradation was largely a matter of the physical conditions in which the lowest orders lived. One "saw inequalities and misery, but souls were not degraded," and so even within the "ignorant and coarse multitude one also found energetic passions, generous sentiments, deep beliefs, and uncultivated virtues."[61] In democratic times, the experience of degradation enters the soul. Consumed by fatigue and doubt, constantly pressed by a felt neediness and insignificance, honored by and honoring no one, even themselves, the inhabitants of democracy grow accustomed to self-contempt. The fact of oppression gives way in democratic modernity to the feeling of impotence, to being dispirited and devitalized, without power and so without "prideful confidence," capable of nothing but servitude.

Along these lines, the idea of man's domestication ultimately becomes the source of Tocqueville's religious terror. Democratic degradation takes the particular form of "tameness," Tocqueville explains, which is not the same as servility: "When we say servility we mean something cowardly, low, someone who has the *consciousness* of humiliation, of slavery, and submits himself with a view to the profit gained by servitude. . . . The almost universal disease of our time is different. *It does not seem shameful and seems almost natural to those who are struck by it. . . .* It is a kind of feeling of a domesticated animal."[62] Like the domesticated animal, uncaged but with broken spirit, democratic man assumes docility as his second nature. In a sense too civilized, democratic peoples sink below the level of humanity not as the wild beasts of anarchy but as a "flock of timid and industrious animals."[63] It is not man-as-wolf that we must guard against in democratic times but rather man-as-sheep.

Following upon the internalization of degradation, the democratic revolution might paradoxically end in what Tocqueville terms the "mild despotism" of a "tutelary power." In the completion of their domestication, democratic peoples welcome any protective power (Tocqueville focuses primarily upon the power of the centralized, bureaucratic, administrative state) that "provides for their security, foresees and takes care of their needs, facilitates their pleasures," and ultimately relieves them entirely of "the trouble of thinking and the difficulty of living."[64] They abdicate all that makes them human for the sake of an extreme sort of assisted living. Born in the epic struggle for liberty and equality, relaxing into a feeble and sleepy mediocrity, democratic peoples might thus end up actually embracing a degree of slavishness never before seen.

For Tocqueville, a simple sense of pride vaccinates us against this democratic despotism.[65] It is hardly an exaggeration to say that Tocqueville's theoretical project amounts to envisioning ways to synthesize in democratic times of mediocrity and docility some semblance of the pride that came as if naturally to the aristocratic actor. Perhaps the central moral imperatives of democratic times, he writes, is to give democratic peoples "a more ample idea of themselves and their species": "Humility is not healthy for them. What they lack most, in my opinion, is pride."[66] The difficulty, of course, lies in inspiring a noble posture in times of equality, after the collapse of the principle that made man's grandeur obvious within a social state that was a theater for acts of great passion, purpose, and potency. Democratic political action-in-association is for Tocqueville the primary vehicle for introducing a quasi-aristocratic manner of being into democratic society. It is by raising ourselves onto and acting on the political stage (whether to vote, build a school, or resist domination) that we might again honor ourselves and be honored by others.

*Domestication in America Today?*

Tocqueville thus takes his place in a critique of "the onslaught of economic man" that runs at least from Rousseau's depiction of bourgeois man through Nietzsche's last man and Marcuse's one-dimensional man to Benjamin Barber's infantilized adult.[67] Whether we are slouching toward a brave new world, amusing ourselves to death, being entranced by our narcissism and consumerism, and on and on, Tocqueville's condemnation of the "universal pettiness," "universal shrinkage," and "universal weakness" of modern man continues to resonate.[68] Whether he represents this as a decline into the childish infatuation with present pleasures, the flaccidity and impotence of old age, or the feminine aversion to hardship and preoccupation with domestic concerns of security and comfort, Tocqueville's depictions seem only to have increased in persuasiveness.[69] While the explanatory reasoning might vary from that of Tocqueville's, the fear of an encroaching domestication remains the same. From worries over the decay of manly assertiveness and "core convictions" to calls for the unruly disturbance of received authority in every walk of life, the specter of tutelary domestication sapping aristocratic or revolutionary possibilities lurks. From the militaristic fascination with the "experience of the front" and the violent reality of "the street" to the provocative celebration of nonconformity and subversive play, from every commercial with an absurdly oversized truck tearing across alkali salt flats and narrated by an unnaturally rugged voice demanding we "man up" to the comic book outlaw-heroism so ubiquitous across popular culture, a sort of bourgeois loathing of bourgeois tameness cries out. Perhaps the pervasiveness of this anxiety helps to explain Tocqueville's often noted appeal to both sides of the so-called culture wars.[70]

Tocqueville argues that this extreme degradation opens up the possibility of a centralization of power into one immense, regulating, coddling state—the vehicle of "tutelary power." This state power "would resemble paternal authority if only its purpose were the same, namely, to prepare men for manhood," Tocqueville writes. "But on the contrary," he continues, "it seeks only to keep them in childhood irrevocably. It likes citizens to rejoice, provided they think only of rejoicing."[71] While the vehicle of tutelary power is often conceptualized today in terms of the market rather than the government—in terms of omnipotent corporations rather than an omnipotent state, a slavish and base consumerism rather than bureaucratism, and a stultifying need for constant entertainment rather than for welfare—the fear that we are being seduced into and pacified by reality-free rejoicing remains largely unaltered.[72] We shall see the most extensive exploration of this new mode of tutelary power when we take up Sheldon Wolin's notions of "postmodern power" and "inverted totalitarianism."

At the same time, can we say that the undiminished force of Tocqueville's theorization of democratic degradation actually proves the limits of its current applicability? If we follow Tocqueville and say that once domesticated, we would not be ashamed or even conscious of our tameness, can we conclude that the ongoing resonance of Tocqueville's warning is itself evidence that we are at least not yet so degraded?[73] Perhaps some proof that we are not descending into either socialism or consumerism lies in the widespread and constant outcry that we are descending into socialism and consumerism. Perhaps some proof that we do not live in a "brave new world" lies in our continued recognition of that world as dystopian. In what follows I argue that Tocqueville himself (even if he is not always fully aware of it) identifies the particular stance from which we in democratic society "face the future with that salutary fear that keeps us vigilant and ready for battle."[74]

## III. Democratic Grandeur: Openness and the Absence of Hierarchy

*Literary Society and Commercial Society*

Thus far we have traced Tocqueville's logic regarding how the experience of degradation is transformed—and pushed to a new extreme—with the disintegration of the aristocratic principle of hierarchy and the rise of democratic equality. But is there a comparable sense of democratic grandeur? Can we speak of a democratic type of nobility and of the experience of elevation within equality, or is democratic society one-dimensional—reducible to "the obsession with material well-being and the congenital flabbiness of bourgeois civilization?"[75] At one end of the spectrum, the deprivations of the serf and the servant in aristocratic times are replaced by the anxieties of the bourgeois individual: even in his wealth he feels himself in constant need; even in his sovereignty he believes himself powerless and insignificant; even in his enlightenment he thinks himself mediocre and small, "lost in the crowd," as Tocqueville often puts it. At the other end of the spectrum, we have this comparison: in aristocratic times, ideas of the "dignity, power, and grandeur of man are widely entertained"; in democratic times, "an ideal and always fleeting perfection presents itself to the human mind."[76] Grandeur gives way to perfectibility. Democratic man imagines sinking below the level of humanity, but he also imagines rising above the level of humanity. The "common man" of democratic times routinely demands of himself that which even the loftiest aristocrats would have found incomprehensible. He is to be a sovereign individual and self-made man.

The full picture of democratic society that Tocqueville presents starts to come into focus here. If democracy's inhabitants are "entranced by a contemptible love of present pleasures," so too are they drawn to an "ideal and always fleeting perfection." To reduce democratic society to the former—to the bourgeois characteristics of the democratic type—is to reduce it to what it is not. In the full picture, democratic peoples' sense of the possible is as limitless as their neediness. Their humility is matched by their hubris, and their fear of insignificance by their passion for individuality. They are as audaciously innovative as they are timid and as adventurous as they are domestic—feeling restless, leaving home, dreaming and striving, narrating their lives as a series of transformative events, daily declaring their independence from even the slightest influence of others.

In Tocqueville's terms, democratic society is part "literary society" even as it is also part "commercial society."[77] Commercial society takes shape around the motive of self-interest, as determined by economic calculations oriented by the bourgeois desire for material profit, pleasure, and comfort. At the heart of literary society is the passion for revolutionary openness—for vital, dynamic, creative potentiality. Tocqueville describes the sense of grandeur intrinsic to the democratic social state as bound up with this literary standpoint. In democratic society, that which we honor, that which we find meaningful and motivating, issues from the revolutionary imagining of an always fleeting or fading state of openness—with the freedom of openness.

And it is from the standpoint of literary society, I suggest, that we still experience certain elements of commercial society as degrading—from the neediness of the consumer to the petty self-interest of the competitor. On the other hand, when commercial society incorporates attributes of literary openness, certain elements of commercial society are affirmed as manifestations of undomesticated freedom—from restless innovation and the open market to unfettered and even savage competition. At the same time, it is from the standpoint of commercial society, with its hardheaded and practical realism, that we scorn the flights of our literary imagination as just so much lofty rhetoric and inexperienced naiveté. Given the economics of our existence, we should just grow up and set aside our utopian projects and projections. It is, in other words, between these parallel lines of literary and commercial society that the democratic social state takes shape. Democratic man is as much artist as businessman, as idealistic as he is materialistic, as much a great dreamer of humanity as a self-interested profit-seeker.

In what follows, I highlight three aspects of Tocqueville's interpretation of the dualism of democratic society. First, this dualism of literary and commercial society is characteristic not only of early French democracy but also of democracy in America. Second, the elevation to which democratic peoples aspire is as limitless as the degradation they fear. And third, there is no intermediate form between these extremes of democratic grandeur and degradation—democratic man imagines himself as either creator or creature, master or puppet, and seldom as anything in between.

*Pilgrimage and Revolution: Making*
*an Idea Triumph in the World*

Tocqueville is perhaps best known for his remark that the disparate courses of American and French democracy follow from the fact that America was born in equality while France had to induce equality through revolution. But this should not obscure a basic similarity between the origins of democracy in France and America. In both countries, Tocqueville writes, democracy arose out of the attempt to ensure the victory of an idea in the world. While he fears that the democratic way of life will eventually narrow into a purely economic way of life, he argues that it issues from a sort of religious striving for transcendence.

Democratic society might culminate in pure materialism and a base pre-occupation with the body, but in France as in America, it originates with a visionary turn toward the unfettered life of the mind and the spirit.[78]

From the very first page of *Democracy I*, Tocqueville describes the advent of democracy in terms of the *disembodiment* of power. In feudal society, "power stemmed from a single source: ownership of land." The status and wealth of aristocracy is essentially "territorial," "materialized in earth," and "rooted in the soil." He continues, "It is not just privilege that establishes an aristocracy and not just birth that constitutes it; it is property in land, passed on from generation to generation." Society was opened to democratic equality with the disincorporation of the "well-springs of power and influence"—when "works of the intelligence became sources of power and wealth," when the clergy, lawyers, writers, and financiers ("men of letters," with their ranks "open to all") took up places of power in society and government. Where the place of power was once "incorporated into the earth and represented by it," then, in democratic society it is rendered immaterial and without place—"intangible and almost invisible."[79] Society takes on wholly new qualities of abstractness and impermanence with the dissolution of power-in-land concomitant to the collapse of hierarchy. In this sense, democracy is intelligible as the social state of openness as much as of equality.

Perhaps Tocqueville's finest description of the disembodiment of power characteristic of democratic times lies in his discussion of modern despotism: "Princes made violence a physical thing, but today's democratic republics have made it as intellectual as the human will it seeks to coerce." And where "despotism tried to reach the soul by striking crudely at the body," tyranny in democratic republics "ignores the body and goes straight for the soul"; no longer represented by "chains and executioners," the violence of despotic power is itself rendered abstract and almost invisible.[80]

The shift from the physical to the intellectual and spiritual orientation of society is exemplified for Tocqueville by the point of departure of American democracy. "It was by no means necessity" that compelled the Puritan flight from their "native land": "They left behind enviable social positions and secure incomes. They did not travel to the New World in the hope of improving their situation or enhancing their wealth. They tore themselves away from the pleasures of home in obedience to a purely intellectual need. They braved the inevitable miseries of exile because they wished to ensure the victory of *an idea.*"[81] Taken up with neither territory nor the pleasures of home, these decidedly undomesticated souls strove to establish a world apart from both aristocratic landedness and bourgeois materialism.

The French men of '89 similarly sought to ensure the victory of an idea in the world. Their means were necessarily different—revolution in the Old World versus pilgrimage to the New World—but their endeavor was in many ways the same. Puritanism, Tocqueville writes, "coincided with the most absolute democratic and republican theories."[82] As such, it "was almost as much a political theory as it was a religious doctrine."[83] The tenets of the men of '89 constituted a religious doctrine almost as much as a political theory. The Revolution, as Tocqueville put it, became "a new kind of religion."[84] Like the Protestant Reformation, the French Revolution served to erase "all the old frontiers from the map" and establish, "above all particular nationalities, a common *intellectual homeland* where men of all nations could become citizens."[85] The Revolution represented a sort of mass pilgrimage to this intellectual homeland, wherein "questions of territory gave way to questions of principle."[86] And like the Puritans, the apostles of revolution were willing to sacrifice material well-being and bodily concerns to reach this homeland. In its religiosity, the revolutionary rupture "tore them away from individual egoism, encouraged them to heroism and devotion, and often made them seem insensible to all the petty goods which we possess."[87]

Whether democracy emerged through pilgrimage or revolution, Tocqueville marvels at the grandeur of democracy's introduction into the world.[88] Whether as departure or rupture, the democratic event stands as a moment of sublime action to make a universal principle manifest in the world. Tragically, the revolution in France ate its young, as it were, largely because this sublime action proceeded absent any sort of practical political experience on the part its leaders. The men of '89 were heroes but not statesmen. This situation was due partly to the administrative centralization of the Old Regime, which monopolized the practice of politics, and partly to the uncompromising idealism of the men who made the revolution, which was willfully deaf to the lessons of experience. In America, conversely, the democratic revolution found its bearings because ideas were conditioned by political and even commercial experience; principle and practice were never entirely divorced from one another. Regardless, the original event by which democracy entered the world was a transcendent moment for all the world and all of history to behold.

As we have seen, Tocqueville's abiding fear is that modern peoples would cease to be moved by democracy's original intellectual principles and spiritual passions, even as they were endlessly agitated by the trivial pursuit of bodily well-being. Tocqueville presents this narrative of decline in microcosm, for instance, when he describes America as devoid of great politics and political parties. "The political parties that I call great are those that dedicate themselves more to principles than to their consequences; to generalities and not to particulars; to ideas and not to men," he writes. Such "parties generally have nobler features, more generous passions, more genuine convictions, and a franker, bolder manner than others." Bourgeois rather than quasi aristocratic or revolutionary, "minor parties are [in contrast] generally without *political faith*": "Because they do not feel ennobled and sustained by any great purpose, their character bears the stamp of self-interest." With the apparent alternatives of noble conflict and base calculation, Tocqueville writes that great parties "stand society on its head; minor parties agitate it": "Great parties tear society apart; minor parties corrupt it. . . . America has had great parties in the past, but today they no longer exist. This change has contributed greatly to its happiness but not to its morality."[89]

I want to suggest a different formulation, one wherein the sense of grandeur Tocqueville describes in democracy's points of departure, and which he associates with the "great parties" of early democracy, is a permanent and determinate aspect of the democratic social state. We perceive this permanence in that the feared or felt absence of principled convictions and passionate boldness in politics is represented as a narrative of decline and experienced as a loss. Even as democratic peoples are preoccupied by the pleasures of home, they continue to inhabit an intellectual homeland, established above all particularities, where the realities of territory give way to questions of principle. Whether born in revolution or in pilgrimage, the democratic project continues to be about ensuring the victory of an idea in the world.

Tocqueville himself occasionally offers this interpretation of democratic society, even as he perhaps more often adheres to the decline-and-fall narrative. In the former, pride, passion, heroism, and the experience of being ennobled by great purpose are not lost to universal banalization and degradation but are instead attached to the possibility of rupture with or departure from the world as it is. Here, democratic man is an imagining animal. Where normative meaning in aristocratic society took shape around the dichotomy of noble and base, normative meaning in democratic society takes shape in the tension between opening ourselves and the world to the democratic idea and collapsing into the domesticating pleasures of home—between the passion for revolution and passionless materialism.

*Ambitious Words: Democratic Abstraction and the Politics of the Impossible*

While it is true, Tocqueville writes, "that a part of the human mind is drawn to that which is limited, material, and useful, another part is naturally drawn upward to the infinite, the immaterial, and the beautiful."[90] The human mind has simultaneously economic and religious leanings. We have seen how the idea of degradation in democratic societies attaches to the belief that an exclusive preoccupation with the economic will come to dominate thought, entirely eliminating the religious. Tocqueville himself expresses the fear that the democratic mind might cease to be fully human, abdicating the human aspiration to transcendence and permitting pragmatic thought full reign. At times, though, he offers the opposite analysis, wherein the idea of grandeur toward which the human mind is drawn is not lost but radically expanded in democratic times. The writers of democracy, for instance, "are always pumping up their imaginations until they become so unreasonably inflated that they forsake the *great* for the *gigantesque*." Combining both strands, Tocqueville writes, "In democratic societies, each citizen is usually preoccupied with something quite insignificant: himself. If he lifts up his eyes, he sees only one immense image, that of society, or the even larger figure of the human race. He has either very particular and very clear ideas or very general and very vague notions; *there is nothing in between*."[91] In this characteristic formulation, democratization does not collapse the dimensionality of the human mind, which is still drawn upward toward the infinite and immaterial—the vast idea of humanity in this case.

Rather, both the down-turned sight and the upturned vision of the intellect tend toward unmediated extremes after the democratic revolution. I shall argue that this tendency of democratic thought—to eliminate everything in between the material and the ideal—as opposed to the tendency of thought to either exclusively abandon itself to economic calculations or lose itself in infinite abstractions, is at the center of Tocqueville's critique of the democratic way of life.

For Tocqueville, the democratic revolution and the works of religion mirror one another in proceeding by way of abstraction from all particulars. "Religions," Tocqueville writes, "consider man in himself, without regard for what laws, customs, and traditions of a country have added to the common base. . . . The rules of conduct which religions prescribe . . . are based on human nature itself." The more a religion maintains this "abstract and general character," the "more it spreads, despite differences of laws, climate, and men."[92] The "political gospel" of the revolution in France, with its rules of conduct prescribed by nature's truth of universal equality and the rights of man, similarly "considered the citizen in an abstract manner, outside of any particular society, . . . independently of time and place."[93]

The difference between religious and revolutionary modes of abstraction is as significant as their similarities, however. Where religion reserved its ultimate abstraction for the divide between this world and the next, between lower and higher, the revolution sought to realize its timeless and placeless aspirations in the here and now. With the revolution's goal of imminent transcendence, the "always to come" logic of the next world gave way to that of the next step—dynamic movement supplanted hierarchical order in salvational thought. The revolutionary project operated, in turn, through the near-total denial of the present world (the world of particular times and places) so as to enact a timeless archaic past/timeless utopian future of unfettered equality, liberty, and fraternity. The revolutionary rupture—whether conceptualized as toward pastoral origins or pristine newness—constituted as much a departure from the conventional world as an attempt to presently establish democratic ideas and principles. From "thick treatise to the popular song," Tocqueville writes of France, revolutionary thought went on a sort of mass pilgrimage from the city of experience to a city of imagination: "Above the real society, whose constitution was still traditional, confused, and irregular, where laws remained varied and contradictory, . . . there was slowly built an imaginary society in which everything seemed simple and coordinated, uniform, equitable, and in accord with reason. Gradually, the imagination of the crowd deserted the former to concentrate on the latter. One lost interest in what was, in order to think about what could be, and finally one lived mentally in the ideal city the writers had built."[94] At an "almost infinite distance" from practical experience, this "literary society" was engineered upon "pure theory," "abstract speculations," and that which filled "dreamers' imagination."[95]

As the French were striving through a program of revolution to ensure the victory of the dream, Tocqueville writes that even "political life was violently driven back into literature."[96] Where political affairs had been conducted by men of action par excellence (aristocrats and statesmen), the politics of revolutionary France was conducted by "men of letters" (writers, philosophers, lawyers, economists). In Tocqueville's telling, these ivory-tower intellectuals' "profound practical ignorance" was matched only by their "taste for the original [and] ingenious." Laboring to put into action a "literary politics" full of "general expressions, abstract terms, ambitious words, and literary turns of phrase," they were impractical as much out of a "contempt for existing facts" as out of inexperience.[97] At once beautiful and terrible, the result is what Tocqueville calls "the politics of the *impossible*"—perfectly ordered, wholly moral and just, universal in scope, purified of any departure from principle by perpetual revolution, constitutively uncompromising, and willfully unrealistic.[98]

With its ambitious words—in the audacity of its abstractions and its sense of impossible possibility—the revolution of which democracy was born founds a pride and purpose as expansive as the neediness Tocqueville saw in democracy's future. This is the society and politics of "I have a dream." In times of hierarchical order, pride attached to the lofty station of man, which presented itself to the eye in the pinnacle figure of the aristocrat. In times of democratic openness, with the collapse of hierarchical order, pride attaches to the (re)creative capacity of man, which presents itself to the mind in the phenomenon of revolution. The aristocrat, in his recognized superiority, judges himself to stand atop society and creation; the democrat, even in his recognized equality, imagines himself to rise above society and creation. Man as commander is succeeded by man as creator. Where the pride of the aristocrat followed from his capacity for action in the world, the pride of the democratic revolutionary follows from his capacity for imaginative abstraction from the world—with the thought of breaking with and remaking the world. Tocqueville calls this the "pride and absolute spirit of makers of systems."[99] Aristocratic elevation is not lost through democratization, then, but rather outstripped by the idea of transcending or overpowering fettering reality—from nobility to perfectibility in "a world astonishingly open."[100]

Thus, while democratic modernity in France might culminate in the timid flock animals of socialism, for Tocqueville, the revolutionary opening of the world to democratic principles was ushered in by no less than a "cult of blind audacity."[101] Indeed, it "became impossible to say what unheard of audacities the minds of the innovators would be led to, liberated at one stroke from all the limits that religion, custom, and law impose on the human imagination."[102] The long narrative arc of the democratic character in France ranged from the heights of the revolutionary creator to the encroaching degradations of the materialistic creature. The story of democracy in France is one of the departure from the scene of great men, great parties, great principles, great passions, great revolutions, and all those quasi-religious aspirations and abstractions of literary society. With the passing of the revolutionary moment, the sensible, practical, unprincipled mediocrity of commercial society was the best that remained. The absurdity of the revolution of 1848 and its aftermath confirmed in Tocqueville's eyes the coming of something much worse.

Tocqueville's interpretation of democracy in America and of democracy as such, however, does not exactly conform to this narrative of democracy in France. Rather, while the equality of conditions renders the *occurrence* of great revolutions rare in established democracies, it would appear that the *passion* for revolution—for the openness inscribed in democracy's revolutionary heritage—might endure. The idealizing imagination might endure. Here, the collapse of hierarchy generates a permanent belief in limitless possibility and indefinite perfectibility as much as a sense of stultifying mediocrity. Tocqueville represents these "literary" qualities as abundant in the America of his time and in the concept of democracy, if not to the unhinged extent to which they were present in the France of his past. Extending Tocqueville's analysis, I shall suggest that democratic society has not taken shape in the arc from revolutionary audacity to bourgeois (much less socialistic) tameness but rather is constituted in permanent tension between these polar opposites. The democratic character sees himself as at once revolutionary creator and materialistic creature.

## The Poetry of Democracy

The contrast Tocqueville draws between French and American democracy is well known. The former is a social state wherein democratic equality is alloyed with the alien presence of violent revolution—warped by first the act and then the memory of revolutionary conflict. The latter is a social state of untroubled equality and so of democracy relatively closer to what Tocqueville considers its natural form. France is a theater of democratic revolution, and America of democracy as such.

The contrast of French and America democracy would seem to map on to the dichotomy of literary and commercial society. As Tocqueville describes it, American life is directed not by utopian men of letters, with their quasi-religious abstractions and reckless idealism, but by pragmatic men of business—makers of things rather than of systems. The settled equality Americans take for granted levels their gaze toward the particular and material things of this world. Absent grand ambitions, Americans—and eventually "all men who live in democratic times"—acquire the "habits of the industrial and commercial classes": "Their minds take on a serious, calculating, and positive cast. They gladly turn away from the ideal and aim for some visible nearby goal."[103] Where France has economists and political philosophers (physiocrats and philosophes), America has businessmen and politicians.

A number of intertwined contrasts follow. Where revolution gave French thought an ideological and uncompromising bent foreign to the egalitarian mind, American thought is empirical and practical—it never has "so blind a faith in the correctness and absolute truth of any theory." Where the idea of revolutionary rupture moved the French to abandon the real world of facts and experience for a world of "general and eternal laws" that "encompass the entire human race," such sweeping generali-

ties "terrify" the Americans, who are "accustomed to concrete calculations" and prefer "common sense" to "genius." In turn, where French
thought is always lunging via abstraction toward universality and so
toward uniformity and systemization, Americans "honor practice above
theory" and are always "correcting . . . ideas through experience." Finally, where revolutionary democracy is inherently nonterritorial and
expansionistic, Tocqueville describes American democracy as utterly local (only at great pains made national). And these qualities of the businessman order other spheres of life beyond the economic. For instance,
scientific study in America conforms to these commercial norms, with
its preoccupation with "the tangible and the real in all things." Tocqueville notes that "in America, the purely practical part of the sciences is
admirably cultivated," while almost no one "devotes himself to the essentially theoretical and abstract aspects of human knowledge."[104]

Democracy is not without its own literary qualities, though. In the full
picture Tocqueville presents, the dualism of literary society and commercial society is hardly less characteristic of American democracy and
of democracy in general than of democracy in France. Americans are as
idealistic as they are pragmatic, they are as taken with the immaterial
and infinite as they are inveterately materialistic, and they are nearly as
liable to lose themselves in vast abstractions as in practical details and
particular facts. And Americans are not just conservative and rooted in
the local; they "have always demonstrated a decided taste for the sea"
and they "already reach well beyond" the limits of their "territory." Indeed, nowhere does the American "perceive the limits that nature may
have imposed on man's efforts," and this renders him "ardent in his desires, enterprising, adventurous, and above all innovative." Amid the
"universal movement that dominates everything else in the United
States," an "American experiences all life as a game of chance, a time of
revolution, a day of battle."[105] The difference between the French men of
'89 and the average American seems here more of degree—or of the direction of revolutionary exertions—than of type.

We have seen how democracy's point of departure in American was
the attempt to ensure the victory of an idea in the world, just as in
France. To some extent, the impossibility of ensuring this victory in
France except through revolutionary rupture was contingent upon French

social and political conditions—the old world had to be erased to make way for the democratic idea.[106] American democracy took shape differently because it did not need to undergo the terrible labor of revolution; born equal into the new world, it need not be born again. At the same time, though, Tocqueville's interpretation of democracy in America demonstrates that the passion for revolutionary rupture is not merely contingent upon French circumstances. Rather, this passion is constitutive of the democratic way of life as such. The grand abstraction of universal equality permanently seats the schism of "literary" idealism and "commercial" realism at the center of democracy, just as Christianity takes shape around the schism of this world and the next.[107] The passion for revolutionary abstraction from the here and now is no less basic to democracy than the desire for material well-being in the present moment. The democratic revolution, we might say, is as temporally unbounded as it is territorially unbounded—as recurrent in time as it is expansive in space.

However much Americans—and the democratic type in general—may prefer the commercial to the literary, Tocqueville makes clear that when they do "dream . . . of what will be," their "imagination knows no bounds": "It stretches and grows beyond all measure." This becomes amply evident when surveying the poetry natural to democratic times. Poetry, on Tocqueville's account, "is the search for and depiction of the ideal."[108] As such, the poetry of democracy highlights the tendencies of the idealizing imagination in the democratic social state more generally. To study democratic society's poetry is to study its normative dimensionality.

On first take, it seems democracy is without sources of poetry. Democratic pragmatism and materialism turns thought toward "conceiving the useful and representing the real," while egalitarian homogeneity "not only discourages portrayal of the ideal but also reduces the number of objects to be portrayed." The age of feudal aristocracy, principled upon hierarchy and based in the locality of landedness, was one of constitutive diversity. This deeply ingrained particularity was reflected, for instance, in the religious practices of aristocratic peoples. What seized the imagination was not the axial resemblance of the faiths but the irreducible differences between the faiths. Consequently, religion in aristocratic times overflowed with all sorts of "supernatural beings," "secondary agents," and "intermediate powers between God and man."[109] The distant grandeur of these various figures, along with the only slightly less distant grandeur of the aristocrat himself, offered the poets of feudal aristocracy a rich and diverse pallet. So what is left amid universal mediocrity and uniformity for the poets of equality to idealize? The very vastness—the unbounded universality—that opens up before the imagination with the democratic abstraction. The democratic sense of grandeur, as Tocqueville puts it, forsakes "the great for the gigantesque."

Initially, this awakens democratic peoples to inanimate nature: "As they lost sight of heroes and gods, they sought first to depict rivers and mountains." Ultimately, though, material nature proves insufficiently oceanic to spur the democratic imagination, which drives on to the *exclusively* immaterial and infinite. In the idea of "indefinite perfectibility," for example, democracy "opens the future" to poetry. Nobility is supplanted by perfectibility, and the heritable past by an indefinite future, as outlets of imagination. Further, the very "similitude of individuals, which makes each of them an unsuitable subject of poetry, enables poets to embrace all in a single image"; thereafter the "nation as a whole" serves as a subject of the ideal. The figurehead of aristocratic command is supplanted by the powerful abstract collective—the father figure by the fraternal. Democratic abstraction does not halt with the nation or the state, however. These ideas fall short, in their remaining particularity and territoriality, of the democratic imagination's reach, which drives on to the idea of merging all nations into "one vast democracy." The democratic abstraction makes it possible for the first time in history, Tocqueville writes, to envision the human race as a single whole. The poets of aristocracy "never *dared* to embrace the destinies of all mankind," looking up only so far as to the relatively trivial actions of passing aristocrats and their particular figures of faith. The democratic imagination is not so timid: "As individuals look beyond their own country and at last begin to perceive humanity as such, God reveals ever more of himself to the human spirit in his full and entire majesty." If belief in intermediate divinities fades, democratic peoples "are nevertheless apt to form a far vaster idea of Divinity itself and to see its intervention in human affairs in a new and brighter light."[110]

Tocqueville thus concludes, "Equality does not destroy all the subjects of poetry; it reduces their number but enlarges their scope." The democratic universe depopulates the heavens and the earth of great poetical figures, leaving nothing in between the insignificant individual facts of reality, including the individual, and the vast timeless and placeless panoramas of oceanic nature, open future, global humanity, and the fundamental Divine. Far from collapsing the poetic into the prosaic, the egalitarian social state pushes these categories toward unprecedented extremes—the sublime and the banal. What remains to democratic thought and belief are inconsequential particulars, meaningful only in gigantesque sums, and the view from nowhere, representations of essentially unrepresentable sum and scope, a grandeur beyond grand. What seizes the idealizing imagination is a sort of *formlessness*—of being without determinate, finite, limiting territory, whether conceptually present to the mind in terms of nature, future, humanity, or God. Opposite ends of the circle, uniformity and formlessness are the promise of equality's revolution. Here again we see the movement toward disembodiment at the heart of the democratic revolution. "Democratic poets will always seem petty and cold," for instance, "if they venture to bestow *corporeal form* on gods, demons, and angels and bring them down from heaven to vie for the earth." Tocqueville continues, "But if they seek to link the great events they narrate to God's general design for the universe [as does Tocqueville himself], and to reveal the sovereign master's *thought* without showing his *hand*, they will be admired and understood, because the imagination of their contemporaries naturally follows this same route."[111]

In the end, Tocqueville writes, the confluence of these tendencies turns the idealizing imagination of democratic modernity toward its ultimate content: man—that is, democratic man, who is taken to be man as such, "apart from time and country and set before nature and God." The human being, individual man, the particular sign of democratic humanity: here is the pinnacle figure of democratic abstraction, of the revolutionary aspiration to imminent transcendence. At once universal and unique, the self supplants the aristocrat as the centerpiece of poetical imaginings. Insignificant as embodied fact of the world, wholly significant as particular sign of humanity, the individual, like God, must be explored in depth, in its oceanic and fundamental nature, before or beyond corporeal form, to rouse the poetics of democracy. The portrayal of the ideal here requires "sounding the depths of [man's] immaterial nature," delving "beneath the surface revealed by the senses to catch a glimpse of the soul itself."[112] Contra the bourgeois individual, the democratic individual is a world apart from materialistic or superficial—the seeker of souls and soul mates.

In representing the ideal, then, a democratic poetry of the impossible accompanies the democratic "politics of the impossible." "Finding no more material for the ideal in what is real and true, poets give up on truth and reality altogether," just as did France's revolutionary men of letters.[113] Democratic idealization is drawn away from the corporeality of the present moment and toward the irreducibly immaterial and infinite. The ideal is supplanted by the utopian. We might follow Tocqueville's reasoning beyond his immediate interpretation, to surmise that the moment even the vast abstractions of democratic modernity (nature, nation, state, humanity, divinity) are given representative form—as soon as they are objectified, conventionalized, and domesticated by definitional borders and boundaries—the idealizing imagination will be left cold and turn elsewhere. Public opinion will be inviolable when voiced from nowhere by "the people" or as "common sense" but will lose its normative weight the moment it is depicted in poll form. State and market "forces" will stand above question until they are materialized in actual institutions, corporations, and persons. The divine will be sapped of its grandeur the moment it is made manifest in particular religious form.[114] In this way, the poetry of democracy drives ceaselessly onward toward the fundamentally unrealizable in its representations of the ideal; that which is realized ceases to be ideal. There is a sort of revolutionary contempt for existing facts that is intrinsic to the idealizing imagination of democracy.

Democracy, then, is far from without a poetical sense of grandeur. The world as experienced in equality, with its correlates of materialism and mediocrity, is lost to poetry. But the world as imagined with the collapse of hierarchical absolutes, with its correlate sense of openness, of being without form or limits, presents a vast canvas for democratic poetry. Indeed, forsaking the great for the gigantesque, the idealizing imagination is animated by ideas so sublime that the poetry of aristocracy seems petty and absurd by comparison. These poles of equality—of prosaic flatness and poetical openness, of uniformity and formlessness, of perceiving oneself as lost in the crowd and as standing as the particular sign of universal humanity—give the democratic social state its dimension-ality, as with nobility and baseness in the aristocratic social state.

Tocqueville thus offers both of the following formulations: "Equality does not destroy the imagination . . . , but it does limit it, forcing it to hew close to the earth as it flies"; and "I have no fear that the poetry of demo-cratic peoples will prove timid or quite mundane. I worry, rather, that it will constantly be losing itself in the clouds and end up depicting worlds that exist only in the imagination." This same bipolarity is reflected in democratic language. With their sober, scientific, commercial cast of mind, democrats favors "plain language" to "bandying about big words." These are the single-syllable words of pragmatic communication, used free of airs and formalities and employed only when even simpler signals do not suffice. At the same time, democratic peoples have "a taste and often a passion for general ideas" and "vagueness," which "manifests itself in democratic language through the constant use of generic terms and ab-stract words."[115] These are ambitious words—the meaning of which transcends their word forms—that struggle to express ideas beyond what language can convey. In these things Tocqueville does not contradict himself. Rather, he envisions the dualism of the democratic social state.

The whole image of democratic society comes into view in a minor but telling chapter from *Democracy II:* "Why Americans Build Such Insignifi-cant and Such Great Monuments at the Same Time." In democratic times, "man's imagination shrinks when he thinks of himself as an individual and expands without limit when he thinks of the state." Reflecting these poles of the imagination in their works, democratic peoples "produce a host of trifling works but also erect a small number of very great monu-ments. Between these two extremes . . . there is nothing."[116]

### The Specter and Prospect of Humanity

Tocqueville is less than enraptured by the literary abstractions that cap-ture the democratic imagination. At times he seems as wary of the dem-ocratic sense of grandeur as of democratic degradation. Interpreters of Tocqueville have long emphasized his warning that individuality and diversity might drown in the experience of the limitlessness that is char-acteristic of democratic times. Forsaking the great for the gigantesque, the individual feels insignificant before the very vastness he idealizes.[117] This phenomenon manifests itself in a variety of ways—as the sense of being "lost in the crowd" amid the monolithic sameness of mass society, as gravitational peer-pressure conformity to public opinion, as the tendency to drain the world of its particular qualities and reduce human perception to quantification and human judgment to accountant calculation: in all things, the more the better—the greater number as the greater as such. Tocqueville fears above all that the democratic abstraction paves the way for centralization and the abdication of individual rights to the "the social power."[118] Transcending territoriality, the democratic movement arcs from the local particularities of feudalism to the uniformity and centralization of socialism.

For all of his praise of the principled audacity and selfless abandon of the revolutionary men of '89, Tocqueville argues that their beautiful abstractions and universal systems only streamlined things for further concentrations of power. Perhaps paradoxically, the passion for revolutionary transcendence fosters centralization, no less than does the passionless need for material well-being. In contrast, Tocqueville praises Americans' clear-eyed if shortsighted conduct of "public business." Close to home, experienced directly rather than muddled by all sorts of speculative representations, American politics "force each citizen to be concerned with government in a practical way, [and to] moderate the excessive taste for general theories in political matters that equality encourages."[119] Carrying the pragmatic, utilitarian, empirical caste of mind of commercial society into political life, Americans check the centralizing bent of the poetical imagination by virtue of firsthand and hardheaded experience.

It would be a mistake, however, to take Tocqueville's wariness as an outright condemnation of democracy's ambitious words and ideas. The "passion for general ideas" follows from both the "inherent virtues and defects" of the democratic mind, and the "great merit . . . as well as the great weakness" of democratic language lies in the "constant use of generic terms and abstract words."[120] Regarding its defects, democratic abstraction leads to obscurity of thought and vagueness of language.[121] More troubling, the passion for general ideas threatens the notion of human agency. In aristocratic times, the "world stage" was occupied by a small number of "leading actors"; the "influence that a single individual [could] exert" upon the human epic was obvious to all.[122] In democratic times, "when all citizens are independent of one another and each of them is weak," society "seems to proceed on its own owing to the free and spontaneous cooperation of all its members." Tocqueville continues, "This naturally prompts the mind to look for the general reason that could have struck so many intellects at once and simultaneously reoriented them all."[123] It becomes, in turn, tempting to believe that human action in general "is not voluntary, and that societies are unwittingly obedient to a superior force, which dominates them"; any cause "vast enough to apply to millions of people at once and strong enough to move them all in the same direction might easily seem irresistible."[124] The aristocratic world of commanding authorities gives way to a democratic world of controlling powers, against which resistance is futile. The stage exit of the aristocratic actor clears the way to explaining human action in terms of the vast, unseen, and impersonal imperatives of, for instance, "the nature of races" or "the spirit of civilization"—of the course of history, fate or chance, subconscious human instinct, choice standardized as generic rationality, the invisible hand of market forces, evolution's genetic programming, and other such general, spontaneous, and insurmountable ordering powers.[125] Sounding the depths of man's immaterial nature in search of the soul, we discover the determinate universal constant that we are, in fact, "98% chimp."[126] In such ways, the grand abstractions of the democratic imagination can be as degrading as the need for comfort, security, and pleasure. Democratic grandeur is not necessarily elevating. The democratic individual might submit to the thought that he "has no power over either himself or his surroundings," that his influence over events and even himself amounts to a drop in the oceanic.[127] Transcending limits and forms, overawed, he stands as free as he is powerless. Lost in the gigantesque, confined to the fatal circle of his own felt weakness, though once he dreamed of transforming the world, he here concedes that he cannot even reform himself. A "false and cowardly" principle issuing from the idealizing imagination, determinism joins socialism as the twin aspects of unwitting obedience—of democratic tameness.[128]

At the same time, though, Tocqueville maintains that the abstract thought and language of democracy captures as much as it obscures of what is true, good, and beautiful. First, general causes really do "explain more things in democratic centuries than in aristocratic ones, and particular influences explain less." Tocqueville identifies his use of the word *equality* "in an absolute sense" and "without applying it to something in particular" as an example of democratic abstraction. Second, for all his praise of Americans' business-minded tendency to check general theories against experience and grand principles through practical application, Tocqueville writes that if "the sources of our enlightenment were ever to die out, they would dwindle gradually," as we "limit ourselves to applications, [and] . . . lose sight of principles." While dissolving individuality and agency into the protean abstractions of democracy "would soon paralyze the new societies and reduce Christians to Turks," abandoning those abstract principles and theories in an exclusive preoccupation with practical concerns would lead to "the singularly static character of the Chinese mind."[129]

Tocqueville's full ambivalence comes into view in his discussion of that vastest of democratic generalities: humanity. In times of equality, man "sees around him only people more or less like himself"; for that reason, "he cannot think of any segment of humanity without enlarging and expanding his thought until it embraces the whole of mankind."[130] Tocqueville fears the swallowing up of individuality in this universal resemblance, with the reductive/expansive power of abstraction dissolving particular identities, leaving only the homogeneous generality of "the mass." At the same time, the recognition of human resemblance proves no less than providential, opening consciousness to generalizations like human rights and human dignity.[131] In predemocratic times, people simply could not conceive of the noble truth that a "common thread" ties "all together into the vast bosom of the human race."[132] Again associating democratic and Christian abstractions, Tocqueville writes that "it took the coming of Jesus Christ to make people understand that all members of the human race are by nature similar and equal."[133]

I suggest, then, that Tocqueville is concerned less with the abstract dimension of democratic thought and speech as such than with the tendency to expand this dimension to exclusive extremes. He never denies that the egalitarian generalization advances the highest human calling of freedom. For instance, the recognition of human equality and resemblance, and so of the universal rights of man, at long last exposed the practice of slavery as an ignoble lie—grossly unjust and based on false doctrines. But this very consciousness of similarity, when taken to extremes, threatens to annihilate the individual and his rights, culminating in the idea of humanity as herd, as one vast, undifferentiated multitude. The prospect of slavery is rehabilitated, expanded beyond all previous forms and limits, and insinuated into the soul itself as domestication, as the individual's loss of humanity. The very condition that enables us to envision totalizing freedom enables us to foresee a totalizing slavery.

*Conclusion: Principle versus Practice in Democratic Society*

Perhaps above all, Tocqueville views the transition to democratic modernity as a transformation in the way we imagine human degradation and grandeur. In his account, degradation in democratic times takes shape as domestication. Tocqueville associates this dissolution of human dignity with the felt powerlessness and insignificance of insurmountable mediocrity and overawing vastness, with the diminution of pride, passion, and purpose, and with the overriding need for material well-being. Compared with the proud aristocrat and the audacious revolutionary, the democratic individual is petty, timid, and soft—self-centered but without the resources for self-respect. At the opposite end of the spectrum, the democratic sense of grandeur takes shape as an idea we struggle to put into words, a sense of formlessness and limitlessness perhaps best represented as "openness." Where modern conceptions of degradation follow from the experience of equality, openness and its concomitant notions of freedom issue from the revolutionary advent of equality, when the hierarchical absolute gave way to the democratic abstraction. The democrat draws his immense pride, passion, and purpose from the aspiration to openness, which imbues the idealizing imagination with thoughts of infinite possibility, indefinite perfectibility, and imminent transcendence.

What Tocqueville shows is that both aspects of democratic society—both its characteristic degradation and grandeur—are principled upon equality, which can be divided out as the dual presence of equality and absence of hierarchy. The leveling of equality is conjoined to the openness of this absence of hierarchy, domestication to liberation. In turn, neither element of democratic society can overcome its other. That which makes indefinite perfectibility conceivable at the same time makes indefinite corruption conceivable. The correlate of the transcendent possibility we idealize is the bottomless need we fear possible. The movement toward one extreme conceptually enables a countermovement toward the other extreme. Thus is Tocqueville's fear of our finally succumbing to tutelary domestication not warranted by his own analysis. Given the normative dimensionality of the democratic regime, the specter of slavery welcomed into the soul is better understood as a *constitutive insecurity* of democracy. Being tamed by tutelary power—whether political, social, religious, economic, or otherwise—is the mode of dehumanization we believe most likely and perhaps in a way most tempting (as opposed to, for instance, evil's seductions). But as the antithesis of openness, with its promise of revolutionary liberation and sovereign independence, this unwitting docility defines our condition as our paramount anxiety rather than as present reality. Indeed, that Tocqueville's fears remain our own attests to the point that we remain not so shamelessly tamed.

Envisioned as a whole, then, the democratic way of life is ordered and animated by a permanent, fundamental tension between the fear of domestication and the aspiration to openness—between sinking below and rising above the human condition. After the democratic revolution, we foresee the collapse of society into the purely economic—into petty self-interest and competition, shallow materialism and consumerism, the meaningless pursuit of bodily pleasures, and so forth: all the world reduced to Wall Street, Hollywood, and Las Vegas. At the same time, *for the same reason* and to a *mirror extreme*, we envision a sort of quasi-religious pilgrimage of moral and spiritual transcendence, abstracting from the fetters of all thing material, bodily, and territorial: all the world democratized, freedom's reign established over global humanity. The character of democratic consciousness and society is captured less by either extreme than by the simultaneous tendency toward both extremes. Here we have the full portrayal of life in democracy: "The same equality that allows each citizen to entertain vast hopes makes all citizens individually weak. It limits their strength in every respect, even as it allows their desires to expand." The same equality "drives men forward and at the same time holds them back, spurs them on yet keeps them tethered to the earth."[134]

No less than in Tocqueville's time, this polarity shapes the faiths and works of democratic society today. Consider, for instance, that greatest of monuments to democratic modernity: the American Dream. Being in essence abstract and having a global constituency, the dream testifies to democracy's dualism—the vision of imminent transcendence, of movement away from home to wide-open lands of new beginnings and limitless possibilities (westward expansion across the plains, which at once signals the return to pristine nature and the drive toward the future), of pilgrimage to the all-inclusive land of an idea, the land of liberty (immigration), a vision that is always just on the verge of being lost once and for all or collapsing into the American Nightmare of unfettered materialism, petty decadence, and docile conformity (the dream of hitting the open road reduced to one of car and home ownership). As another iteration of dualism—one which is well situated to exemplify the democratic affinity for extreme and mutually exclusive notions of degradation and grandeur—consider the debate surrounding today's so-called genetics revolution. We hear that it is possible "to view genetic engineering as the ultimate expression of our resolve to see ourselves astride the world, the masters of our nature."[135] Molecular biologist Robert L. Sinsheimer plainly states the Promethean resolve of the genetics revolution: "As we enlarge man's freedom, we diminish his constraints and that which he must accept as given. . . . We can be the agent of transition to a whole new pitch of evolution. This is a cosmic event."[136] Ethicist Julian Savulescu offers an even more immoderate formulation of this revolutionary aspiration. With our newfound biotechnological powers, the "next stage of human evolution may be rational evolution, where we select children who not only have the greatest chance of surviving . . . , but who also have the greatest opportunities to have the best lives."[137] Evolution need no longer be a pitch of the die at all. The choice is ours: "the natural lottery or rational choice."[138] Savulescu concludes that "our future is now in our hands, whether we like it or not"—failure to exert ourselves over nature "is to be responsible for the results of the natural lottery."[139]

Even as innovations in biotechnology allow us to entertain vast and lofty hopes, however, we apparently take ourselves to be ever more firmly tethered to the earth. Regarding statements like Savulescu's, political philosopher Michael Sandel worries that the power to rewrite our genetic constitutions will produce an overawing extension of responsibility. As we "attribute less to chance and more to choice," he argues that "humility gives way [and] responsibility expands to daunting proportions."[140] Yet, as new modes of genetic mapping and brain imaging have recently seized the imagination, the very concept of personal moral responsibility is called into question.[141] We have the power to reprogram our nature, but we are powerless to escape our material hardwiring. We slide between the images of ourselves as creature and as creator—far beyond the capacity of the aristocratic commander, as the masters and originators of the reality we inhabit, and as puppets on evolutionary strings.[142] As Tocqueville theorized, we paradoxically take ourselves to be without power and without limits, in a wholly determined world where everything is becoming possible. Amid the "cosmic event" of the genetics revolution, we think ourselves always on the brink of both rising above and sinking below the level of humanity—of collapsing into dehumanization and leaping into the "posthuman." In a single stroke, the lines are blurred between man and God, and man and animal.

To return to the question with which we began: how might we understand the simultaneous waxing of democratic principles and waning of democratic political practices? Building upon Tocqueville's works, I argue that this contrary movement is inscribed in the democratic social state itself. It issues from the more general divergence of the "literary world" of ideas and speech (which takes shape in a sort of this-worldly transcendence of the here and now) and the "commercial world" of action (which is reduced to purely economic rationalities and formations). When we think and talk about democracy, we are prone to flights of poetical idealism. We dream of a world reordered exclusively in accordance with democratic principles—a world of openness and revolution, of universal freedom-in-equality, where anything we can imagine is possible. As I take up in the following two chapters, this open world seems as natural, as given and inevitable, as the hierarchical world once seemed. Any sort of authoritarian walling up of self, society, or world is presumed destined for the ash heap of history. At the same time, we are prone to cynically degrade the prosaic world within which we act—whether politically or otherwise—to the status of wholly unprincipled. Within the confines of the material world, the "real world" where power rules, we are experienced enough to know that ideas are decidedly immaterial, talk is cheap, deliberation is a naive waste of time, and arguments are just "spin" meant to manipulate. This sort of world seems natural too—real, factual, given, and inescapable. Taken together, the victory of democratic principles seems as inevitable as the basic practices of democracy seem impossible. The key here is that we are not just exceptionally cynical, or exceptionally idealistic, but that we are both exceptionally cynical and exceptionally idealistic, and for the same reason. Limitless idealism and bottomless cynicism are intrinsically linked, polar opposite expressions of the same faith in equality. Our cynicism becomes fully intelligible not as disappointment at failing to achieve our ideals but as the worldly articulation of an idealism principled upon openness.

With this dualism of the world we imagine and the world we experience—of thought and action, principle and practice—democratic society harbors two polar opposite characters. There is the man of business, the executive decider, the practical man of action who just gets things done. And there is the man of letters, the dreamer and artist who speaks for hope and change and the promise of future generations. What is most revealing of democratic society, though, is not the simultaneous predominance of these two types but that their synthesis or mediation appears inconceivable today. The dreamer is all principle and no practice, the businessperson is all practice and no principle, and there is nothing significant in between. In relation to the latter, the former seems uncompromising and/or impotent; in relation to the former, the latter seems calculating and corrupt.[143] The choice is between meaninglessness and powerlessness. The blending of principle and practice by the statesmen gives way to the split between the sell-out politician just "playing politics" to gain power and the moralistic and/or naive political preacher.[144]

Principled upon openness, then, democracy is essentially a politics of the impossible. A contempt for existing facts, including the facts of actual democracy, is not contingent upon conditions and events but intrinsic to democratic society. To give openness form, to embody it in our practices and conventions, is to place limits upon and so degrade openness. In a sort of politics of buyer's remorse, any determinate representation bounds and domesticates revolutionary possibility. We can never quite realize the victory of the democratic idea in this world; by remaining a world apart, democracy's victory is assured. Further, progress toward the idea is potentially experienced as regression. Tocqueville famously wrote that the "inevitable evil that one bears patiently seems unbearable as soon as one conceives the idea of removing it."[145] In times of democratic openness, we conceive the idea of removing every evil, of indefinitely perfecting the world and ourselves. Those evils that inevitably remain—those inequalities, injustices, immoralities, and limits to our freedom—are more frustrating precisely because they seem more contingent and slight. In Tocqueville's words, "The weight, although less heavy, seems then all the more unbearable."[146] As openness is thought natural, given and inevitable, every restriction, boundary, and material necessity is thought aberrant, arbitrary, and so intolerable. The persistence of imperfectability is taken not as a meaningful aspect of the human condition but as something simply inexplicable and absurd. If there is a cure out there to every sickness, how do we make sense of our continuing ill health? The politics of the impossible is, in turn, also a politics of impatience. Sensitive to every limitation, flaw, and deficiency, we may see even the steady democratization of America as the steady transformation of America into a more authoritarian, antidemocratic society.

CHAPTER **2**

# Civilization without the Discontents

*Tocqueville on Democracy as the Social State of Nature*

> Democratic peoples often hate the repositories of central power, but they always love the power itself.
>
> —Tocqueville, *Democracy in America*

## I. Freedom, Equality, Power

*Freedom's Meaning: Mastery and Escape*

In America today, freedom has taken on two polar opposite meanings. This is the conclusion put forward recently by moral psychologist C.Fred Alford, based upon a series of interviews he conducted with primarily young Americans. Alford finds that most of the people he spoke with associate freedom with "the possession of money and power, or they devalue freedom compared to money and power." The formal freedoms embodied in the Bill of Rights, for example, are largely dismissed as "effete" and "mere symbols"; "real freedom" requires "total control," and control requires power and money. Being permitted to say what one wants means little relative to the power to do what one wants. Alford writes, "The view of freedom that comes closest to that of young people is the ancient Greek view of freedom as *autokratôr.* . . . The difference is that for the ancient Greeks the term *autokratôr* generally (but not always) referred to the freedom of the polis, a city state with sufficient power to govern itself. . . . For most people I spoke with, each individual is or would be his or her own city state." As one of Alford's respondents put it, "Freedom is being the CEO of my own life."[1]

This notion of "freedom as mastery" issues not from any will-to-power, though, or from a self-affirmative aspiration to extend one's dominion but rather out of the fear of being victimized and dominated amid ceaseless competition. The drive to power is born of felt weakness; one must be predatory lest one is preyed upon. Seeing "civilized society in the terms, if not the extremes, of Hobbes's state of nature," Alford writes, what is "desired above all else is the power to protect oneself against the incursions of others. Insulation becomes freedom." In a world where I am vulnerable and everyone else is aggressive, I must preemptively control others so that I am not subject to a will not my own. The level of untouched independence we expect, desire, and feel we require is secured only in mastery. In turn, feeling under siege and trapped in a sort of arms race, "the mastery that most young people seek is not *idealized* as much as it is *regretted,* as though there were no other choice." Alford continues, "They wish they did not have to trade freedom for power, but dare not refuse, lest they end up with neither."[2] Given our notion of freedom-as-independence, the drive for power becomes a pressing necessity.

And out of this very same logic follows a second norm of freedom, seemingly the opposite of mastery, which we might call freedom-as-escape. Freedom here is not about the exertion of power *over* others but about the retreat into a power-free space *away from* others. The alternatives are autocracy and isolation. Alford describes this second dimension as the freedom of "losing control of oneself," of "letting go of one's need to control the world" in the darkness of sleep, hot baths, and relaxation, when "the cares of the world, all the constraints and demands of the day, slip away, and one is free to just be, subject to a part of oneself kept under lock and key during the day."[3] This is the part of the self that is unleashed—set free to stretch out and roam about, to play and dream—either when one is asleep or when everyone else is asleep. It is the freedom not of sovereign independence but of unfettered liberation. It is desired in reaction to the fatigue of endless competition but moreover as an end in itself—as freedom in its pure and ideal state. Where we regretfully settle for power, we aspire to escape.

An alternative experience of freedom-as-escape follows from "relaxing with friends," when one is with others but without the need to "monitor" oneself.[4] This is the experience of informality, of being at home with others. Where freedom that is experienced as power over others aligns with the "sex object" mode of human relations discussed in the previous chapter, freedom experienced as power-free relaxation with friends is the "soul mate" formulation. Only from the relational positions of being on top or being alone can I feel free. The socialized alternative to these two positions lies in the experience of "being by myself with others." The line between "I" and "we" is blurred here, whether in the frictionless communion of lovers or friends, in the authentic community of one's culture, or in facile communication across humanity.

It is, of course, impossible to tell the extent to which these notions of freedom actually predominate today, beyond the conclusions Alford draws from those he interviews. To what extent do the pursuit of power and the retreat into privacy define our consciousness of freedom and in turn our norms of human association? This is the question we explore in this chapter, as I continue to draw upon and extend Tocqueville's theory of democratic modernity. Insofar as these poles do constitute the dimensionality of modern freedom and society, Tocqueville's interpretation of the democratic social state helps us recognize ourselves along a number of lines.

First, the experiences people associate with freedom have just as much to do with the democratic principle of equality. Freedom takes shape as mastery and escape within the normative context of equality. Alford suggests that the power to get what one wants has apparently become the sole conceivable "medium of moral exchange in a world in which all values are equal." When competition between equals replaces hierarchical command as the immanent ordering principle of social relations, *success* supplants *excellence* as human action's standard of judgment. Freedom's meaning in turn adheres to the power requisite for the former rather than to the recognized authority that frames the latter. By the same token, freedom as mastery and escape is embraced in an egalitarian world where dependence of every sort is seen as degrading. "Not having to ask permission turned out to be a leading example of freedom," Alford writes, because "having to ask permission reveals the power differential between the parties, and it is the knowledge of that differential that is humiliating." Further, the passion for equality is evidently turned inward when freedom is experienced as relinquishing self-control, as "letting go" and not having to "monitor" oneself—freedom as the absence of internal hierarchy.[5]

Second, as with democratic norms of elevation and degradation, freedom-in-equality tends toward exclusive extremes. Alford interprets his interlocutors as suggesting that there is no intermediate point between "the extremes of all and nothing at all": "If they can't be completely free, then they want none of it." The possible practices of freedom *in* society and the world are cynically devalued in relation to the idealization of freedom *from* others and the world. A cynical contempt of existing freedoms is inscribed in the impossible promise of modern freedom's absolutism. Most people expect their freedom to be "real, . . . complete and total"; they "assume that they should be able to do what they want." Here again we encounter the idea of a sort of commonplace rising above the level of humanity. The middle-class people of democracy simply assume a measure of mastery to which few kings throughout history aspired. When this proves impossible, the experience is of being wholly unfree, degraded below the level of humanity. The wellspring of perpetual indignation, every limitation of freedom, every compromise or need to ask permission seems an outright negation of freedom. Along these lines, Alford identifies the same duality of idealization and devaluation that was discussed in the previous chapter. Alford attributes this "borderline" quality of freedom to the fact that his respondents "have grown up in a consumer society in which the commercial media panders to narcissistic fantasies of total control" in "a world without boundaries or limits."[6] I have argued that we must look to the larger whole of society after the democratic revolution—of which consumer society is but a derivative part—to understand our passion for the idea of limitless control. The commercial media is the creature rather than the creator of modern society and consciousness. It panders to rather than produces the narcissistic sex-object and soul-mate fantasies that take shape within a society principled upon democratic openness—upon the freedom that rises from the collapse of hierarchy.

And third, Alford makes clear that even as people imagine absolute freedom, they don't believe their ideas have any impact upon the workaday world. Living in the world with this ideal of freedom, they feel equal parts indignant and impotent. The "economic world they live in . . . is harsh, competitive, and relatively unforgiving, like Hobbes's state of nature." Consequently, they "do not expect their imaginations to have any influence on the world, or the world on their imaginations." Alford continues, "Rather, imagination and material reality belong to separate categories of existence that never meet." The same divergence of *powerless* thought and *meaningless* action detailed in the previous chapter recurs here as freedom's dualism. In principle we are entirely free; to approach this freedom, we must retreat from the present world into isolation or transcendent intimacy—into a "literary" world of our own making. In practice freedom is immaterial; we are entirely subject to forces and necessities beyond our control. Alford picks up a hint of this, reporting that when informally talking about experiences of freedom, people spoke in terms of respite and relaxation; when asked to actually define freedom, people spoke of mastery, money, and power.[7]

*Freedom-in-Equality: Competition and Intimacy*

Tocqueville is perhaps best known for his argument that modern democratic peoples might sacrifice freedom in their overriding obsession with equality: "They want equality in liberty, and if they cannot have it, they want it in slavery. They will suffer poverty, servitude, and barbarity, but they will not suffer aristocracy."[8] For all of Tocqueville's renowned powers of prediction, though, this one seems furthest from the mark today. Far from being our principal passion, equality may be something no one even cares about anymore. We certainly don't hear much about it in these times of great and growing inequality. If anything is held to be self-evident today, it is that "the rich get richer while the poor get poorer."[9] In contrast, freedom is constantly invoked as "an all purpose word for everything that is good about our way of life."[10]

However, we can account for this situation from within Tocqueville's theory of democracy. What is affirmed as everything good about our way of life is freedom of a particular sort, freedom-in-equality, in the absence of stable hierarchical absolutes. This is the freedom of what we can call "democratic openness." Equality of authority is the unnoticed background picture we accept silently, as neither advocates nor adversaries, like the course of the sun and the succession of the seasons. And it is against this background picture that freedom comes into relief as everything good. Even while freedom and equality are at times in tension, equality is the very precondition of the freedom we celebrate; the latter is inconceivable absent the former. In this sense, democratic freedom is to the principle of equality what aristocratic command was to the principle of hierarchy. While we are animated by the spirit of freedom, we are oriented by the principle of equality.

Of course, as Hobbes makes so clear, the equality of authority is also a precondition of the competition for power, and so of the inequality between winner and loser. Like freedom-as-openness, competition would simply not make sense outside the context of equality. Modern material inequality as much as modern freedom are conceptually and ethically warranted by the principle of equality, as excellence and command are warranted by hierarchy. The inequalities of power produced by open competition supplant the inequalities of authority that justify command. Inequality thus persists (even thrives) in democracy, but hierarchy does not.[11] Tocqueville himself draws on such a distinction, as above, when he distinguishes between servitude and aristocracy.[12]

While Tocqueville clearly accounts for the inequalities that issue from the equality of conditions, he at times neglects the inextricable link (exposed by his own theory) between democratic equality and democratic freedom—that both are sourced in the absence of authority. I argued previously that Tocqueville's own work can be read to explain how equality does not subvert the *passion* for revolution (even if it does make great *political* revolutions rare). Similarly, equality cannot subvert the passion for freedom (even if, as we shall see, it does make freedom's political expression seem impossible). I argued further that the democratic social state, constituted by the presence of equality/absence of hierarchy, takes shape in the ineffaceable tension between extreme notions of human degradation and grandeur—between the fear of collapsing into domestication and the revolutionary aspiration to transcend the fetters of the material world and realize the impossibility of possibility without limits. I extend this analysis here, arguing that freedom-in-equality takes on its "borderline" characteristic against the fear of domestication. We respond to the prospect of domestication severely, by striving for mastery and escape; relative to independence and liberation without limit, every narrowing of freedom seems to signal encroaching domestication.

Alford describes how many of the people he interviewed saw society as simply a less extreme version of Hobbes's state of nature, the implicit logic being that the social compact just reduces the natural war of all against all to a sort of cold war hostility. This view should not surprise us.

The social state of equality cannot but mirror many of the features of the natural state of equality. Hobbes's state of nature is characterized by the absence of authority and the irreducible potential for force in every human interaction—with no basis for command comes a constant struggle for control. This condition of insecurity and defensive aggression may be attenuated in society but never eliminated. The notion persists that, once we get past all the fancy and fanciful talk and down to the brute truth of the matter, human relations are just power relations. While I may no longer fear for my life in society, I feel constantly vulnerable to being overpowered by others—economically, intellectually, emotionally, and so on. Insofar as I internalize this insecurity and come to perceive myself as weak, such domination threatens to end in my domestication.[13]

Moreover, as Locke recognizes, the construction of new social, political, and economic power centers and systems actually introduces a whole new level of threat—the wolf is replaced by the lion. In society I am subject to far vaster concentrations of power than were present in the state of nature. And insofar as I perceive these powers as conventional or personalized, as the embodiment of human intentions rather than as natural or supernatural (when "market forces" become "corporate power," for instance), I encounter them as the power of another's will over me. The experience of both controlling and being controlled is thus greatly expanded in the socialized state of nature. In the zoo that is society, the threat of death is supplanted by the specter of domestication. And in the zero-sum struggle for "alpha male" status, every influence of one person over another may seem to signify the loss of freedom.[14]

As we have seen, though, the struggle for mastery is often viewed as a regrettable necessity of the world in which we live. In an extension of Alford's representation, if his respondents feel trapped in Hobbes's state of nature, they imagine escaping into Rousseau's state of nature. Circumstances force conflict and the striving for power, but what people really want is a different sort of freedom, a different sort of wildness—the pastoral freedom of privacy or utter intimacy. This nature is a power-free state apart from the economic necessities and power drives of material reality. Here, I need fear neither death nor domestication. I am free to let down my guard and relax into inaction, to just stretch out and dream.

In what follows, I argue that these two notions of wildness—the Wild West and the unspoiled frontier—frame central norms of human relations within the democratic social state. We often take a watered-down version of Hobbes's state of nature as a truth we would be naive to deny in our open society. At the same time, we affirm socialized aspects of Rousseau's state of nature as all that is potentially good and beautiful about our open society. We might say that democratic society rejects the terms of the liberal contract under which certain aspects of liberty are traded for security, holding that even in society insecurity is inevitable, and that liberty is properly unlimited. In turn, democratic society tends to be represented both as a market (a social construct, of course, but one that is taken to be natural, a mirror of the Hobbesian—or Darwinian—way the "real world" works) and as a community (another social construct, but one that mirrors the "authentic" blood bond of family resemblance). What captures the imagination in democracy are those relationships wherein we feel together as one or feel in competition with others.[15]

I conclude that democratic politics comes to seem paradoxically alien to democratic society, which is taken as at once a preconventional state below politics and a postconventional state beyond politics. Political argument is represented accordingly, not as the debate between citizens but as either a powerless word game or an interfamily "war" between "cultures." I suggest that Tocqueville's most prescient concerns are most precisely formulated not as the threat to freedom in equality, then, but as the threat to democratic politics in democratic freedom-in-equality. We should be less concerned with the despotism born of equality than with the depoliticization born of democratic openness—with the view that the practice of arguing in association with equal others toward the collective use of power is basically an incoherent idea, out of place in the modern world. As Tocqueville explains, the devaluation of political argument is significant beyond the political sphere, in that the practice of democratic politics provides perhaps the sole remedy to the fight-or-flight pathologies of the open society.

## II. The Freedom of Openness

*Savage and Slave*

At the close of *Democracy I*, in his story of the savage and the slave, Tocqueville offers something of an allegory of modern freedom's dimensionality of mastery and escape as against domestication. Tocqueville writes of how, "while traveling through the forests," he encountered an "Indian woman . . . holding the hand of a little girl of five or six, of the white race. . . . A Negro woman followed along behind." In appearance and demeanor, the savage and the slave were mirror opposites. The "savage women," who "was not married," looked "free, proud, and almost fierce." The "Negress wore European clothing that was almost in tatters" and exhibited neither pride nor ferocity but only "a servile fear." For her part, the child "displayed a sense of superiority that contrasted oddly with her weakness and her age." Yet, alone together in the wilderness, the group was like a family, the two women showing an "almost maternal attachment" to the little girl. There was, Tocqueville recounts, something touching in this scene of "nature . . . striving to bring them together" in a "bond of affection," despite the "vast distance that prejudices and laws had placed between them." Tocqueville ruined it all, though. Upon noticing his presence, the Indian "abruptly stood, rather roughly pushed the child away, and with an irritated glance in [Tocqueville's] direction set off into the forest."[16]

We can think of these two types—the savage and the slave—as theoretical markers of our own understanding of freedom and its loss in democratic times. The slave represents the possibility of utter domestication made possible not by the brute fact of enslavement but by the consciousness-shaping social institution of slavery. Tocqueville writes that while violence has deprived the slave "of nearly all the privileges of humanity," his "habituation to servitude has given him the thoughts and ambitions" of a slave. He has "learned only how to . . . obey his needs." The modern slave does not have to be physically constrained, punished, or really even manipulated; slavery enters the soul, and he "enjoys all the privileges of his baseness in tranquility."[17] In his contented if needy servitude, he is not unlike the tame and timid creatures of our supposed brave new consumer culture. As the consumer is habituated to bourgeois thoughts and ambitions, disposed to abdicate individual identity and human capacities, the purchasing-power freedoms of the consumer amount to the slave's privilege of wearing his master's clothing.

The savage's reaction to the intimacy-shattering presence of power represents the alternatives of mastery and escape. Tocqueville writes that where the "Negro exists at the ultimate extreme of servitude, the Indian [exists] at the outer limits of freedom." As opposed to the slave's reflexive baseness, the "Indian's imagination is filled with the supposed nobility of his origins." The Indian "lives and dies amid dreams inspired by his pride"—not unlike the revolutionary men of '89. Where the slave "finds his joy and pride in servile imitation of his oppressors" and "aspires, by imitating them, to become indistinguishable from them," the savage "is afraid of resembling the Europeans" and "clings to his opinions and to the least modicum of his habits with a lack of flexibility unparalleled in history." The "Negro [is] the proprietor of nothing, not even his own person," while the "savage is his own master from the moment he can act." Tocqueville says of the Indian, "He has never bowed to the will of another man. No one has taught him to distinguish between voluntary obedience and shameful subjection, and he knows nothing of law, not even the name. For him, to be free is to escape from nearly every social bond." The Indian revels in his "barbarous independence," unwilling to "sacrifice any part of it" and Tocqueville concludes that "civilization has little purchase on such a man."[18] Whether in mastery or escape, the noble savage's prideful pursuit of all-or-nothing independence in isolation perfectly capture the borderline norms of freedom characteristic of democratic openness. Where the slave is consumed by social conventions that he takes as natural, the savage, reacting to the slave's domestication, obstinately denies society's influence upon him in his fugitive quest to remain unbowed and untouched—to pursue the outer limits of freedom. Totalizing notions of freedom and of unfreedom proceed hand in hand.

I argue in what follows that democratic society's two most characteristic traits in Tocqueville's account—individualism and materialism— both take shape around these poles of the slave and the savage.[19]

*Democratic Individualism: Sovereignty and Insignificance*

Tocqueville's metaphor for the organization of aristocratic society is that of a long chain linking all together from peasant to king. Born into their stations within an immutable network of *influence* and *service*, each member is bound to his place and to those members in the places above and below him. Association is obligatory. Aristocratic society is thus the public society par excellence: "Men who live in aristocratic centuries are almost always closely tied to something outside themselves and are often disposed to forget about themselves." Democratic society is organized not as a chain but via revolutionary rupture: "Democracy breaks the chain and severs the links." This is in part a consequence of the revolutionary path by which equality was introduced into the world. Revolution is a violent teacher, and the hatreds it generated drove people apart. Further, postrevolutionary society is populated by those intoxicated by their newfound independence and made overconfident by their newfound powers. Most significantly, though, the breaking of the social chain is a consequence of equality itself. While "democratic revolutions encourage [people] to shun one another," democratic equality "tends to make men unwilling to approach their fellows" lest the influence of one over another threatens the return of hierarchy.[20] Competition is warranted by equality; influence and service are not. Even as equality makes people more similar, then, it causes them to keep their distance. Human relations as such become problematic, as most every encounter is a stage for one or another inequality. The public world is an inhospitable environment for equality.

Even in revolution-free America, democratic man thus follows the maxim "In everything that regards himself alone, he remains master." One must rule oneself lest one be ruled by another: self-sufficiency alone honors equality. If we extend this logic, one must ensure one's mastery by involving oneself only in things that regard oneself alone. This maxim first takes root at the level of the republican political unit but is eventually adopted by each individual within democratic society. In relationships between family members, citizens, and Protestants, what Tocqueville terms the "dogma of popular sovereignty" becomes the "law of laws." For perhaps the first time in human history, the utterly audacious idea of being one's own exclusive authority presents itself to each member of society—every man a king, even if only of a very small territory. As Tocqueville puts it, "Equality fosters in each individual the desire to judge everything for himself." In the absence of a recognized external authority, "each man seeks his beliefs" and his "rules of judgment solely from within." Ultimately, people are even "pleased to think that their fate lies entirely in their own hands."[21] These norms of self-sufficiency and personal sovereignty constitute one aspect of democratic individualism. And as between sovereign states, the rules of international relations govern relations between democratic individuals.

We might say that the other-oriented members of aristocratic society are supplanted by the self-centered individuals of democracy. Tocqueville writes, "All men [in aristocratic times] are connected with and dependent on one another. All are linked by a hierarchical bond, which helps to keep each individual in his place and enforce obedience in the body as a whole." In democratic society, a disobedient, savage streak persists: "Accustomed to subjecting his movements to no rule other than his personal impulses," the democratic individual "finds it difficult to bend to rules imposed from outside." And this inflexibility, which takes root with the republican political principle, self-subvertingly rebounds to make collective self-government more difficult. Even if the democratic individual "consents to join with others in pursuit of a common goal, he wants at least to remain his own master, cooperating in the common success as he sees fit."[22] The self remains always the standard reference and standard of judgment. Democratic society, in turn, becomes the private and personal society par excellence; democratic man is never disposed to forget about himself.

This proud and powerful stance of sovereignty is only one aspect of democratic individualism, though. The reverse side of the self-made man is the sense of being just one small and insignificant self, lost in a sea of innumerable other individuals—"as alone amid the crowd as the savage in his woods." Being independent vis-à-vis other individuals and maintaining self-sufficiency by standing outside all particular networks of influence, the democratic individual ends up helpless before the influence of the mass and the events of the world. Having "neither superiors nor inferiors" means being without the service of "habitual and necessary associates." In this dissociation, the individual sees himself both as master and as powerless. He ends up the CEO of a company of one, under constant threat of losing controlling interest. Not unlike Hobbes's state of nature, then, the experience of individualism in the social state of equality is one of being independent but vulnerable: "Equality of conditions makes men aware of their independence but at the same time points up their weakness."[23] And their impotence feels to them as limitless as their independence.

In turn, Tocqueville argues that aristocratic influence is supplanted by democratic conformity—the rule of the particular supplanted by the rule of generality. Because democratic individuals are desperate for intellectual, spiritual, and emotional guidance and support but too proud to admit any sort of dependence upon their equals, the overt command that is characteristic of aristocratic society gives way to covert control by democratic society; no one commands but everyone submits. "In democratic countries it is common for large numbers of citizens to make for the same point," Tocqueville writes, "[even as ] each one . . . flatters himself that he does so . . . wholly of his own accord." The democratic individual never forgets himself, but he does end up losing himself— "lost in the crowd and easily swallowed up in the common obscurity."[24] Inflexible pride inverts to soft neediness as each person realizes he is not up to the task of transcendent self-sufficiency and goes in search of some external but impersonal authority compatible with equality. The sovereignty of the savage inverts to the slave's "servile imitation," not of particular others, which would violate equality, but of the abstract other of the greatest number. "Don't tread on me" inverts to obedience to some commanding voice, so long as that voice honors equality with its every word. Wildness inverts to domestication. This is the other aspect of democratic individualism.

In their individualism, Tocqueville concludes, democratic peoples "are constantly wracked by two warring passions: they feel the need to be led and the desire to remain free." As we shall see, Tocqueville argues that to combat the need to be led, democratic peoples must combat the desire to remain free, at least insofar as the exclusivity of the desire to remain free subverts itself, turning into powerlessness—into the experience of isolation and insignificance. To remain free, the inhabitants of democracy must be "*forced* to know and accommodate one another." The democratic individual must be awakened from the dreams of mastery inspired by his pride to see that he is not as independent as he imagined and that it is often "in his own interest to forget himself." To remain free, he must resist his natural, savage, revolutionary inclination to escape from nearly every social bond and instead practice "the art of joining with his fellow men."[25] This, for Tocqueville, is an essentially political practice—the art of arguing together, of political freedom—wherein power is shared rather than fought for or fled from. Here, the disposition of the citizen displaces those of the master and the stranger.

*The Heroic Materialism of Democratic Times*

We see a similar dualism in Tocqueville's description of the material-ism characteristic of democratic society. In Tocqueville's account, the democratic individual's need for "material well-being" renders this indi-vidual ultimately docile and submissive. Potentially more domesticated animal than human being, the petty desire for a modicum of material wealth saps the democrat's loftier passions and purposes, while the ob-sessive need for bodily pleasure, security, and comfort strikes at his pride. Oriented by their "commercial mores," democratic peoples end up excessively conservative, timidly opposing "revolutionary instincts" with "conservative interests," "impetuousness" with "inertia," and "adven-turous passions" with "homely tastes." But this is only half the picture of democracy's commercial society. In America, democrats display a cer-tain wildness in their materialism—a "commercial recklessness" and "audacity" along with a "boldness in industry." Far from only opposing revolutionary instincts, they have a passion for acquisition and profit, along with a love of chance and risk, all of which stimulates a passion for revolution *within* their commercial mores. Whatever homely tastes and conservative interests commerce as a way of life inculcates, commer-cial mores also harbor an adventurous spirit of "intense competition [and] endless experimentation." Indeed, Tocqueville identifies a preda-tory passion in American materialism that exactly opposes the stultify-ing need for material well-being. With Americans hardly resembling the timid sheep that might lie in democracy's future, Tocqueville writes that it is "difficult to describe the avidity with which the American hurls himself upon the immense prey that fortune offers him." A "passion stronger than the love of life constantly spurs him on" to, for instance, "fearlessly brave the Indian's arrows and the maladies of the wilderness" for the sake of indefinite future gain.[26]

In full view, then, the American sacrifices his material well-being for the sake of a passion that manifests itself in the striving for material well-being. Like all those who "live amid democratic instability," Tocqueville explains, Americans have "the image of chance constantly before their eyes, and eventually they come to love all undertakings in which chance plays a role." Tocqueville continues, "Hence they are all propelled toward commerce, not only for the promise of gain it affords but also for the *love of the emotions* it occasions." Democratic peoples love the gamble more than the gain. They love the excitement of the competitive game—the chance of rising and even the risk of falling—an excitement that reflects, in their economic pursuits, the open-ended uncertainty and revolutionary flux of the democratic way of life. In this sense, commercial society takes shape and is affirmed as an aspect of the democratic mode of being. Materialism is as much an opportunity for adventure, mobility, and innovation as it is a doctrine of timidity, submission, and neediness. Tocqueville goes so far as to say that there is "a kind of heroism" in the entrepreneurial American's "avidity for profit"; there is "something heroic about the way Americans do business, . . . not just responding to a calculation but obeying the dictates of his nature." There is even something of the Napoleonic spirit of the French in American businessperson: "What the French did for victory, they do to cut costs." Their commercial norms manifest closer to imperialism than consumerism as they leave home and risk all on the front(ier) to master the world or make something grand out of nothing. It is this sort of reckless, warrior, pioneer materialism—this bourgeois heroism—that "fires the imagination of the crowd" in democratic times.[27]

For Tocqueville, then, there is a duality to both democratic individualism and democratic materialism. Whether lost in the innumerable crowd or lost in the consumerist herd, whether in isolation and insignificance or in the need for material well-being, democratic man may suffer a boundless loss of freedom and power. The opposite path of individualism and materialism leads toward an equally boundless sense of freedom and power—whether of the self-sufficient and sovereign individual or of the bold soul who hazards uncharted and unpredictable waters with the view that the risk is the reward. This freedom, the residue of democracy's original revolutionary impulse to unconditional independence and liberation, takes shape as restlessness within the social state of openness.

### Democracy's Compulsive Restlessness

Tocqueville argues that France's revolutionary sequels, particularly of 1848, were sentimental imitations of the original rupture of 1789. Even as these sequels violated the original intent of '89 by pushing France toward socialism, and even in the episodes of reaction against the Revolution, it was clear that a faith in revolution was written into modern France's genetic code. Analogously, I suggest that what Tocqueville describes as the characteristic "restlessness" or "restiveness" of American democracy can be understood as an ongoing reenactment of America's founding rupture of pilgrimage to the New World. Restlessness, openness, and freedom are intertwined in America's migratory epic. The acts of leaving home or being born again, the pursuit of the original and the new, the notion of never being bound to place, the passion for innovation and improvement: these become the animating spirit of the lives of Americans, of their economics, their religion, and their politics. Tocqueville, as we shall see, develops this picture in what is perhaps his master trope of the different freedoms of aristocratic hierarchy and democratic equality: in aristocracy, freedom means having a place to stand; in democracy, freedom means having space to move.

For Tocqueville, the democratic rupture seems the precondition for imagining change in the world. It is almost as if the very concepts of newness and possibility come into the world with modern democracy and its elements of revolution and equality: "[In centuries of hierarchy] conditions seemed fixed forever, and the whole society seemed so static that no one imagined that anything could ever stir within it. In centuries of equality the human mind takes on a different cast. It is easy to imagine that nothing stays put. The mind is possessed by the idea of instability." Democratic equality is the milieu of open-mindedness. And this shift in the mode of thought leads to a shift in the aim of action; value shifts with fact. Tocqueville writes that "aristocracy seeks to maintain things as they are rather than to improve them"; in democracy, the "improving spirit" rules and there "exists an urge to do something even when the goal is not precise, a sort of permanent fever that turns to innovation of every kind." This fever manifests itself perhaps most pointedly in the fashionism of democratic expression: "In aristocracies, language inevitably partakes of the general ambience of repose. Few new words are created, because few new things come to pass." Conversely, "the perpetual fluidity that is so prominent a feature of democracy is forever reshaping the face of language," with democratic peoples sometimes feeling "a desire to change words even when there is no need."[28] Change becomes valued for its own sake.

This same basic contrast of repose and restlessness runs throughout Tocqueville's writings. Aristocratic society is dominated by a stillness that would seem like death in democratic times. Democratic society is dominated by a flux that would seem like Pandemonium in aristocratic times.[29] There is a more basic constant we should not overlook, though. In democracy as in aristocracy, the accepted order of society and the perceived order of the world reflect one another. Norm and nature, ought and is, take the same shape. Before the revolution, Nature and regime mirrored one another in their hierarchical solidity, which was considered at once given and good. Change signified corruption, and the idea of the old was coupled with that of the proper. In America, in contrast, where "everything seems to be in constant flux," Tocqueville remarks that "every change seems to mark an advance": "Hence the idea of the new is coupled . . . with the idea of the better."[30] In Tocqueville's account, the order of the democratic social state seems as natural to its inhabitants as the aristocratic social order had seemed previously. The principle of openness is accepted as a fact of reality after the revolution, just as the principle of hierarchy was once accepted absolutely, as the Truth. Today, the natural world is as full of dynamic change and unpredictable newness as the social world is full of dynamic change and unpredictable newness, and perhaps providentially this means not decay and corruption but vitality, innovation, evolution, beautiful mystery, even indefinite progress. "In the midst of the universal movement that surrounds him," the American considers "change . . . the natural state of man" and comes to "love change for its own sake."[31] All come to "consider society a body in progress and mankind a changing tableau in which nothing is or should be fixed forever."[32] That which is at rest, immobile, or static seems an unnatural, unhealthy aberration amid democracy's oceanic movements.[33]

As much as the material bounty of the New World shaped this view of society and the world, it doesn't appear for Tocqueville limited to America. At the time of the Revolution, the French too had a taste for instability and risk. The difference lies in Tocqueville's assessment of this passion for change. As we shall see, the consequences of this passion in the openness of the New World are mixed. Amid the long-established inequities and crowded accretions of the Old World, restlessness becomes wholly ugly and dangerous. It turns into "the revolutionary disease"—

the "disgust at and horror for rules and authority, even for rules one has made and authority one has established." The love of change in the French context was pressed into a lust for violence, and the taste for instability into reflexive insubordination. Tocqueville makes clear that while the symptoms of this disease will never be as acute as in the immediate wake of revolution, they will henceforth be chronic. They find permanent purchase in the society that revolution built: "[The] illness finds itself with living roots in the permanent social state, the habits, ideas, and lasting mores that the revolution has founded. . . . Therefore some of it will necessarily remain, even after the revolutionary period is completely over. This something will be a certain disquiet and chronic instability, and a permanent disposition to relapse easily into the revolutionary disease."[34] A residual passion for revolution persists as habitual rebelliousness—a condition between revolution and restlessness. In France, as in America, the founding event resonates; neither people should ever be expected to fully settle down.

This new sense of possibility and mobility—of being able to take to the open road—gives rise to what Tocqueville describes as the *compulsive* restlessness of democratic society. "Equality," Tocqueville writes, "allows anyone to go anywhere." But this opportunity turns into an imperative; able to move, the democratic individual feels enjoined to move. To stand still when everything is in motion and everyone is on the move, to stay at home when one can go anywhere, is to appear unfree, somehow constrained, even in a way not fully alive. This restlessness—this "universal tumult"—is as inescapable and normatively determinate in democracy as settled tradition was in aristocracy. Where aristocratic man could never move, democratic man feels like he can never stop; he persists in a "state of constant agitation." Democratic society settles into its determinate form as amorphous—as a *"permanent state of transformation."* Restlessness becomes the new rule. "Democratic centuries," Tocqueville concludes, "are times of trial, innovation, and adventure," but they are not times of chaos or anarchy. All is in motion, but all motion is animated by the same spirit and governed by the same principle. The experience of life in the flux and fluidity of democracy is not so much of being left adrift as of being "daily swept along and buffeted about by the impetuous current that carries all things before it."[35]

This habitual restlessness drives the spiritual as well as the economic lives of Americans. In his obsessive pursuit of material wealth and well-being, the American demonstrates a "fervent ardor" not at all akin to rational choice: "He grasps at everything but embraces nothing and soon lets things slip from his grasp so that he may go chasing after new pleasures. . . . He settles in one place only to leave it a short while later to pursue his changing desires elsewhere."[36] His experience of well-being lies in the pursuit more so than in the state of well-being; his pleasure lies in the chase; what he desires is change in itself. Tocqueville thus famously concludes, "No one can work harder at being happy than Americans do."[37] In the pursuit of happiness, the American is as neurotic as he is optimistic. Interestingly, Tocqueville argues that the "vast competitive arena" arising when "everyone is constantly seeking to change places" causes democratic society to uncomfortably take on a sort of aristocratic stillness: "Having destroyed the obstructing privileges enjoyed by some of their fellow men," democratic peoples "run up against universal competition." He continues, "The form of the obstacle has changed, but the obstacle remains."[38] The open society's principle of competition generates a tense immobility functionally similar to the repose engendered by the closed society's principle of caste. One is obstructed not by one's better but by one's equal.

As Tocqueville describes them, Americans forsake bodily needs and comforts in their feverish quest for material well-being, abandoning what they have today in pursuit of what they will abandon tomorrow. A parallel recklessness manifests itself when they turn away from the material world and toward matters of the soul. This transcendent enthusiasm manifests itself in eruptive moments of religious reawakening, when the soul, feeling "imprisoned within limits that apparently it cannot transgress," seems "suddenly to cast off all material bonds and fly impetuously toward heaven." In this anxious flight, Americans neglect "even their most pressing bodily needs." Not at home even in their own bodies, restlessly seeking independence even from their own fettering materiality, they incorporate the spirit of revolution into their religion. Given how they imagine freedom in the social state of openness, the opposite poles of materialism and spiritualism take shape similarly, in the transgressive striving to escape or overcome the limits of the here and now—whether through innovation or conversion, science or faith, the aspiration is regeneration, to be born again. The "fervent ardor" that characterizes American's entrepreneurial pursuit of material well-being is thus mirrored by their "impassioned, almost wild spiritualism."[39]

## Pilgrimage into the Wild

We saw previously how Tocqueville interprets the founding pilgrimage to the open territory of the New World as motivated not by any material need but by promise and principle. He describes America's ongoing westward migration in analogous terms. Marching together toward "the same point on the horizon," millions of Americans "depart the place of their birth to create vast estates for themselves in far-off places": "[They] left their original homeland in search of the good life. They left their second homeland in search of a still better one. . . . They long ago broke the bonds that attached them to their native soil and have formed no bonds since." And while this emigration from birthplace and settled territory "began as a need . . . today it has become a game of chance, which they love as much for the emotions it stirs as for the profit it brings."[40] The American vocation is restlessness, as that of the French is rebelliousness; the passion for revolution is constant, although adapted to different social, historical, and physical environments.

Along these lines, Tocqueville writes that the shift from aristocracy to democracy is largely constituted by the shift from landedness to openness as the ordering, animating virtue of society—from homeland to breaking the bonds of territory. It is in this sense that he writes of the American West as "democracy pushed to its ultimate limit"—a sort of instantiated ideal type of democracy in its permanent state of transformation, in perpetual flight from the fatherland. It is primarily in the West that one encounters the "wild spiritualism" and "bizarre sects" of American religion. And it is in the West—where society was "organized only yesterday [and] is still but a swarm of adventurers and speculators"—that one encounters the full extent of American's wild materialism. Across these open lands, upon which people don't so much settle as restlessly pass over, freedom-in-equality—the freedom of mastery and escape—is pushed to its ultimate limit: "The Americans who flee the Atlantic coast and rush headlong westward are adventurers impatient of discipline of any kind. . . . They arrive in the wilderness as strangers to one another and find there nothing to restrain them—not traditions or family spirit or examples. The law has little power over them, and mores even less." These adventurers portray the ideal of democratic individualism in action—sovereign, self-sufficient, isolated, insignificant. Although previously socialized in the "civilization of their fathers," they live the life of savage independence, "born in the woods," where men "barely know their neighbors" and so can exert "little control over one another." Having "escaped the influence" of authority—whether paternal or traditional, of enlightenment or virtue, of artificial or natural aristocracy, formally instituted or informally observed—the pioneer and frontiersman live the authentically undomesticated life.[41]

In the perpetually new and natural world of the West, with its unrefined surplus of freedom and equality, and with its deficit of public life, the idea of democratic openness comes close to being realized in the world. And it is this freedom-in-equality of the frontier that still seems to grip the American imagination: freedom as the insecure power-reality of the "Wild West," where we know ourselves to live once the comforting words of polite society are stripped away; freedom as the escape from power and external influence into the untouched wild. This is the freedom of the state of nature—of life in the irreducible conflict of Hobbes's crowded state of nature, of life on one's own in Rousseau's state of nature.[42]

*Freedom's Meaning: From Place to Space*

Thus far I have argued that for Tocqueville the compulsive restlessness evidenced in American individualism and materialism, and in sharper form in the habitual rebelliousness of the French, follows in large part from the idea of freedom inscribed in democratic equality. This is the freedom experienced when reality is thought of as in flux and one can/must move about ceaselessly, without constraint, obstruction, or inhibition. Tocqueville is of two minds about this notion of freedom. In a description that aligns freedom with democratic restlessness, and the lack of freedom with aristocratic repose, Tocqueville writes that in a free country "bustle and activity are everywhere," while in an unfree country "everything seems calm and still." He goes on to exalt the "universal movement that dominates everything else in the United State, the frequent reversals of fortune, the unforeseen shifts in public and private wealth": "All of these things combine to keep the soul in a sort of febrile agitation, which admirably disposes it to effort of all kinds and keeps it above the common run of humankind." This elevating uncertainty shapes not only the private industry of Americans but also their religious doctrines. And this same dynamism flows from politics into civil society: the practice of democratic government "spreads throughout society a restless activity, a superabundant strength, an energy that never exists without it, and which, if circumstances are even slightly favorable, can accomplish miracles." Dominated by universal movement, moved to a miraculous ingenuity, American freedom produces "an image of strength, a little untamed, to be sure, but full of vigor; and of life, not without mishaps, to be sure, but also dynamic and energetic."[43] Messy but vitalizing, the freedom of the democratic way of life seems here synonymous with being healthy. To be restlessly active is to be fully alive.

By the writing of *Democracy II*, Tocqueville comes to argue that American's universal movement is actually insufficiently audacious, a timid restlessness that "disturbs and distracts the mind without stimulating or elevating it." Horizontally ubiquitous but not at all deep, democracy's state of agitating doubt causes waves of great frequency but minor amplitude. The same uncertainty and perpetual transformation that permits social mobility, and even enjoins mobility, ends up stifling true revolutionary questioning and change by disorienting the minds and sapping the energies of democratic peoples. Openness proves a necessary but not sufficient condition of vital thought and action. Tocqueville writes, "[A] perpetual motion is ubiquitous in [democratic] societies and rest is unknown, but that agitation is confined within certain limits that are seldom exceeded. Men in democracies change, alter, and replace things of secondary importance every day but are extremely careful not to tamper with things of primary importance."[44] A certain clinging veneration of primary things goes hand in hand with an unmoored fashionism in secondary things.

In contrast to this potentially self-subverting quality of the experience of democratic freedom, Tocqueville identifies and to a degree embraces what he describes as the freedom specific to aristocratic times. While democratic freedom is about having space to move, aristocratic freedom is about having one's own place to stand in public. The latter freedom takes shape not so much as acting and speaking without constraint but as being seen and heard—it is less universal, more exclusive; less formal, more effective. In times of democratic equality, Tocqueville explains, "all are insignificant and none stands out from crowd." Democracy, in turn, offers the freedom of anonymity, of being nobody in particular, invisible in the audience rather than up on stage. This is the freedom of the frontier—or of the big city—where everyone is a stranger and one barely knows one's neighbors, neither influencing nor being influenced. Mobile, the traveler escapes power and evades surveillance (thus, the compulsive restlessness of his freedom). Tocqueville describes this in one of his finest passages: "Men living in the democratic centuries upon which we are now embarking have a natural taste for independence. They are naturally impatient of rules; the permanence of the very state they prefer tires them. They like power, but they are inclined to scorn and hate the man who exercises it; and their very minuteness and mobility makes it easy for them to evade his grasp. These instincts will always be found because they stem from the depths of the social state, which will not change. For some time to come they will prevent the establishment of any form of despotism."[45] Here is Tocqueville's picture of democratic freedom, painted in its entirety.

In contrast, aristocratic peoples prevent the establishment of despotism through visibility rather than mobility. "Among aristocratic peoples," Tocqueville explains, "all ranks are different, but all are also fixed. Each individual occupies . . . a place that he cannot quit, and he lives among other men similarly moored all around him. In such nations, no one can either hope or fear that he will not be seen. No man is placed so low as to be deprived of a theater and likely to escape blame or praise by dint of obscurity."[46] In turn, one derives strength and service from the permanent group within which one is stuck. There is an unquestioned sense of fellowship and mutual obligation (rather than otherness) in aristocracy, and one simply cannot slip from one's station into anonymity, isolation, and insignificance. Moreover, one is influenced—almost forced—to be free as a matter of what in democratic times would be belittled as "keeping up appearances." Always on stage, one is going to be judged, and so one seeks to be judged well by putting on a noble show of freedom. Aristocratic man is an actor in every sense of the word. And the felt potency derived from being judged well, both from above and below, effectively decentralizes power away from any potential despot.

In times of democratic equality, freedom is precisely about being un-influenced by the judgments of others—or at least about putting on a show of being uninfluenced, in order to be seen as authentic. In aristocracy, freedom is driven by the pride born of being honored, and in democracy, by pride in being undomesticated. Freedom attaches not to being seen as noble but to being untouched and unseen. Power in democracy is not distributed hierarchically via judgment but left untouched in the egalitarian flight from judgmentalism. The experience of freedom occurs in privacy rather than publicity, even as the experience of power cannot but remain in public life, when one is with others rather than in isolation and insignificance. With the devaluation of public life, freedom and power part ways. Liberated from and independent of others, democratic man is as effectively powerless as he is entirely free.

In aristocracy, then, freedom takes shape as having a place upon which to stand up to power, rather than as being able to evade power. In this sense, aristocratic freedom follows from that social state's generative fact/principle of "landedness." Owning actual property is one aspect of aristocratic standing, with property serving as the basis for a public platform rather than for walls that insulate the property owner from the incursions of the public.[47] But Tocqueville also offers a more figurative sense of having a place to stand. The bourgeoisie of the old regime, for example, had a sense of standing and an "independent mind" because the "old construction of society had made each profession . . . a little stage."[48] There "was no one, whatever his rank, who did not believe that he had a certain part to fill, a certain place to occupy, and spectators to judge his attitudes and his acts."[49] Further, the legal rights and privileges that the bourgeoisie enjoyed both "made of them a pseudo-aristocracy which often showed the pride and spirit of resistance of real aristocracy" and ensured that the bourgeois individual could not "lose himself in the crowd and hide his cowardly subservience. Every individual found himself on stage, in a very small theater."[50] As with their property, the rights of certain classes were less a form of private insulation than a public platform.

Of course, aristocratic freedom is not without its downside in Tocqueville's account. The democratic individual tends to get lost in the very space that constitutes his freedom. The aristocratic actor is locked into the place that belongs to him, and to which he belongs. He is bound to a public station and a public role that he cannot quit and bound to others

by a chain of mutual obligations. As we have seen, this social arrangement can end up very much devoid of the freedom and vitality of openness—ossified, still, and stagnant (like the New World aristocracy of the
slave-holding American South). Moreover, Tocqueville writes that the
freedom-in-hierarchy of the Old Regime was reduced and deformed:
"There was much more freedom then than in our day: but it was a kind
of freedom that was irregular and intermittent, always contracted within
the limits of a class, always linked to the idea of exception and privilege,
and almost never went so far as to furnish the most natural and necessary guarantees for all citizens."[51] Aristocratic freedom was as noble as it
was unjust, politically beneficial but less natural than democratic freedom. And it was linked to the accretion of the immutable inequities of
class privilege and division, which paved the way for the revolutionary
collapse of aristocratic society. No less than democracy, aristocracy contains its own internal flaws and self-subverting elements.

As is usually the case, Tocqueville takes up the cause not of returning
to the conditions of aristocracy but of incorporating select features of aristocracy into the democratic social state. Democracy is made better
than itself, its self-subverting excesses moderated, when alloyed with
the elements of aristocracy that can be synthesized by egalitarian means.
For instance, Americans do well to reproduce the sense of public place
and standing through the use of newspapers, which "give visibility" to,
and so empower, otherwise anonymous people and ideas.[52] Similarly,
democratic political public associations potentially replicate the standing the aristocratic actor held in society, at once generating and decen-
tralizing power. In all such cases, Tocqueville argues, democratic society
must identify places, reasons, and resources within itself to reconstitute
something of the political public life of aristocratic society and thereby
to open the way for reuniting the experiences of freedom and power.

## III. Norms of Association in Democracy

*Political Bonds and Natural Bonds*

Thus far I have argued, building upon Tocqueville, that freedom in times
of democratic openness manifests in the shadow of revolution, as a sort
of compulsive restlessness. In what follows, I argue that association in

times of democratic openness takes shape around norms of *informality* and particularly in terms of *intimacy* and *competition*. The key, as Tocqueville explains, is that democracy weakens the political bonds of society while strengthening those bonds that seem natural.

We would be mistaken to conclude that democratic freedom leads exclusively to the fragmentation of so-called atomistic individualism. Disassociation captures at best half the picture of human relations in the democratic social state. Viewing democratic freedom from a broader perspective, we see that the individual distances himself from others in his pursuit of a sort of savage liberty but also comes together with others in ways that seem in accord with such liberty. The individual feels free when by himself but also when by himself with others. This is the "soul mate" norm of human relations discussed previously—of being together-as-one, without effort and without mediation or compromise, in a way that feels spontaneous, authentic, and natural. In such a relationship, one enjoys the liberty of the savage without suffering his isolation, loneliness, and insecurity.

I shall argue that two types of association generally convey this experience of being alone with others: the imperceptibly tight ties of family (or of the extended family of one's "culture" or "community") and the imperceptibly loose ties that unite all humanity (our "global village"). Along with aspirationally independent individualism, the blood bond of family and the blood bond of species constitute the central norms of human relations in the democratic social state. Such are the ways of being free in the open society—of being in society without civilization's discontents. Along these lines, I argue that democratic freedom leads not to dissociation and the dissolution of society (as if such a thing were possible) but to new norms of association that are best understood as apolitical or antipolitical. Democratization dissolves the political element of human association—the element of arguing together with free and equal others to address common problems and formulate common purposes.

To unpack this a bit, we might say that association in democratic society takes shape around two intertwined paradoxes. First, the inhabitants of democracy are as fixated upon resemblance and unity as upon individuality and uniqueness. Whether in terms of our biology or our morality, our faith or our fears, that we are all basically the same is as celebrated as that we are all different and diverse. And second, as democratic peoples seize upon relations that seem natural (power free and spontaneous, outside human intentions and interventions) as a way of experiencing freedom and belonging at the same time, the principle of inheritance again takes center stage, trumping the principle of democratic choice. Locke above all sets forth the modern, liberal project of banishing from social and political thought the norm and the fact of filial inheritance—of replacing paternalism with consent as authority's source. Yet relations based upon choice remain problematic in democratic society because intention implies the exercise of power (whether legitimate or otherwise). To live under social arrangements or with social relations that are the product of choice (even when one is among the choosers) is to live under the sway of others, by another's leave. Conversely, to live within social arrangements that are inherited as the product of impersonal nature (or of traditions so distant and transcendent as to seem impersonal second nature) is to live freely, at least in relation to others The norm is of a union that is neither arranged nor contracted into but rather "born into," "destined" or somehow simply "meant to be." Perceived as natural, such bonds are worn lightly. One might feel at home with others—and so free to be oneself—in the so-called tribal relations of lovers, family, friendship-as-extended-family, community and so forth. There remains the individual, the community, and nothing in between. These relationships transcend or delve beneath the need for mediating words; unspoken, such communion is embraced as properly intimate and authentic.

In this context, we should revisit the argument of Tocqueville's with which we began, that democratic peoples will accept servitude before inequality. Perhaps to be free in relation *to* others while remaining *with* others, to be free of every inequality of power in society, democratic peoples are prone to collectively abdicate power to a common master. To honor equality, and so to maintain the experience of democratic freedom, this locus of power would have to be wholly impersonal and abstract—literally superhuman. All too human and so to speak personifiable, the state does not suffice. Democratic peoples like power, but are inclined to scorn and hate those who are seen to exercise it. In the parlance of the moment, the government is all too easily exposed as having an "agenda" that is being "crammed down our throats."[53] Rather, for the open society to be sustained, power would have to be relocated to those determinates considered natural or "higher": the market, evolution, God, chance, fate, and so forth. Governance by meta-Leviathan is the solution to securing the socialized state of nature. Along these lines, the desire for freedom-in-equality requires a sort of servitude.

### Democratic Associations: The Family and Humanity

Tocqueville makes clear that, along with the idea of the independent individual, the idea and obligations of humanity occur naturally to the democratic imagination. In aristocratic times, "the general notion of 'one's fellow man' is obscure, and little thought is given to devoting oneself to one's fellow man for the sake of humanity. . . . By contrast, in democratic centuries, . . . the duties of each individual toward the species are far more clear."[54] This dual movement toward individualism and humanitarianism—toward the desire for separation from each other and toward the idea of being bound to every other—is born of democratic equality and the recognition of one's similarity to others that follows. This recognition of resemblance, of being surrounded by those like oneself, neither superior nor inferior, facilitates mass conformity, compassion, and a facile communication within and between democratic societies—the elements of what is today celebrated and scorned as "globalization." It also facilitates the opposite phenomena: the ostentatious display of uniqueness, competitiveness, and the sense of being strangers to one another.

We have already touched upon the conformity, and the reaction against conformity, produced by freedom-in-equality. In times of equality, one takes pride in not depending upon one's neighbors. At the same time, independence is a difficult test, and one is prone to clandestinely go with the flow of what seems to be the prevailing opinion. Isolated, the individual has the desire but not the ability to maintain his individuality. Consequently, insofar as one can make it out, the authority of all humanity will be felt as overwhelmingly weighty on the one hand. On the other hand, as in the story of the savage and the slave, the more one's resemblance to one's neighbors is recognized, the more widespread, vehement, and even rebellious will be the reaction against resemblance. Feeling lost in the human crowd, the individual is compelled to declare his independence—that is, his original personality—and make a conspicuous show of his freedom. As with the attitude of the savage, "pride will always impel individuals to escape the common level." Conformity and the pursuit of authenticity thus advance together. With democracy, Tocqueville writes, for "the first time in history, the features of the human race become clearly visible." At the same time, to avoid individuals' being "confounded in a common mass, a host of artificial and arbitrary classifications arise, and individuals use these to set themselves apart lest they be dragged against their will into the crowd."[55] This is what Freud would later term the narcissism of minor differences.

Moreover, Tocqueville argues that diversity can only be shallow in times of equality and mobility. With the collapse of the principle of hierarchical difference and with the dissolution of the principle of landedness and the separation between distinct places, diversity cannot but diminish to idiosyncrasy. In a passage that must seem bizarre to modern sensibilities, Tocqueville writes that the era between the Roman Empire and the empire of democracy was a golden age of diversity and individuality. The advent of equality, in contrast, gave rise to the tendency toward assimilation: "The Middle Ages were times of fragmentation. Each people, each province, each city, each family had a strong tendency to assert its individuality. Today, an opposite tendency is apparent: peoples seem to be moving toward unity. Intellectual bonds join the most remote parts of the earth, and people cannot remain strangers to one another for a single day or ignorant of what is taking place in any corner of the globe." In democracy "uniformity reigns," and "diversity, like liberty, is vanishing day by day."[56]

The recognition of human similarity facilitates more than conformity and freedom's reaction against conformity, though. Democratic people, Tocqueville argues, will also be compassionate—as compassionate in their humanitarianism as they are competitive in their individualism. And again, resemblance is the source of both sides of the apparent opposition. When all are equal and similar, Tocqueville explains, the possibility of climbing up (and falling down) the social and economic ladder is "open to all," with the result being that "all citizens are secretly at war with one another." But even as the democratic individual has one foot in this socialized version of Hobbes's state of nature, the other foot is planted firmly in Rousseau's. Tocqueville writes, "[When all are equal and] everyone thinks and feels in almost the same way, then each person can judge everyone else's sensations in an instant: all he has to do is cast a quick glance at himself. . . . No matter if strangers or enemies are involved: his imagination instantly puts him in their place. . . . In democratic centuries, men rarely sacrifice themselves for one another, but they do exhibit a general compassion for all members of the human species."[57] Compassion, no less than competitiveness, is born of the mixture of self-centeredness and equality.

Finally, the recognition of similarity facilitates unfettered communication within and across peoples but also a sense of distance between people. In democratic times, the members of the human association cannot remain strangers—thought circulates freely, as everyone is "in constant communication with one another." Mobile, people "are constantly changing places, and inhabitants of different countries mingle with, see, listen to, and borrow from one another."[58] But in Tocqueville's account, this mingling represents achieved unity less than given uniformity. People and nations associate less as distinct and differentiated parts of a whole than as homogeneous additions to a general mass. And as in the American West, constant mobility renders communication shallow. Like tenants in an apartment building—right next door but transient— the inhabitants of democracy are increasingly able and increasingly disinclined to converse with disparate others; "hi" and a smile become the custom. Everyone speaks the same language, as it were, but no one talks.

These, then, are the bonds that unite individuals in human association. They are ties that divide as much as they bind, whether in reaction against homogenization, in competition, or in the feeling of being among strangers. Given and universal, these ties seem natural, as normal and spontaneous as caring about oneself. They bind everyone equally and are worn lightly, without effort or compromise, never constraining or obstructing the freedom of the individual. Communion is given, vague, vast and only occasionally experienced in conscious reflection. It is a product of the native and abstract resemblance of individuals, of a time when "each person looks at himself and instantly sees everyone else."[59] In this sense, the human association is unspoken, a sort of association of one, beyond the need for mediating words. Talking with other members is as shallow and as intimate as talking to oneself in the mirror.

The idea of association via the Internet exemplifies this bond of shallow intimacy—of a bond one clicks out of as easily as it is taken on, wherein emotions are exchanged largely through pictures and symbols ("emoticons") with similar strangers around the world (one's "friends"), in a manner that conveys the sense of being at home and by oneself with others. In this sense, the Internet constitutes the social state of nature par excellence, the perfect marriage of privacy and recognition, freedom and belonging. It is the perfectly open society one creates above the world one actually inhabits.

Tocqueville writes that with democratization all "bonds of race, class, and country are becoming looser; the great bond of humanity is growing tighter." There will come a day when there is but one people in the world, "all equal to one another, all members of the same family." But universal humanity is not the sole mode of association Tocqueville describes as inscribed in democracy. The familial association is just as central as the human association. More precisely, a single norm of association—association based upon native characteristics, whether understood as pre- or postconventional—shapes democratic society in its opposite extremes. While human beings are tending to see each other as "members of the same family," Tocqueville sees a future when each individual, "withdrawn into himself, is virtually a stranger to the fate of all the others": "For him, his children and personal friends comprise the entire human race. As for the remainder of his fellow citizens, he lives alongside them but does not see them. . . . He exists only in himself and for himself, and if he still has a family, he no longer has a country."[60] There is the exclusive family, inclusive humanity, and nothing in between.

The equality of conditions thus both expands and contracts the orbit of social relations—one is connected to everybody in the world and disconnected from one's next-door neighbor. But even in dissociation the individual does not retreat into isolation. Instead, individualism "disposes each citizen to cut himself off from the mass of his fellow men and withdraw into the circle of family and friends, so that having *created a little society for his own use,* he gladly leaves the larger society to take care of itself."[61] We saw how the French attempted through revolution and literature to create the society they imagined above the one they inhabited—an effort at mastery and escape in a single stroke. Here, the American exemplar of democracy creates a little society outside the one he inhabits, a little society where he feels at home, by himself with others. The French envisioned politics as a vehicle for their literary idea of perfectly free, egalitarian, and fraternal pubic life, of an expansively open society liberated from Old World hierarchy and landedness. Americans envision private family life as a venue for their literary idea of an intimate, power-free society liberated from the disagreeableness of public and political life. Bound by nature, the democratic family is a little society that can do without politics.

Tocqueville addresses the influence of democracy on the family in a single chapter, which can be read as a microcosm of the entirety of *Democracy II*. For Tocqueville (and as we shall see, for Claude Lefort as well), democratic society takes shape around the disappearance of the *figure* of the father—the representative figure who speaks on behalf of authority, whether of God, the sovereign, or tradition. In aristocracy, the father is the present embodiment of the distant ruler (who himself is the present embodiment of a distant God). As the "natural and necessary bond between the past and the present" the father "is the organ of tradition, the interpreter of custom, the arbiter of mores." With an oedipal resonance, democracy is born into the world with the revolutionary beheading of the father figure. This, of course, transforms the family as much as it does society. The aristocratic father as ruler of the domestic polity, as head of the household, established aristocracy as the paternalistic society par excellence. Democracy's egalitarian revolution destroys the barriers and distances that once demarcated father from family: "Paternal authority has been if not destroyed then at least impaired." This tendency is taken to its extreme in America, where "the family—taking the word in its Roman and aristocratic sense—does not exist." The American parent "enjoys the unchallenged domestic dictatorship" that the vulnerability of the child necessitates, but as the "young American approaches manhood . . . the bonds of filial obedience grow looser": "He first becomes master of his thoughts and soon thereafter of his conduct." The order of the democratic family thus perfectly mirrors that of democratic society in general: with the dissolution of the right of command, the distance between people decreases and the bonds that hold them to-gether soften.[62]

In Tocqueville's account, the democratic family coheres around the intimacy this new closeness brings: "As mores and laws become more democratic, relations between father and sons become more intimate and tender. Rule and authority are less frequently encountered. . . . The master and magistrate have vanished; the father remains." Fraternity supplants paternity even in the relations between father and son. There is such an ease and sweetness to this new bond of affection that the appeal of the democratization of the family becomes irresistible. Democratic family mores, Tocqueville famously concludes, are so seductively "mild that even partisans of aristocracy find them attractive, and after savoring them for a time they are not tempted to revert to the chilly and respectful formalities of the aristocratic family."[63]

With this newfound intimacy, all that is formal in the relationship dissolves, leaving only a warm and familiar informality: "As power slips away from the aristocracy, we see *all that was austere, conventional, and legal vanishing* from paternal power . . . , and a kind of equality establishing itself around the domestic hearth." There remain few "external signs of respect" surrounding the father, and no "recognized formula for addressing him." Thus, for instance, the style of the domestic correspondence of aristocratic times "is always correct, formal, rigid, and so cold that the heart's natural warmth can barely be felt through the words. Among democratic peoples, by contrast, every word that a son addresses to his father bears the stamp of something that is at once free, familiar, and tender."[64] Aristocratic language is like the formal and often uncomfortable suit and tie one is expected to put on in public, while democratic language is what one relaxes in around the house. Democratic communication is direct and "from the heart," liberated from the rigid and repressive confines of mediating social rules, forms, and conventions. Aristocratic communication, conversely, appears more concerned with propriety of style than authenticity of expression. Words are a facade, more affectation than affectionate, whereby one presents oneself to public court rather than open oneself up to others. The son of aristocracy is recognized through posturing etiquette and in a sense concealing himself, what in democratic times would be considered repressing himself. The son of democracy is recognized through revealing himself, what in aristocratic times would have been considered degrading himself.

Tocqueville concludes that the modes of association in democratic society mirror that of the democratic family: "The natural bond seems to grow tighter as the social bond relaxes."[65] Generally, all those relationships that are taken to be rooted in family resemblance are strengthened; associations that seem held together merely by social conventions are weakened. The former—whether conceived of in terms of family, humanity, nationality, culture, race, gender, and so forth—accords with democratic freedom-in-equality by conveying the experience of what Tocqueville calls "collective individualism."[66] In such relationships—born into rather than constructed, inherited rather than intended, given and spontaneous—power is located outside the brotherhood community, in nature, and thereby one is permitted to feel by oneself with others, collectively at home together without the fear of being domesticated. In one's "tribe," one need not compromise or ask permission. Recognizing oneself in others, one can let go and "act naturally," forgetting oneself without risk of losing oneself. In this sense, the experience of individual liberty in democratic society is as much enabled as threatened by community. Conversely, all those looser but less comfortable associations wherein the individual is conscious of being with equal others—all those relations necessarily framed by conventional or institutional mediation, which are seated in conversation rather than unspoken communion— are undermined as artificial.[67] Between the cold reality of market competition and the warm authenticity of family intimacy, the artifice, formality, and public posturing—"political correctness" or politeness— required of such interactions cannot but seem absurd, meaningless, and unfree.[68] Relative to the intimacy that democratic openness makes possible, argument goes the way of aristocratic etiquette as a medium of human association. Democracy thus "brings kin closer together while at the same time driving citizens further apart."[69]

### Democratic Informality: Association without Mediating Conventions

In the years leading up to the French Revolution, Tocqueville writes, people were "simultaneously immensely proud of humanity and exceptionally humble with respect to their own time and country": "The idea of the greatness of man in general, the omnipotence of his reason, the unlimited extent of his intellectual abilities, penetrated all minds and filled them; with this proud notion of humanity as a whole there was combined an unnatural contempt for the particular time in which they lived and the society of which they were part. . . . Everywhere people spoke of nothing but institutions' weakness, their incoherence, the absurdities and vices of contemporaries, society's corruption, its rottenness," and they constantly made "predictions of a coming catastrophe."[70] Man in abstract and humanity in general were idealized as figurations of limitless potency and true grandeur; all things pertaining to the particular situations of actual people were devalued as weak, corrupt, and absurd. The pride people felt in relation to the democratic abstraction was matched only by the contempt they felt for their own present time and place.

I have argued that this duality of idealization and devaluation was not contingent upon the facts preceding the French Revolution but rather is intrinsic to the democratic social state born of revolution. Relative to the transcendent ideas that seize the imagination with the collapse of hierarchy—of the expansive liberty of the savage, of a society potentially ordered and animated by fraternal intimacy and humanitarian compassion, of the union of such natural liberty and natural love—the world we inhabit can only seem rotten and incoherent, always verging upon catastrophe. Catastrophe and transcendence seem at the same time and for the same reason imminent. Relative to the indefinitely perfectible self, society, and world of democracy, the particular practices and institutions of the here and now can only seem a theater of the absurd: a play full of trite, clichéd, nonsensical jargon that obstructs authentic expression and meaningful communion: an unsatisfying play where nothing happens while we perpetually await the revolutionary opening onto the natural, whether imagined in terms of the past or the future.

Perhaps the most significant iteration of this duality arises in our view of democratic politics today. On one hand, democracy is idealized as the grand political revolution of humanity spontaneously coming together in a transterritorial movement toward peace and prosperity for all. Or democracy is idealized as synonymous with freedom, the "seeds" of which will spontaneously spring up to transform the world over, once obstructing artificial power formations have been cleared away, whether by means of revolutionary or military action. Or democracy holds the promise of the new transpartisan politics that we are all awaiting but which never seems to come—regardless of which plainspoken, Washington-outsider, agent-of-change president next appears on the horizon. On the other hand, the present democratic political system is precisely a theater of the absurd, wherein everyone is "playing politics" in a routine that seems contemptibly disconnected from real world concerns. And try as we might, we can never revolutionize, escape, or transcend the fettering rottenness of this system, the institutions and conventions of which obstruct the way to authentic democracy. Despite the immense pride we take in our democracy, we are exceptionally humble with respect to our own democratic political practices: everywhere people speak of nothing but institutions' incoherence, the vices of contemporaries, and society's corruption, with predictions of coming crisis. The democratic movement seems given, inevitable, and entirely meaningful. The democratic political systems, processes, and organizations that are supposed to be a vehicle for this movement seem entirely— indeed constitutively—beyond reform.

Ultimately, the gap between principle and practices proves not contingently but intrinsically unbridgeable. In the democratic social state, where openness—the freedoms of openness (mastery and escape) and the associations of openness (market competition and family intimacy)—is deemed natural (realistic and authentic), whatsoever is perceived as conventional is devalued as such, precisely in its conventionality—as artifice and artificial. Openness cannot by definition be put into conventional form—it cannot be domesticated—and so conventional form is left without substance, as norm without normativity, the always false "conventional wisdom." Openness cannot by definition be located in time or place, and so that which is of temporal or particular human contrivance is devalued as obstructing or confining artifice, an arbitrary barrier keeping us from the real and the possible.[71] While the principle of democratic equality subverts hierarchical conventions, then, the concomitant principle of democratic openness subverts the conventional as such. "Democracy," Tocqueville thus writes, "destroys or obscures nearly all the old social conventions and prevents men from easily settling on new ones."[72] The result is democracy's constitutive, compulsive restlessness.

In the transition from aristocracy to democracy, the collapse of conventionality manifests itself in the dissolution of manners and etiquette. In aristocratic societies, Tocqueville writes, "outward relations among men are subject to mostly stable conventions," wherein the "customs of the leading class . . . serve as a model for all others." The stability of hierarchy is mirrored by the stability of aristocratic conventions, and the visibility of authority is recognized in the "precise signs" of etiquette and the complex "rules of politeness" that mediate every association. Aristocratic society is the society of artifice par excellence—that which is meaningful are the outward forms, the formalities and manners, that constitute all relations. Equality levels all these models, signs, and rules, and promises a mode of association liberated from all such rigid and encumbering conventionality. What had been thought to facilitate now seems to fetter, and what had been meaningful now seems superficial. Should the inhabitants of democracy chance to encounter one another, their approach is "natural, frank, and open." People are no longer bound to meet by reciprocal obligation, but when they do meet, their interactions are easier and relaxed. Tocqueville explains that the inhabitants of democracy are too equal and too mobile to "allow some group of them to establish and enforce a code of etiquette. Each individual therefore behaves more or less as he pleases . . . , rather than conforming to an ideal model held up in advance for everyone to imitate." In turn, where aristocratic manners display the virtues of "regularity and grandeur," democratic manners display "simplicity and freedom"; where aristocratic manners "adorn and hide what is natural," draping "human nature in beautiful illusions," democratic manners are "more sincere," a "thin and poorly woven veil, through which each person's true feelings and individual ideas can easily be seen." Aristocratic social conventions constituted a sort of noble lie, revealing what was considered most significant by concealing certain aspects of nature; democratic society disdains such hypocrisy (the public pretense to superiority) and demands openness, in which nature is honored by the disavowal of pretense and the removal of all adorning masks. The shift is from persona to personality, and nobility to intimacy. Authenticity of expression (confession) thus supplants formality of presentation in facilitating association. Where the aristocrat was recognized by acting out intricate rules of etiquette, democratic peoples recognize one another by considering "the feelings and ideas rather than the manners of the people they meet," and they "attach more importance to the substance of actions than to the form." In the end, Tocqueville writes, "it is fair to say that the effect of democracy is not precisely to give men certain manners but to prevent them from being mannered."[73]

As in the case of the dissolution of manners, the collapse of conventionality manifests itself in the dissolution of codes of honor. As opposed to moral laws, which are universal and based on "the permanent and general needs" of humanity, honor is, according to Tocqueville, "nothing other than a particular rule based on a particular state that a people or class uses to assign blame or praise." Refusing to fight a duel or a war, for example, might be objectively moral but deemed dishonorable by the feudal aristocracy because, "born in war and for war," they honored martial courage above all. The characteristic rules of judgment are no less particular and arbitrary in America, which was born in and for labor—where there is "no door that work cannot open." Courage is still honored, but in terms of boldness in industry rather than valor in war; what would have once been considered "servile greed" is now called "noble and estimable ambition." But as the democratic abstraction effaces particularity and distinctions, in codes of honor no less than in codes of etiquette, democratic honor ceases to be distinguishable from the generalities of human morality. Were there to come a day when "all the peoples of the world had the same interests and needs and no characteristic features any longer set them apart, then people would cease to ascribe any conventional value to human actions altogether," and the "general needs of mankind, revealed by consciousness to every man, would be the common measure."[74] In democracy's expanding empire, the conventional forms and rules for assigning praise and blame are no less particular than those of hierarchical society but are increasingly perceived as natural and universal; generality—the individual's humanity—is recognized and honored at the heart of every particularity.

Tocqueville thus portrays the shift from aristocracy to democracy—from etiquette and manners to openness and intimacy, from particular rules of honor to the universal law of morality—as a shift from formality to informality as the governing norm of human association. The more simply and directly one conveys one's ideas and feelings to others, the more open and heartfelt one is in one's relationships, the more one is authentic and at home with others, the more meaningful is the experience of association. Informality is taken as natural, and the formal is dismissed as "mere formality." All the requisite procedures and regulations, all the rituals and ceremonies that one must abide by, come to seem trivial and absurd, obstacles to both recognizing the truth (whether ugly or beautiful) and to performing effective and efficient action. That which defined aristocratic society is today's red tape and superficiality— what we need to get above, beneath, or outside to realize democratic freedom-in-association.

In a theme he returns to time and again, Tocqueville writes that in politics, religion, and thought in general, "nothing is more repugnant to the human mind in ages of equality than the idea of submitting to forms." This is due in part to the popular sovereign's or sovereign individual's impatience with all barriers and constraints. Democratic peoples harbor an "instinctive" disrespect for settled rules, regulations, and procedures because such things "continually slow or halt the realization of their designs." Forms impede power and slow action. The "arrogant disdain" for forms therefore proves one of the greatest dangers of democratic times, particularly when this aspect of democracy's revolutionary disease carries over into politics, where minding one's political manners serves as a barrier "between the strong and weak, the governing and the governed, slowing the former while allowing the latter time to take his bearings."[75]

Tocqueville identifies a second, more subtle, reason why forms arouse the reflexive contempt of democratic peoples. Beside inhibiting the free exercise of power, conventional forms obstruct the desired immediacy of understanding and experience. The American mind aims "beyond form at substance," striving to be "free of the systematic spirit," and to "seek on one's own and in oneself alone the reason for things." To this end, Americans "strip away as much of the outer husk as they can, remove anything that stands between them and the object of their attention, and eliminate whatever is hiding the thing and preventing them from getting a good, close look. This habit of mind soon leads them to despise all outward forms, which they regard as useless and inconvenient veils placed between them and truth." The external form of something is a facade, its physical embodiment or public image, which masks its true nature; the form is a lie, the truth is assumed to be inner, deep, and private. Seeking "the real in all things," down below the thin surface of particular and passing conventionality, the democratic individual wants to base his "opinions on the very nature of man." Tocqueville concludes that the democratic revolution, beyond destroying hierarchical conventions, "cannot fail to destroy what is purely conventional and arbitrary in forms of thought," resulting in an "uncultivated, almost savage vigor" coming to "dominate thought."[76] The democratic mind will be as restless as the democratic body.

With this characteristically impatient manner of pursuing unfettered power and freedom, and of pursuing the power and freedom that lies in exposing the unvarnished truth hidden by outward social forms, democratic association takes shape both below and beyond the need for mediating conventions. Familial and humanitarian relations take on great normative weight precisely because they do not seemed mannered or bound by etiquette. They are pure and spontaneous expressions of intimacy or compassion, respectively, that delve beneath or transcend the rules of social grammar. They are relations premised upon free and natural communication. And so they are experienced as real and meaningful, not contingent upon the arbitrary and artificial conventions of any particular time and place. In his cast of mind, Tocqueville argues, the democratic individual seeks to remove anything that stands between him and the object of his attention; in his relationships, we might say he seeks to remove anything that stands between him and the object of his affection. As when he is alone, he feels at home in such informal relationships.

### The Separation of Democracy and State

Of all the spheres of thought and activity effected by the democratic norm of informality, Tocqueville argues that religion has perhaps the most to fear—and to gain. Insofar as organized worship amounts to a sort of religious etiquette, to a detailed code of particular observances, hairsplitting doctrines, and ritual practices, it will come under suspicion and risk being dismissed as absurd. Whatsoever seems merely ceremonial will be deemed without significance, a world apart from the utterly significant voice of conscience. And in their religion, as in their lives more generally, democratic people are "impatient of figurative images. Symbols strike them as puerile artifices used only to veil or embellish the truth that it would be more natural to present openly."[77] Conversely, insofar as faith transcends all organized institutional and conventional forms, religious beliefs, practices, and associations will stand as among the most meaningful in democratic society. Where religion sheds its fettering externalities in favor of directly and vehemently engaging ideas and emotions—as the path to highest truth and deepest intimacy—it will join the competitive and laborious pursuit of profit and opportunity as the second great passion of democratic peoples. The pilgrim and the pioneer will plunge into the wilds of the New World with the Bible in one hand and an axe in the other, as Tocqueville puts it. A sort of undomesticated fundamentalism—a revolutionary return to untouched original source—will capture the democratic imagination as much as does the expansive openness of globalization.[78] Fundamentalism drops below and rises above the artifice of conventional forms; globalization moves beyond the constraining borders of conventional forms. Both are born of a contempt for the particular time in which one lives and the society of which one is a part.[79]

We saw previously how democracy's revolutionary movement overflowed all territorial boundaries and spread like a religious conversion. The modern democratic abstraction, mirroring the monotheistic and above all Christian abstraction, transcended all particularities and distinctions. In the ancient world, Tocqueville writes, there were "as many gods and human species as there were nations. . . . Several religions kept particular social or political institutions . . . , like slavery, which made them inadmissible in countries which did not accept these institutions." The Christian religion, conversely, "placed itself absolutely outside particular institutions which can exist among men, social or political, and all legal conventions, in order to consider the human species as a single whole, composed of similar individuals, all subject to the same moral law." The democratic social state is similarly based "on principles so general, so natural, so much founded on the nature of human society outside any particular society, that it can be understood and adopted by all people." Democratic society appears as society as such—society in its natural form, taking shape around natural laws and human nature alone. It is for this reason that the empire of democracy "has been able to aim at conquering not only one people, but all humanity." Indeed, the open and egalitarian empire of democracy makes the very idea of humanity—of humanity as an association—conceivable. Like the Christian religion, then, the "political gospel" of the democratic revolution considers "man in the abstract," with "prescriptions . . . that claim to regulate the relations of men between themselves, independently of the positions these men occupy in each society. These are the natural relationships; those of father to son, son to father, brother to brother, men to men."[80] As with Christianity, democracy's tenets speak directly and solely to the family and the species.

In an argument that continues to resonate, Tocqueville writes that the authority of religion, like that of democracy, lies precisely in its distance from conventional forms and temporal powers. The separation of church and state is to the benefit of the former. Religion cannot seek "the support of worldly interests" without becoming as "ephemeral" and "fragile as any temporal power," nor can religion "share the material might of those who govern without incurring some of the hatred they inspire." The continued vitality of religion in America, for instance, is due to the fact that members "of the clergy . . . steer clear of power voluntarily and take a sort of professional pride in having nothing to do with it." Paradoxically, then, "diminishing a religion's apparent strength . . . [makes] it more powerful."[81] Beyond the separation of church and state, the same logic would seem to hold true for the separation of religion and church, at least insofar as the institution of the church is itself in any way temporally bounded or wields worldly power. Establishing a house of religion can only diminish that which is properly universal, infinite, and immaculate—boxing the transcendent into the here and now, bringing it down into present but passing conventional form, getting religion's hands dirty. Along these lines, the often-heard notion of "spiritual but not religious" seems the logical extension of the separation of church and state.

Democracy founds its modern moral empire in precisely the same fashion. To ensure the victory of the democratic idea—the idea of openness, of the freedoms and associations of openness—democracy must cast off all particular, embodying, encumbering forms. Democratic society aspires to universality and so must forsake affiliation with all temporal and material power. Democratic society aspires to naturalness and so must forsake all conventional establishment. In this sense, the secret of democracy's expanding monopoly of authority lies in its pristine powerlessness. Diminishing democracy's apparent strength makes it more powerful. We might say that the continued vitality of democracy depends upon the separation of democracy and state, and ultimately of democracy and politics—at least insofar as by "politics" we mean a practice organized within particular conventional forms and institutions. To house democracy thusly is to domesticate democracy's promise. Where the spiritual impulse is strengthened by its distance from religious realization, the democratic impulse is strengthened by its distance from political realization. "Spiritual but not religious" has its logical cognate in "democratic but not political."

### Conclusion: The Political Atheism of Democratic Society

In a letter to Eugène Stoffels, Tocqueville writes, "You speak of what you call *your political atheism,* and you ask me if I share it. On this we must understand each other. Are you disgusted only with parties or also with the ideas they exploit? In the first case, you know that such has always more or less been my way of thinking. But when it comes to the second, I am no longer your man in the least." Wary of such a dualistic formulation, though, he goes on to write, "I am trying not to construct two worlds: the one moral, in which I am still enthusiastic for what is beautiful and good; the other political, in which I lie down flat on my face in order to smell more at my leisure the dung on which we walk. . . . I am seeking not to divide what is indivisible."[82]

The democratic revolution in the principle of authority, I argue, founds just such a two-world construction of politics—of ideas versus parties, of the still good and beautiful moral world versus the political dung heap. In democratic times the world of ideas is transcendent, with the universal moral law of freedom-in-equality elevated far above all particular and arbitrary codes of honor—from honor to human rights. This world presents to the imagination the promise of revolution, of overcoming the insignificant and fettering world of conventional norms and forms, to arrive at a social state of nature—the open society. The democratic promise is as grand as the Christian, and in a way grander in that transcendence is to be imminent. Conceived of as an innocent and unpolluted past lost to us despite efforts at return and renewal, and as a dreamt-of future that seems tantalizingly inevitable yet impossible to realize—as the untouched primitivism and the unlimited promise of the New World—the idea of democratic openness frames the possibility of being in the world and with others without compromise or mediation. The norms of freedom and association inscribed in New World openness frame a way of life as compelling as it is impossible, compelling *because* it is impossible, incorruptible because it is by nature before and beyond the material powers and conventional embodiments or representations of our particular time and place. Regarding the politics of compelling impossibility, the standards of judgment involve universal morality and human rights, humanitarian compassion and the familial intimacy of mutual trust and recognition, freedom-in-security and individuality-in-community, world peace and world prosperity, authenticity, and all that private life has to offer in public. This is a politics that aspires to every good imaginable.

Such democratic faith goes hand in hand with political atheism. The principle of openness cannot be realized or materialized in conventional form; relative to the essentially external principle of openness, present practices and institutions cannot but seem compromised, degraded, and absurd. Emptied of any internal standards of judgment—of any way to be honored—the second world of politics is conceived of solely as the partisan power play of petty self-interest and unprincipled opportunism. The separation of church and state intimates the fusion of state and economics, so to speak. Never wholly moral, politics in the open society is assumed to be wholly amoral or immoral, evaluated exclusively in the economic terms of power's accumulation, effectiveness, and efficiency. The politics of "realism" goes hand in hand with the politics of the impossible. The great and abiding paradox of democracy is that under its reign fact and value never seemed further apart—or closer together. Nature as fact and nature as norm are both conceptually manifest in the principle of openness, even as the principle of openness, in its overwhelming naturalness, cannot be put into conventional practice. There is the real and the right, and conventionality in between.

Tocqueville describes the second world of actual politics in 1840s France, and for us today: "We all consider the greatest evil and the greatest danger of the present situation to be the profound indifference into which the country is falling. . . . There are many causes of this evil; but surely one of the principle ones is the belief that . . . political life is no more than a game in which each person seeks only to win; that politics has nothing serious in it but the personal ambitions of which it is the means; that there is a sort of gullibility and almost stupidity and shame in growing impassioned for a game that lacks reality and for political chiefs who are only actors not even interested in the success of the play, but only in that of their particular roles."[83] This image of politics as just a game, played by self-serving frauds before an ignorant, apathetic or foolishly fanatical, crowd is immediately recognizable today—in the assumption, for instance, that "politics" is at bottom just staged photo ops and sound-bite spin (advertising), driven by unprincipled partisans to manipulate a dumbly apathetic electorate into unreasonably fanatical support (brand loyalty). There is a sense in which political cynicism tends toward its logical end point here, not so much in the assumption of politics as corrupt (which would presume that there is something meaningful to be corrupted) but in the assumption of politics as simply absurd (recognized by all as meaningless). Liberal democratic politics— the politics of organized parties and suit-and-tie representatives, of formal institutions and procedural mechanisms—seems as artificial and out of place today as would an intricate code of etiquette, and for much the same reason. No wonder today's political satire has such an easy time of it, barely needing to exaggerate the mannerisms everyone already recognizes as ridiculous. *The Daily Show* is just CNN with a studio audience. At the same time, the disappointment, frustration, and anger people express (along with their ridicule and resignation) when politics predictably follows this teleprompter script to the letter demonstrate that there is another world of politics, a pre- or postpartisan world apart from this one, which remains always good and beautiful.

The political atheism of democratic society, Tocqueville holds, is no less than tragic. Contrary to a prevailing opinion of democratic times, he argues that democracy needs a robust politics even more so than did previous social states. The health of democratic society is inextricably bound to the vitality of its politics, even as the inhabitants of democracy tend to consider politics secondary to their economics, religion, law, art, and so forth. The practice of democratic politics—of coming together in argument to act in association with free and equal others—serves as a remedy to the pathologies of democratic consciousness and culture. The politics of arguing together is the medium for a type of freedom removed from the idea of savage liberation and independence, and for the exercise of power sharing in between the aspirations to mastery and escape. And such a politics is the venue for a type of association in between that of individuals in market competition and that of the collective individualism of familial and human resemblance. Political society stands in between the extremes of commercial society and literary society; the citizen occupies the social space in between the businessman and the dreamer.

Man is a social animal, in Tocqueville's account, and so public life is largely an end in itself: "Feelings and ideas are renewed, the heart expands, and the human spirit develops only through the reciprocal action of human beings on one another." The "science of association" is, therefore, "the fundamental science" and an ever more important science in times of democratic individualism and materialism: "If men are to remain civilized, . . . they must develop and perfect the art of associating to the same degree that equality of conditions increases among them." Being uncomfortable in public, feeling anxious to avoid the influence of others, viewing public life as a locus of artifice and hypocrisy, democratic man must nonetheless cultivate and inhabit a public persona in public places. Above all, he must be open to persuading and being persuaded in turn. In addition to being an end in itself, public association also serves as a means to obstructing administrative centralization, the political and social tyranny of the majority, and the despotism of the state. Such associations serve not only as a venue for the exercise of judgment but also for the exercise of collective power; in public, citizens can argue together and they can act together. In this sense, associations replicate in democratic society something analogous to the aristocratic actor, above the undifferentiated mass of insignificant individuals: "Ordinary citizens, by associating can constitute very opulent, very influential, and very powerful entities—in a word, they can play the role of aristocrats. . . . A political, industrial, commercial, or even scientific or literary association is an enlightened and powerful citizen that cannot be made to bow down at will or subjected to oppression in the shadows."[84] Like the aristocratic actor, the democratic association is always seen and heard and so can stand up to the exigencies of power. In terms of both judgment and action, nothing less than human dignity hinges on the possibility of public association in democratic times.

For Tocqueville, a very large part of freedom is indeed an endless meeting. As valuable as is most any public association in this regard, the specifically political public association is the real key in Tocqueville's account.[85] These associations convey the experience of political liberty, which for Tocqueville is the most integral means to the end of human dignity found in democratic times.[86] Political associations are those wherein divergent people (not only people of like minds) must learn to exercise power together (in addition to merely obstructing power). Tocqueville writes, "It is through political associations that Americans of all walks of life, all casts of mind, and all ages . . . see and speak to one another" and potentially "come to a common understanding."[87] In political associations, actual people, equal and similar but with differences, must attempt to reach an understanding of one another by means of conversation and argument rather than by presuming some more basic or abstract sameness of identity or interest. Understanding association as potentially based in the act of arguing together helps stave off the excessive notions of both sameness and difference characteristic of democratic society. These associations bring people out of silent isolation, but not by means of the spontaneous and unspoken relations of either the community or the "special interest" group. And these associations teach citizens not so much how to trust one another, nor even how to cooperate exactly, but rather how to accept the possibility of persuasion and to take that possibility seriously despite their belief in and passion for freedom-in-equality. In this sense, they teach the democratic individual a most difficult lesson in the art of uniting with those like him.

"Unfortunately," Tocqueville writes, "the same social state that makes associations so necessary in democratic nations makes them more difficult to achieve there than anywhere else."[88] In aristocratic times, people were bound and obligated to be together. They were habituated to political incorporation as a sort of second nature.[89] In the open society, free and equal individuals have every opportunity but no inclination to associate, to come together beyond their private circle of immediate friends and family. What they find most meaningful cannot be had in public life, and what they most fear and deride seems inherent in public life. In turn, Tocqueville argues, the inhabitants of democracy must at first be *forced* to associate and so to be free—to exercise their political rights and liberties and more generally their human capacities for judgment and action. Only over time will they become habituated to life together with others and to the modest but real and significant freedoms and powers this life makes possible. Here again, the specifically political practice of liberty in associations is vital to the health of democratic society. "In civil life, anyone may . . . persuade himself that he is capable of meeting all his own needs," Tocqueville argues. "In politics, such a thing is unimaginable." When citizens are "forced to concern themselves with public affairs, they are inevitably drawn beyond the sphere of their individual interests, and from time to time their attention is diverted from themselves."[90] Acting in the role of the citizen, the democratic individual learns that he is neither god nor beast, neither self-sufficient and sovereign nor dumbly domesticated to a life of private self-interest, neither autocrat nor idiot. Simply, the practices of democratic self-government are "constant reminders to each and every citizen that he lives in a society."[91] The exercise of political liberty thereby to some extent inoculates citizens against both the individualism and the materialism of the democratic equality of conditions. Political liberty "alone can effectively combat the natural vices of [democratic] societies," Tocqueville writes: "Only freedom can bring citizens out of the isolation in which the very independence of their circumstances has led them to live, can daily force them to mingle, to join together through the need to communicate with one another, persuade each other, and satisfy each other in the conduct of their common affairs. Only freedom can tear people from . . . the petty daily concerns of their personal affairs . . . [and] substitute higher and stronger passions for the love of material well-being, . . . and create the atmosphere which allows one to see and judge human vices and virtues."[92] Where the resources to satisfy self-interest lie in commercial society, and those to accommodate self-expression in literary society, the resources for self-respect reside in political society. The cure to the ills of democracy is a more political democracy.

In Tocqueville's account, the absence of the habits of political life and liberty is primarily what divided the course of democracy in France from democracy in England and America. With the political and administrative centralization produced by the French Old Regime, the various classes were deprived of the opportunity for political association and action. With the government and bureaucracy taking every initiative, the classes "no longer felt the need to come together and reach agreements," and ultimately they "never met except by chance in private life."[93] In England, conversely, "freedom always forced them all to stay in touch with one another, in order to be able to reach an understanding when necessary."[94] And America proves to Tocqueville that over time political association might become, if not entirely natural to democratic peoples, then at least familiar and desired. Only "politics generalizes the taste for and habit of association. It takes a crowd of men who would otherwise have lived alone and makes them want to unite, and it teaches them the art of doing so."[95]

In all of these ways, politics is for Tocqueville a place for the mediation of democratic extremes. Political associations draw—or force—citizens together from out of their private lives in such a way that they might both recognize and mediate their differences.[96] From a broader perspective, politics serves as an intermediary between principle and practice. It is in the act of collective self-government that citizens temper their ideals by having to put them into particular practices, and elevate their particular lives out of the trivialities and shadows of isolation, insignificance, and felt powerlessness. In the practice of politics, Tocqueville holds, the demands of morality and expediency may moderate one another, imagination is made to meet experience, and the sense of limitless possibility is tested against necessity. Today's tendency toward representing politics as either religion/morality or economics by other means erodes this unique and uniquely important place of politics in democratic society. Every "I believe" sermon about "core convictions" delivered in strident voice by today's politician-preachers, and every cynically knowing assertion that to really understand the way politics works, one need only "follow the money" or recognize that "it's the economy, stupid" erodes the place of democratic politics.[97] Pulled toward these opposite poles, the middle place—the mediating place—of democratic politics cannot hold.

More so than mere disassociation, for Tocqueville this depoliticization of society is the great source of democracy's tragic discontent. The democratic revolution is an essentially political movement—a revolution in the principle of authority, from unquestioned hierarchy to self-evident equality, from the embodiment of authority in the present paternal figure to the openness of authority and the restless compulsion to place authority safely apart from the actors and institutions of the here and now. Aristocratic society gave form to authority at every link in the long chain from Nature to convention to nature; democratic society breaks each link in the chain, leaving authority without representative form. Authority in aristocratic society was heard and seen; it was a society of command. Authority in democratic society is rendered abstract; it is a society of informality, of unfettered competition and unfettered intimacy. With the chains of hierarchy broken, the democratic consciousness comes to recognize two distinct worlds—one of power absent authority, the other of authority absent power. The former is the real world of hard truths and cold fact; its inhabitants strive for mastery, for fear of succumbing to the slave's domestication by some illicit power formation, whether overt or conspiratorial, personal or impersonal. The latter world is the potential world of beautiful truths and authenticity; its inhabitants strive for escape into the untouched and uncompromised wilds of savage liberation and independence. With the collapse of hierarchical divisions and mediations, the relationship between democracy's two natures seems one of imminent transcendence and irreconcilable difference. In principle, everything is and should be possible except the realization of possibility.

In between these polar norms of nature, the realistic and the authentic, the practice of politics cannot but seem debased as unnatural—a vestigial aberration or anomalous presence in the open society. Insofar as politics involves particular people, exercising power within the mediating confines of formal institutions and procedural mechanisms, under an authority that is purely conventional, politics cannot but appear out of place in either nature. Relative to the power play of Hobbes' state of nature, democratic politics seems a charade, a public pretense that masks the way things really work. To accommodate this nature's norm of realism, politics must reduce to just another iteration of market competition and consumption—of equal and independent individuals pursuing private self-interest in public. This politics is as noisy as it is silent—cacophonous in the constant sparring of politicians and "special interests" to secure power through electoral advantage, silent in that argument (and mediating speech more generally) is dismissed as manipulative talking-point strategy or naive waste of time. Relative to the power-free play of Rousseau's state of nature, democratic politics seems shallow, a petty and ugly necessity of life that obstructs the way things should be. To accommodate this nature's norm of authenticity, politics must aspire to the beautiful union of community—of the spontaneous, informal, heartfelt political movement that displays naturalness in its "grassroots" quality, and emotional intimacy in its choked-up, confessional anti-politicians. This politics is as noisy as it is silent—cacophonous in the family-feud clash of private authenticities and identities in the "culture war," silent in that argument (and mediating speech more generally) are taken as petty partisan bickering and a sad reminder of an absent national intimacy. Between the open society's poles of self-interest and self-expression, the possibility of persuasion—and so, Tocqueville argues, a critical basis of human dignity—is lost. The democratic individual is left self-centered without the resources to generate self-respect. What democratic society needs most, then, it denies itself, as democratic politics is devalued and taken to be the mere epiphenomenon of something more significant, meaningful, real, and natural—whether understood as higher or deeper, in the past or in the future. Originally political, the democratic revolution ends up tragically subverting the politics of democracy.

The fate of politics in democratic society can be summed up in the proposition that democratic man does not consider himself a political animal in a dual sense. First, democratic man imagines himself as at once transcending the need for politics and as being so beastly as to be incapable of the practice of politics. Second, political life is thought of as properly standing above the economic world of material needs and powers or as being so beastly that it best be avoided. A politics that does not reflect the privatism of the market or the privacy of being at home finds no place in democracy's social states of nature. In its openness, the democratic way of life takes shape not through argument and persuasion but rather in the dual pursuit of unconditional power and unconditional love. In either case, democracy dissolves the political element of human association.

# CHAPTER 3

# The Regime of Revolution

*Claude Lefort on History, Nature, and Convention after the Democratic Revolution*

They are like travelers dispersed in a great forest in which all the paths lead to the same point.

—Tocqueville, *Democracy in America*

## I. Democracy as Natural

*The Democratic Third Republic*

Conventional wisdom holds that from the end of Reconstruction to the start of the Great Depression a "laissez-faire orthodoxy" reigned in America.[1] More a way of life than merely an economic system, capitalism was taken as the ordering and animating principle of society. Market competition and the liberty of contract constituted a symbolic order within which all spheres of life were represented and evaluated. The contract stood, historian Eric Foner writes, as "an all-purpose metaphor for proper social relationships" and no less than "the *embodiment* of free will and voluntary action," the liberty of contract was elevated "from one element of freedom to its very essence," and the "market, not democratic politics" was considered "the true realm of freedom."[2] William Graham Sumner, for instance, went so far as to claim that questioning the market order was tantamount to attacking "the foundations of civilization"—socialism in particular was "anti-social and anti-civilizing."[3] Conversely, the free market was thought the vehicle of most everything that is of value: freedom, justice, wealth, peace, progress. In sum: "Man became economic man, democracy was identified with capitalism, liberty with property and the use of it, equality with opportunity for gain, and progress with . . . the accumulation of capital."[4]

With its currency among the courts (most notoriously in the 1905 Supreme Court case of *Lochner v. New York*), this worldview was insinuated into the very constitution of the American polity. Today, *Lochner* symbolizes a national identity so distinct as to be considered its own "constitutional regime"—the "second republic" of "laissez-faire constitutionalism," as Bruce Ackerman writes.[5] The revolutionary collapse of this order with *West Coast Hotel Co. v. Parrish* (1937) is cast as a "paradigm shift . . . of the most fundamental kind. In Robert Jackson's words, it signified the disintegration of 'the older *world* of laissez-faire.' "[6] In a sort of national identity crisis, what had been unquestionable became unconscionable.

This narrative helps us understand modern democracy, I suggest, although not in the ways usually supposed. The *Lochner* era's free-market orthodoxy is typically put forth as the antithesis of the characteristic openness of modern democracy. In this context, the "world of laissez-faire" epitomizes the tendency to represent a particular conventional settlement as grounded in the universal order—as "social arrangements decreed by nature."[7] As Cass Sunstein puts it, "The Court took as natural and inviolate a system that was legally constructed."[8] Moreover, as this free-market second nature—guided by an "invisible hand"—was synthesized with Protestantism, nature was reaffirmed as Nature: "It must be born in mind that [this order] was a mixture of three intellectually powerful currents of Western thought: the Protestant ethic; classical laissez-faire economics; and the principle of natural selection."[9] Uniting religion with economics and science in a single normative/descriptive representation of the world, the "national creed" of laissez-faire came to stand under "a sort of cosmic seal of approval."[10]

Just as laissez-faire was itself defined and defended against the paternalistic and putatively natural order of slavery, "democracy" is often formulated against the tendency to "naturalize" or "essentialize" our socially constructed world—to endow historically situated conventions with the character of universality. More than just a form of government, "democracy" here represents a governing ethos, a way of life in which almost nothing is sacrosanct, repressed, or incontestable—everything is at least in principle questionable. Every convention and identity is recognized as a social construct, and every construct is subject to being deconstructed. Thus is Justice Holmes's declaration that "the Fourteenth Amendment does not enact Mr. Herbert Spencer's Social Statics" celebrated today as a great democratic dissent, exposing the truth of laissez-faire as mere opinion, contingently situated in the here and now.

Against this notion of democracy as the essentially open society, I weigh the possibility that we tend today to think of democracy itself as natural—that modern democracy is more analogous than antithetical to the laissez-faire orthodoxy described above. Specifically, I argue that democratic *openness* is today what free-market *competition* once was: the simultaneously descriptive and normative fact/value of our way of life.[11] Democratic openness stands as the normative principle of the sole social order that we accept as good and legitimate, an order in which paternalism is excluded and everything is subject to endless questioning. At the same time, openness describes the modern condition of uncertainty and worldly contingency that we find ourselves born into, where the absolute is excluded and everything is subject to endless change. Consequently, the democratic social order seems inscribed in the order of the world—if not decreed by a now silent nature, then singularly in accordance with the flow of nature's unpredictable movements. In nature as in society, hierarchy has collapsed and revolution rules. Perhaps providentially, the state of openness is both that which we willingly (even passionately) affirm and that which we simply cannot deny. If this analogy holds, democratic openness would serve today as an all-purpose metaphor for proper social relationships. Democracy would be taken as not one element of freedom but as its essence, and as the good from which most others (freedom, equality, justice, wealth, peace, progress) follow. We would live in a time when man has become democratic man and when capitalism is identified with democracy, liberty and equality with democratic openness, and progress with democratization.

What follows is an exploration of how democracy, through its association with the state of openness, might come to seem natural. To this end, I turn to the writings of Claude Lefort.[12] Perhaps beyond any other contemporary theorist of democracy, Lefort offers a way to conceptualize the inherently abstract idea of openness. His work illuminates both how modern democracy is fundamentally connected to the principle of openness and how this *political* principle is constitutive more generally of a social form—a regime—within which are embedded signature modes of belief, judgment, and action across the spheres of politics, economics, religion, the arts and sciences, law and morality, and so forth. As we shall see, Lefort fruitfully interprets the characteristic openness of modern democratic society by exploring its genesis in the democratic revolution, the original phenomenon of opening, which he describes as "the dissolution of the markers of certainty."[13] Through this analysis, we are better able to see what Tocqueville occasionally overlooks: the advent of equality is inextricably intertwined with the collapse of hierarchy, and so the passion for equality is inseparable from the passion for revolution—from the freedoms of openness. Paternalism—Tocqueville's tutelary despotism—is as an anathema to democratic peoples as it is to aristocracy, and for the same reason.

At the same time, Tocqueville helps us see what Lefort fails to theorize: even as the principle of openness introduces an element of uncertainty and restlessness into modern existence, it is affirmed in such a way as to shut down argument and contestation regarding the principle itself. Like the capitalist economics of laissez-faire before it, the democratic culture of openness is inhabited as second-nature.[14] After the democratic revolution, Lefort argues, our notions of both freedom and nature take on an open or "historical" quality: existing necessarily in the unpredictable and open-ended flow of time, no body can legitimately claim to have the last word on matters of truth and right. Principled upon openness, democratic society, which Lefort terms the "historical society par excellence," seems both basically and ultimately free and natural—inscribed not in the immutable hierarchy of Nature but in the indeterminate openness of history. No longer can anyone speak in the name of Nature, but to oppose democracy would be to stand against history. Thus is the social state of openness underwritten by history's endlessness, warranted by the revolutionary nature of historical time.

Through a critical interpretation of Lefort's work, then, we shall see how the principle of democratic openness itself might constitute a sort of orthodoxy, although—and this is crucial—one without authoritative interpreters. In democratic modernity we are like Tocqueville's travelers: unled but nonetheless ending up at the same point. I go on to argue that the consequences of this faith in openness are not the blatant injustices and inequities of the laissez-faire orthodoxy, absurdly encoded as natural and justified as good, given, and inevitable. Rather, I argue that whatsoever is perceived as part of the present world of conventional norms and forms is devalued—not so much opened to questioning as undermined *as such*, without question (not unlike the political regulation of the free-market economy in the laissez-faire order). Meaning and authority, I conclude, determinately coincide with the idea of that which cannot be represented or embodied, enclosed and incorporated, in conventional norms and forms—with the idea of formlessness or informality.

Before returning to Lefort in Part II, I frame the notion of "democratic society" against the more common notion of "market society" and then take up some recent works of democratic theory that demonstrate or invoke the connections between "democracy" and "openness."

*Market Society or Democratic Society*

Conventional wisdom holds that we in America (and beyond) once again live in a fundamentally "market society" and "consumer culture"—a neoliberal, laissez-faire third republic. In our age of globalization, in the words of Thomas Frank, the "reigning economic faith . . . is merely a souped-up version . . . of the market-as-nature."[15] Moreover, this economic faith is supposedly taken as our faith as such (in the odd synthesis of "neoliberal" capitalism and "neoconservative" Christianity).[16] We hear that the corporation, like "the Church, the Monarchy, and the Communist Party in other times and places, . . . is today's dominant institution," with CEOs as the "heroes" and "high priests" of our time.[17] The "status of the market," this analysis runs, is "something close to a global theology": "Market society is no longer simply a metaphor. . . . It is a living reality . . . [wherein consumption] has become existential, the veritable badge of identity. As we consume so we are."[18] Even more strikingly: "Economics, as channeled by its popular avatars in the media and politics, is the cosmology and the theodicy of our contemporary culture. More than religion itself . . . it is economics that offers the dominant creation narrative of our society, depicting the relation of each of us to the universe we inhabit [and] the relationship of human beings to God. . . . This understanding . . . now serves as the unquestioned foundation of nearly all political and social debate."[19] In turn, "One cannot think of a single area of American life that does not define itself proudly and brazenly by the bottom line. Books are judged on sales; movies by the first weekend's gross; Broadway, of course; sports, the size of the contract."[20] Beyond oligarchy (which is only one principle of rule among others), we live, as Sheldon Wolin puts it, in an exclusive and all-embracing "economic polity."[21]

Is this the case, though? Can we think of any contemporary representation of a CEO as a hero (much less a high priest)? Do we really *judge* books and movies by their sales (or, conversely, do we usually regard the best seller and blockbuster as at best "guilty pleasures")? Do we *proudly* identify ourselves in terms of consumerism (or, conversely, do we assume that while we ourselves are not so shallow and materialistic, most others are)? Do we still represent our relationships with others via economic metaphors (for instance, marriage as a sort of business contract)? Has economics become our religion, with the shopping mall as our place of worship and Christmas the high holy day of commercialism (or does the very fact that we talk so much of "commercialism run amok" suggest something less than dogmatic adherence to tenets of creedal capitalism)?[22] Perhaps no recent incident is said to be more regrettably indicative of our market society than President George W. Bush's call for citizens to "go back to work" and "go down to Disney World in Florida" (which was widely paraphrased as a call to "go shopping") as the nation longed for unity, purpose, and meaning in the wake of the tragedy of September 11, 2001.[23] But the very fact that this incident is so widely and deeply regretted attests to the possibility that we are not so inured to a consumer consciousness. If we seek to make sense of how we live today in any sort of robust sense, we must attend to this second dimension of our representation of market society—that traveling to Disney World was a (vociferously rejected) metaphor for freedom and courage and family unity. That consumerism captures the imagination to such an extent attests at least as much to its status as a sort of constitutive insecurity of our society as to its present or looming reality—symbolizing less something we find meaningful than our fear of meaninglessness. If consumer culture carries religious implications, it is as our purgatory.

I offer an alternative interpretation of contemporary American society. Insofar as we can make such general claims about our "society," "culture," or "age," I suggest that ours is rendered more fully intelligible as a "democratic society"—a democratic "social state," to use Tocqueville's phrase. This means that we tend to represent and judge ourselves and our society primarily in terms of democratic openness—the freedoms promised by the collapse of hierarchy and the rise of equality. Consumerism and competition, for example, are taken as significant only insofar as they seem either iterations of the principle of openness or violations of that principle. Allow me to illustrate this essentially abstract idea by way of a movie from 1998 titled *Pleasantville*, a strikingly adept allegorical depiction of openness.[24] Over the course of the movie, the characters literally burst out of their closed, hierarchical, secure, unnaturally peaceful, domesticated, routine, predictable, black-and-white existence (no roads lead out of town) and into color as they come to restlessly question inhibiting social norms and conventions, express themselves intimately and authentically, and experience (even savor) the previously repressed uncertainties of life. By the end, every character inevitably awakens to the truth, the good, and the beauty of a colorful/open existence (even, at last, the politician). They learn to take the world as it really is deep down, below what they had been led to believe, and they are set free. The heroes are the artist and the outsider, self-expression is a veritable badge of identity, and the re-creation narrative is one of revolutionary rupture with rigid formality and paternalistic authority. The movie ends with its characters laughing lightly, not knowing what is to come.

To what extent does this allegory of democratic openness resonate with our own understanding of life in modern society? To what extent do we ultimately affirm as both fact and value—and so perhaps blindly—the "colorfulness" of the world? One sign of this symbolic narrative's standing might be that *Lochner* no longer makes sense even while *Griswold v. Connecticut* (1965) still does. Another sign might lie, as we shall see, in the continuing appeal of and quest for the natural, understood as spontaneous, organic, authentic, and undomesticated.[25] Yet another sign might lie in our very fascination with such impossibly general and abstract notions as "market society" and "democratic society," as Tocqueville argued. Most significantly, in such an interpretation it becomes explicable that while we do indeed affirm the free market as normative, even natural, we do so only insofar as it can be depicted in the vivid colors of democratic openness. Capitalism is itself sold as democratic revolution, empowerment, and freedom. Think, for example, of the immensely popular works of Thomas Friedman, wherein the flat world of capitalism and globalization is advertised in terms of its promised openness (he approvingly cites ads like "E*Trade. Now the power is in your hands" and "Sooner or later, all tyrannies crumble. Those that keep putting their customers on hold tend to crumble sooner").[26] At the same time, we are able to account for the other half of the picture: "economics"—insofar as it signifies either the power concentrations of corporatism (Big Oil, Big Tobacco, etc.) or all that falls under "bourgeois materialism"—is hardly the "unquestioned foundation" of our society, much less our cosmology and theodicy. We cannot ignore the fact that "market society," "consumerism," and so forth are invoked precisely so as to question them, rather than as legitimate or aspirational, and that the standard by which we question (and likely condemn) them is that of openness. Along these lines we render intelligible the full picture of our love-hate relationship with capitalism and globalization in democratic society.

*Unpacking Democratic Openness: From the*
*Rule of the People to the Death of God*

Democracy has been associated with openness of one kind or another at least since the time of Pericles, whether in his *Funeral Oration* description of democratic Athens as a "city open to all" or in the Corinthian description of the seafaring Athenians as "lovers of innovation" and "never at home." And of course there are senses of openness inherent in the very idea of democracy as the rule of the people: inclusive and open government, transparent and accountable, operating out in public as opposed to behind closed doors. Increasingly, though, there seems a tendency to take "democracy" as synonymous with "openness" and to formulate openness in a particularly expansive sense. Here, democratic freedom and equality are combined within, conceptualized in terms of, and reduced to openness—democratic openness as the liberty of the late moderns. Illustrative of this association, the first result of an April 2007 Google search for "democracy" was "Democracy: the free and open-source internet TV platform . . . built on open-standards." A nonprofit group advertises that "there's now an opportunity to create a television culture that is fluid, diverse, exciting, and beautiful," as opposed to "the same narrow, top-down cultural stagnation that we see on traditional television."[27] Freedom, open-source equality, organic spontaneity, the opportunity for revolutionary recreation, formlessness, inclusiveness, unpredictability, and beauty, as opposed to hierarchical immobility and stale conventionality: here are most all the elements of democratic openness.

Radicalizing the characterizations of "lovers of innovation" and citizens "never at home," today's expansive sense of openness is taken to mean a great many things (uncertainty, indeterminacy, contingency, spontaneity, open-endedness, fluidity) and to imply the possibility of a great many more (questioning, contestation, pluralism and diversity, integration and communication, radical action, the event of beginning). As Patchen Markell outlines it, radical openness takes shape within a matrix of oppositions between "rule," "stability, order, . . . and continuity" and "freedom," "change, interruption, . . . and novelty."[28] These oppositions are often summed as "democracy" versus "absolutism," "totalitarianism," "fascism," and increasingly "fundamentalism." While this sense of openness is frequently associated with one side of an academic discourse about democratic theory and categorized as postmodern, poststructuralist, and/or agonistic, it is more prevalent than that. Hardly the voice of postmodernism, Thomas Friedman again offers the perfect example in his characterization of the post–cold war order—radically disrupted and rendered fluid by "the democratization of technology," "the democratization of finance," and "the democratization of information"— as one in which "walls fell all over the world" and which "grows . . . more open every day."[29] Insofar as we believe—probably without much difficulty or doubt—that a walled-up world is unfree and unnatural, we are adherent to the principle of openness associated with democratic equality and revolution.

In his valuable recent work, Alan Keenan goes a great deal further in clarifying the affinities (and tensions) between democratic openness and democracy as the rule of the people. He identifies two senses of openness right at the surface of the logic of collective autonomy. First, there is "the openness of *inclusion* and *generality*": for it "to be the people who rule, rather than some faction or special class of the people, the process of making decisions must be open to all members of the community affected by them." Second, democratic self-rule requires the openness of "debate, argumentation, questioning, and revisability": it must be "the people . . . of today who rule, not that of yesterday, or of tradition," and they "must be able to revise their decisions, institutions, and practices as they wish or need."[30] Notice an immediate tension: open decision making necessarily limits the possibility of questioning; open-ended questioning precludes final decision making. Every decision being a closure, a power settlement, and a limitation on the range of potentiality, deciding comes with a sort of democratic buyer's remorse.

At a deeper level, Keenan identifies a third kind of openness, beyond those of the people's identity in space and over time—that of the grounds and standing of the identity of the people. This is "the openness of *incompletion* and imperfection" of "the democratic 'we' ": to be able to either question or decide, " 'the people' must take on an identity whose relative clarity and stability depend on particular foundations, traditions, and institutional forms that cannot be fully general or fully open to question." Yet, since there are "no external, nonpolitical, non-self-generated standards for judging the 'correct' vision of the people," any institutionalization of the people is to some degree arbitrary, illegitimate, and undemocratic. The "vicious circles" of "the people's self-foundation"—that the first cause of the people cannot be the people themselves and that they must perform a Munchausen-like bootstrapping of themselves into existence—embeds openness and uncertainty in the very definition of democracy as the rule of the people.[31] That democracy's source cannot be fully general or fully moral—that democracy cannot perform this politics of the impossible—generates a permanent state of restless discontent, an awareness of imperfection, within the democratic regime. Giving form to democracy is to betray its promise; democracy's birth into the world signifies its limitations.

Keenan thus exposes openness along all three democratic axes— horizontal (generality), forward and back in time (revisability), and vertical (foundations)—as well as at the core of both democratic action (to rule as both to decide and to question) and the democratic actor (the identity of the people who are to rule). Even further, Keenan identifies "the form of openness that in some way lies behind all the other forms of democratic openness": "[This is] the constitutive, even ontological, openness and fluidity of democratic and political freedom."[32] The "democratic spirit or imaginary is fundamentally one of questioning," and this "fundamental . . . democratic openness and uncertainty" warrants "both the " 'positive' openness of generality and revisability" and the " 'negative' openness of democratic . . . incompletion."[33] In other words, the openness of freedom/questioning/uncertainty/indeterminacy lies behind both that which we affirm as the norm of democratic legitimacy and that which we simply cannot deny or escape, the given of our late modern condition.[34] Already we begin to see how, via its association with "ontological" openness, the democratic social order might seem not only good and right but also in a sense natural, not unlike the old laissez-faire order of competition.

In a striking formulation of this connection between "ontological openness" and "democracy," George Kateb writes that "the hidden source of modern democracy may always have been the death of God," and that the "death of God was . . . slyly at work in the founding of modern democracy."[35] For Kateb, modern democracy rests upon the "sense of inessentiality and indefiniteness" born of the death of Father and King—of the collapse of divine hierarchy and so of the paternalistic-command society warranted by this hierarchy. Absent appeal to some higher authority, to the determinate guidance and guarantees of metaphysical absolutes, we are left on our own to navigate the open frontier into which we are cast. For Kateb, democracy is a matter of both coping with and celebrating this necessary self-reliance. William Connolly sums the point thusly: democracy is "grounded in a matrix of uncertainty"—in the "modern pressures to problematize those final markers (God, natural law, the divine right of kings, the natural basis of traditional identities, a fictive contract) that might have governed" us in the past.[36] Ungoverned, our democratic way of life is essentially without final solutions or final destinations. Insofar as we affirm the ethos of openness, we might complete the line: God is dead, and it is good.

Along these lines, Wendy Brown describes democracy as "politics without banisters," without the support of settled convictions and fixed certainties: "Conviction—as Truth or as principle—was never the right modality for belief within a democratic polity. A politics of Truth is inevitably totalitarian, and conviction in the sense of principle converges far too easily in liberal democracies with individualist strains of moral absolutism."[37] To check the comforting appeal of such colorless certainty-in-Truth, Bonnie Honig argues that we must resist the seductive and inevitably illusory longing for peace—for the reassurance and security of "the dream of a place called home," a place that is "free of power, conflict, and struggle."[38] Rather, we must foster a virile "democratic ethos"—"an affirmative cultural/political response to the problematization of final markers that helps to define the late-modern condition."[39] We must, in short, learn to celebrate the uncertainties of leaving home and all the possibilities that come with it. Such a "culture of democratization," Connolly writes, has "at its very center" the "periodic *denaturalization of settled identities and conventions*" and the "disturbance" of the "particular patterns" of "previous settlements."[40] As Peter Euben puts it, democratization is about "naturalized conventions periodically confront[ing] their conventional status."[41] The problematization of final markers requires the problematization of conventional settlements—our proper posture amid the fact of unsettling uncertainty is one of restless questioning.

The political and social upshot of this ontologically open way of life is that no person or group can rule or speak in the name of God, Truth, Nature, History, Reason, Law, or even the People. In democratic times, inequalities surely persist but hierarchy cannot; question supplants command. The properly democratic lexicon replaces the hierarchy of the sanctified Capital Letter with the circularity of the self-hyphenation (self-reliance, self-rule, self-creation, self-foundation, self-determination, and the like). Here we have one of the most common invocations of democracy today. We hear, for instance, "The NFL draft is great because it's democratizing. No one has the slightest idea what will happen, so all opinions are *equally invalid.* . . . And the fact The Experts [who try to predict which college players NFL teams will select] are constantly wrong is democratizing."[42] Beyond Keenan's notion of "revisability," modern democracy here signifies the innate limitation of *any* claim to authority due to chastening uncertainty. No one can legitimately claim final answers because there are no final answers; amid irreducible unpredictability, certainty and conviction are never warranted. And it is within this context that equality (we are all ultimately unsure and insecure, even The Experts) and freedom (there is no basis for command, no unquestionable rule, no reason for absolutism or totalitarianism) take on their specifically modern democratic character and fuse into the principle of democratic openness. In the social state of openness, it is as if we remain in a state of nature; to remain there undomesticated, we must resist the inclination to make up and impose Leviathans.

But how open is this openness? In the account above, "democratic" describes a state of affairs in which social arrangements cannot be massively affirmed as deduced from nature. Grounded in our state of *uncertainty*, democracy justifies the act of *questioning* settled conventions and identities. Is there a sense, though, in which this uncertainty and questioning might come to be massively affirmed as natural? Notice that the "ontological" openness discussed above seems no less descriptive than normative—the death of God as both fact and value, true and good. We necessarily live under openness-as-uncertainty; the freedom and equality expressed in openness-as-questioning is embedded in this condition; hence we are necessarily free and equal. Given the "reality" of our experience of openness—that the world is mysterious and subject to radical and unpredictable changes—the legitimacy of the open society seems simply self-evident, obvious in a way the competitive society of laissez-faire probably never was. Conversely, hierarchy and absolutism seem as much illusory as illegitimate.

Are there, in turn, fixed norms of identity inherent in democratic openness that are taken for granted and closed off from questioning? For example, do the psychological and emotional capacities to cope with the anxiety and frustrations of uncertainty constitute a standard of democratic maturity, even courage, below which we sink into our childish dreaming of places called home? Given uncertainty, does the "questioning self" stand as normative and natural? To cease questioning under conditions of ontological openness, it would seem, is akin to cease believing under conditions of ontological closure (before God's death), or to cease competing under conditions of survival of the fittest. In this sense, perhaps we are less permitted than ethically enjoined to question ourselves, others, and the world we inhabit. In a world defined as being without final answers, what choice do we have but to question things? Contestation becomes freedom's imperative. The liberty of contract was perhaps once cast as an ethical standard of judgment in the capacity to contract (in the dichotomy between competition and paternalism). Is the freedom to question cast as the capacity to question today (in the dichotomy between question and paternalism)? How would we judge one who insists upon clinging to a black-and-white world or one who stands still while all else is in motion?

In this context, how are we likely to judge previously settled conventions that are "made to confront their conventional status"? The evidence for our evaluation seems contained within the proposition that one is seldom "made to confront" something reaffirming. We would judge them harshly, precisely because they are previously settled, closed conventions (as in the negative connation of "conventional wisdom," which is always wrong, as opposed to, for instance, "common sense," which is usually right). At the same time, "unconventional" would strike us as in some way good (not bound by or conforming to convention, innovative, free thinking, original). Things need not be "made to confront" their unconventional status. There seems a certain superficiality to democratic contestation here, a preordained quality wherein every choice amounts to more or less of the same basic good—more or less openness.[43] While we are uniquely permitted to call the conventional world into question, it can only be according to the normative standard of openness. Questioning becomes an end in itself.

To advance this line of inquiry, I turn to the writings of Claude Lefort. Exploring his phenomenology of democracy in Part II of this chapter, we see more clearly than so far possible the origins and dimensions of democratic openness. At the same time, I suggest in Part III that through a close reading of Lefort's work, we come to notice a self-subverting quality of democratic openness. Here, its full factual/normative gravity becomes apparent; the order of openness (or, as we shall see, the rule of history) is no less determinate than the order of Nature.

## II. The Revolutionary Phenomenon of Opening

*The Theologico-Political Form of Society*

"Democracy," Lefort writes, is fully apprehended only as a "regime" or *"politeia"*—a term that signifies not only a "constitution" and "form of government" but also a "style of existence" and "mode of life." These last two phrases should "evoke everything that is implied by an expression such as 'the American way of life,' namely, those mores and beliefs that testify to the existence of a set of implicit norms determining notions of just and unjust, good and evil, desirable and undesirable, noble and ignoble." Best comprehended as a *"form of society,"* democracy above all generates certain notions of "proper relations between human beings." And this *"shaping"* of a people's *"manner of being in society"* defines the regime's "permanence in time, regardless of the various events that may affect it." Democratic society has an identity in that it is united "as a recognizable whole despite its internal divisions" and differentiated "on a fundamental level from other forms of society" by characteristically democratic norms of justice, the good and the right, human association, and a life well lived.[44] We might take this as Lefort's revision and restatement of Tocqueville's notion of democracy as a "social state."

Lefort distinguishes this way of approaching social phenomena from more mainstream methods of the social sciences. He argues that we can neither understand nor evaluate our "form of society" analytically, by reducing it to its internal aspects (whether to its structural components like state and civil society; its "spheres" of economics, politics, law, science, religion, and so forth; or its various groups, classes, and interests). For example, there can be no adequate study of our beliefs and actions in terms of self-interest and rational choice independent of an interpretation of the unifying social-symbolic milieu within which we become conscious of "the individual" in terms of a "self" who is naturally (really and properly) "interested" and who has both the right and rational capacity to "choose" from a menu of options made possible and constrained by the social form itself. To begin with the self-interested actor is to put the partial and derivative before the whole and generative, to explain by that which itself requires explanation. Nor can we approach human association as the epiphenomenal consequence of either economic necessity or economic choice. Social relationships are not experienced solely as, and so cannot be understood solely as, material relationships. Rather than "following the money," as it were, below the public appearance of things, we must follow the trail of that which is publicly represented as meaningful—as something orienting and motivating, a right or a cause, a source of pride and dignity, and so forth.[45] Realistically speaking, we cannot interpret behavior absent meaning, and we cannot interpret meaning absent its public presentation. In turn, the centrality of notions like economic necessity and choice in our society would raise questions such as: What form of society is prone to represent itself, to stage its fears and aspirations, in terms of economic necessities and choices? How have these come to be taken as signs of significance?

For Lefort, what is overlooked in any reduction of the overall schema of society to its empirical components is the "religious" dimensionality of society—the regime-specific mode of articulating the universal and particular. "Religion," as Lefort employs the term, "is a mode of portraying or dramatizing" those relations people establish with something beyond empirical time and space, and "by which they in turn recognize a principle of proper relations with one another." That the inhabitants of a social form identify that form as cohering over time and in space, as a recognizable and meaningful way of life, reveals the "religious sensibility" of the beliefs, attitudes, and representations that order the social, even if "the agents concerned do not relate them to any dogma" or "fidelity on their part to a church" and even if "they may, in certain cases, go hand in hand with militant atheism."[46]

Lefort goes on to argue that to interpret this quasi-religious articulation of the transcendent and the mundane, we must look primarily to the genesis narrative of the regime—how a particular form came into being from and continues to relate to the eternal and infinite: "The space called society . . . cannot in itself be conceived as a system of relations, no matter how complex we might imagine that system to be. On the contrary it is . . . the *particular mode of its institution* that makes it possible to conceptualize . . . the articulation of its dimensions, and the relations established within it between classes, groups and individuals, between practices, beliefs and representations. If we fail to grasp this *primordial reference* to the mode of the institution of the social, to the *generative principles* or to an overall schema governing both the temporal and the spatial configuration of society, we lapse into a positivist fiction." We can think of this coming into being of a coherent social form in terms of the "enigma" of a "division which institutes a common space," of "a break which establishes relations." It is from the "primal division" between the here and now, on one hand, and the quasi-religious dramatization of something beyond the empirical, on the other hand, that society takes meaningful shape for its inhabitants. When we envision modern society, for instance, its characteristic separations between state and society or public and private occur if, where, and how they do—they make sense—in reference to the particular ways in which we perceive modern society's originating, primal separation. As Lefort writes, the "fact that [social] space is organized as one despite . . . its multiple divisions and that it is organized as the same in all its multiple dimensions implies a reference to a place from which it can be seen, read and named." As we shall see, for Lefort we name ourselves democratic via a generative break that is largely oedipal.[47] The particular mode of democratic society's institution is the revolutionary beheading of the king.

But why think of our social gestalt, with its particular founding mediation of the transcendent and the empirical, as fundamentally democratic? Why privilege the language of politics when thinking about the "religious dimension" and "mode of institution" of society? Why "democratic" rather than, for example, "market" or "Christian" society? For Lefort, the interpretive key to the character of any society, to its characteristic norms of human relations, is the way in which power is represented as legitimate. The key to any social form is how power within that form is taken to bridge, or fail to bridge, the primal division between particularity and the universal. Society, Lefort writes, is put into form by the specific way in which power "makes a gesture towards something outside" the material world, toward an "externality," which, if "projected . . . on to the real . . . would no longer have any meaning for society."[48] We glimpse our social form in those instances when power is represented as authority rather than interpreted as naked power. The figurative presence of such a power, capable of explicitly or implicitly obtaining societal allegiance through a gesture toward transcendence, reveals the particular articulation of the social order.[49] In this sense, Lefort concludes, the symbolic status of power makes visible and intelligible the form of social organization, and this social form conditions the way reality is apprehended; the symbolic precedes the empirical.[50]

When speaking of power in this symbolic register, we are dealing with what Lefort terms the "political form" of society, or simply "the political" *(le politique)*. He distinguishes this from "politics" *(la politique),* which is a matter of the "exercise" and "functioning" of power (as opposed to the prior matter of its representation).[51] A regime's politics is revealed in the partisan struggles of competing interests or classes and is analyzable in the terms of the social sciences. The political, conversely, is "revealed, not in what we call political activity, but in the double movement whereby the mode of the institution of society appears and is obscured": "It appears in the sense that the process whereby society is ordered and unified across its divisions becomes visible. It is obscured in the sense that the locus of politics (the locus in which parties compete and in which a general agency of power takes shape and is reproduced) *becomes defined as particular,* while the principle which generates the overall configuration is concealed."[52] Once enmeshed in the empirical and material practices of power, we lose sight of the principle by which such practices came into meaningful being. We might say that "politics" refers us to an "economic" notion of power and so to the divisions and conflicts internal to a social form, while "the political" conveys the "religious" dimension of power whereby power potentially attains the status of social principle. The former refers to power as effective, the latter to power as legitimate, meaningful, and generative of a social-symbolic way of life—of a social state that carries with it a recognized, defining, and affirmed name.[53] One cannot, as Lefort puts it, "separate the elaboration of a *political form*—by virtue of which the nature and representation of power and social division (divisions between classes and groups) can stabilize, and by virtue of which the various dimensions of the human experience of the world can simultaneously become organized—from the elaboration of a *religious form*—by virtue of which the realm of the visible can acquire death, and by virtue of which the living can name themselves with reference to the dead."[54] The connection here is such that Lefort terms society's form fundamentally "theologico-political."[55]

By way of example, we can say that for Lefort (as for Tocqueville) revolutions are caused not exactly by misery or suffering but by the collapse of the constitutional dimension of power, of the political form of society within which material misery and suffering might be symbolically encoded and endured.[56] More religious than economic, so to speak, revolutions "are not born of an internal conflict between the oppressed and their oppressors; they occur at the moment when the transcendence of power vanishes, and when its symbolic efficacy is destroyed."[57] Revolution is thus the product of felt meaninglessness, of the incapacity of power as legitimizing representation to give unified form to—to stage in a meaningful way—social divisions and conflict.

*The Democratic Revolution as the Disembodiment of Power*

What, then, characterizes the democratic theologico-political form of society? What characterizes its symbolic political milieu, wherein power is represented as authority? What is the democratic mode of mediating the particular and the universal? For Lefort, democratic society is like any society in that it can only be interpreted as taking shape within a theologico-political matrix. At the same time, Lefort argues that we must recognize the fundamental transformation of this matrix, a transformation that occurs with the democratic revolution. In an oft-quoted passage, Lefort writes, "Democracy is instituted and sustained by the *dissolution of the markers of certainty*. It inaugurates a history in which people experience a fundamental indeterminacy as to the basis of power, law and knowledge, and as to the basis of relations between self and other, at every level of social life (at every level where division, and especially the division between those who held power and those who were subject to them, could once be articulated as a result of a belief in the nature of things or in a supernatural principle)."[58]

Lefort concurs with Tocqueville that democracy should be understood capaciously, as an encompassing social state or form of society. Here we have Lefort's key departure from Tocqueville's theorization of democracy: the dissolution of the markers of certainty supplants the equality of conditions as the generative fact and generative principle of the democratic regime. The central question for Lefort is, therefore, what "style of existence" is instituted and sustained by this dissolution? What social form, with what principle of proper human relations, is generated by the experience of a "fundamental indeterminacy" precisely as to the principle of proper human relations?

The first thing we can say is that, in Lefort's account, we are tempted to misinterpret the revolutionary *transformation* of our theologico-political social form as its *collapse* into fragmentation—into a formless "economic" materialism and "scientific" empiricism. As we shall see, the incorporating form of modern democracy is elusive precisely because its inhabitants do not see, and so deny, it. Modern democracy, represented as assuming its openness with the death of God (the collapse of religious dimensionality), is taken as the society without form—simply a congregation of individuals (usually represented as a market). This is not Lefort's interpretation, though. With the democratic revolution, the theologico-political form of society does not collapse but instead takes on an unprecedented openness or formlessness of form. We might put it this way: for Lefort, the "hidden source of modern democracy" is not the death of God but the death of Christ—the worldly figure of the sovereign father. The disappearance of the corporeal *figure* or *form*—not the collapse of the *dimension*—of transcendence opens space and time to the democratic abstraction. Lefort thus represents the democratic revolution as the dissolution of the material markers of authority and so of certainty.

On the one hand, then, the "essentials remain unchanged: the theologico-political is revealed in the deployment of a system of representations . . . whose oppositional principle"—"between the particular, which is . . . organized spatially and temporally, and the universal, which is still related to the operation of transcendence"—remains constant.[59] On the other hand, we should not let this continuity obscure the radical nature of the dissolution of the markers of certainty. For Lefort, as for Tocqueville, the democratic revolution is the singularly pivotal event of human history. It inaugurates modernity by rendering problematic the articulation of the particular and the universal, the mortal and the divine. Like Tocqueville, for whom there are really only two basic regime types (aristocracy and democracy), Lefort sees all prerevolutionary social forms (from ancient Greece to the ancien régime) as fundamentally alike, as are all postrevolutionary forms (whether, as we shall see, democratic or totalitarian).

This pivotal quality becomes apparent when we look at the theologico-political form the revolution overturned. "Under the monarchy," Lefort writes, "power was embodied in the person of the prince. . . . The prince was mediator between mortals and gods or . . . the transcendental agencies represented by a sovereign Justice and a sovereign Reason."[60] The physical presence of this Christ-figure king made visible both the union of natural and supernatural, and the division between them: "[The king] condensed within his body, which was at once mortal and immortal, *the principle that generated the order of the kingdom.* His power pointed towards an unconditional, other-worldly pole, while at the same time he was, in his own person, the guarantor and representative of the unity of the kingdom. The kingdom itself was represented as a body, as a substantial unity."[61] Moreover, the properly hierarchical order of the realm was instantiated in the head-body image. In this body politic, the universal could, as it were, speak for itself, in determinate and commanding voice.[62]

Literally, then, the "democratic revolution, for so long subterranean, *burst out* when the body of the king was destroyed, when the body politic was decapitated and when, at the same time, the corporeality of the social was dissolved."[63] In full view, the revolution signifies the "dissolution of the monarchical focus of legitimacy and the destruction of the architecture of bodies."[64] Democratic society, in turn, is instituted as a society without a body; it remains a recognizable whole, but without any determinate, visible representation of itself as a whole. Democracy is a form of society, but a uniquely abstract or formless one—literally, the informal society. Just as Tocqueville argues that democracy takes shape with the dissolution of the feudal principle of landedness (of authority incorporated in the land), Lefort argues that democracy is defined by the absence of physical, objective, perceptible definition—the land without territory, the land of imagination. After the revolution, the transcendent can no longer be made manifest in the material world, power can no longer be vocalized as commanding sovereignty, and so society can no longer be put into form via the Christian mode of *embodiment*. Henceforth, we search without precedent for a new way of articulating the religious dimensionality of social existence—of mediating the universal and the particular. Understood as such, the democratic revolution is "a political event" with no less than "a metaphysical significance: the collapse of an unconditional authority which, in one or another social context, someone could claim to embody."[65]

## Emptiness, Openness, and the Rule of the People

This extraordinary phenomenon of disincorporation is, for Lefort, the instituting mode and genesis moment of modern democracy. The democratic regime is given form precisely, if paradoxically, by the "indetermination that was *born from the loss* of the substance of the body politic."[66] Herein lies the most basic sense of democratic openness, the generative opening of the democratic theologico-political. The democratic political form is *constitutively* open in that "the locus of power," once occupied by the figure of the king, "becomes an *empty place*."[67] After the revolution, power cannot be transubstantiated into authority by means of symbolic incorporation; authority can no longer be present in the flesh, as it were. Sovereign power becomes essentially problematic in that no individual, group, or entity is recognized as representationally consubstantial with it. The people, nation, state, or humanity might assume the status of universality, but none of these are substantial entities. Their representation is always reliant upon open-ended contestation, a matter of inter-subjective discourse rather than objective decree. The principle of hierarchy and the place of command collapse with the destruction of the architecture of bodies. The seat of power remains forever vacant as power must seek out and make an argument on behalf of, rather than simply speak in the name of, truth and right. The claim to legitimate authority is thus conjoined to the legitimate questioning of authority. Of "all the regimes of which we know," Lefort concludes, modern democracy "is the only one to have represented power in such a way as to show that power is *an empty place* and to have thereby maintained a gap between the symbolic and the real. It does so by virtue of a discourse which reveals that . . . those who exercise power do not possess it; that they do not, indeed, embody it."[68] It is in this empty, open space that the democratic way of life restlessly takes shape.

This is not to say that the people are not sovereign in democracy but rather that the people cannot perform their sovereignty. Unlike the self-sufficient king, the people cannot speak and act on their own behalf. The abstraction of "the people" can never be unproblematically identi-fied—located in time and space—and so can never be present in such a way as to occupy the seat of power. In turn, there is always a gap be-tween popular sovereignty and its representation—between symbolic and real, principle and practice. Question supplants decree as the politi-cal's mode of operation. Even as "the people will be *said* to be sovereign," their "identity will constantly be open to question," and so it will re-main ultimately "latent."[69] This latency of sovereignty—this constitutive absence of the father figure—is the beating heart of modern democracy for Lefort. It is, as we shall see, the meaning of freedom in democracy.

Following Lefort further, we can say that this relationship between sovereignty and absence is more than coincidental: the people will be said to be sovereign only *on condition* of their identity remaining latent. The sovereignty of the people is unconditional precisely because it is immaterial. The people's authority being made manifest would actually signify a diminution from potential universality to actual particularity. Lefort writes that by its very instantiation in the here and now power would be "exposed to the threat of *falling into particularity*" and so of arousing something "more dangerous than hatred, namely, contempt." Any descent from universality and power "runs the risk of . . . falling into collective representations at the level of the real," and so of the contingent, arbitrary, and fleeting. At the moment power is wielded, by the very condition of its being taken up and exercised by "mere mortals," as Lefort puts it, it is itself rendered merely mortal.[70] With the democratic revolution, the use of power is necessarily accompanied by a reduction of authority, by its assumed abuse—effectiveness implies a touch of illegitimacy. Democratic peoples love the power itself but hate the repositories of power.

Notice that democratic openness—the emptiness of the place of power—is actually maintained by the idea of the sovereign rule of the people. The people themselves cannot rule, and the thought of a sovereign people ensures that no one else can rule either. The sovereignty of the people, absolute but abstract, guarantees that the seat of power can never be substantially occupied. Democracy, Lefort writes, "combines these two apparently contradictory principles: on the one hand, power emanates from the people; on the other, it is *the power of nobody*. And democracy thrives on this contradiction"; whenever it is resolved, "democracy is either close to destruction or already destroyed."[71] The rule of the people is thus quite literally the rule of no *body*, whether personal or institutional. When power belongs to the people, "no one can take the place of the supreme judge: 'no one' means no individual, not even an individual invested with a supreme authority, and no group, not even the majority."[72] While "no artifice can prevent a majority from emerging *in the here and now* or from giving an answer which can stand in for the truth . . . the fact [is] that every single individual has the right to denounce that answer as hollow or wrong."[73] Intrinsically unrealizable and unrepresentable, the people fall silent the moment some person, group, or institution presumes to speak in their name.[74] In its impossibly all-inclusive *generality*, the popular sovereign cannot *will*. A sort of impotent Leviathan, with a power that is at once unconditional and immaterial, popular sovereignty cancels itself out—limitlessly legitimate but effectively powerless. As Lefort puts it, in democracy "the negative is effective"—democracy as the silence of the voice of the people.[75]

For Lefort, then, the rule of the people is ultimately less a matter of collective decision making and self-government (which, in any case, presumes a nonexistent collective self) than of the exposure of the particularity and so contestability of any decision made in the people's name—democracy not as self-rule but as the rule of no-body. The rule of the people is the operation of negativity. To "return power to the people," as the common mantra demands, is not to empower the people but to debase those who exercise power. The principle of democracy becomes a wholly critical standard. When the people reign, no one rules; therein lies the openness of democracy. We might say that the democratic rule of the people, on Lefort's account, actually serves many of the functions of the liberal rule of law. The *latency* of the people replaces the *immutability* of rights as a check upon the legitimate exercise of power. A constitutively *absent* sovereign replaces *higher* law as the repository of an authority beyond our grasp. And the *generality* of the people replaces the *impartiality* of the law as a safeguard against tyranny.

## The Rule of Revolution

For Lefort, the political shapes the social. The representation of power, the symbolization of its locus, is constitutive of the various elements of social space and of the relationship of those elements to one another. After the democratic revolution, the emptiness of the political form generates the openness of our social form. Lefort describes this democratic political/social form in a key passage: "Democracy invites us to replace the notion of a regime governed by laws, of a legitimate power, by the notion of a regime founded upon *the legitimacy of a debate as to what is legitimate and what is illegitimate*—a debate which is necessarily without any guarantor and without any end." This open-ended debate, wherein by definition nobody has the last word, is the essence of democracy. Where the social order could once be articulated as a result of a belief in the stable nature of things, after the revolution a restless and unsettling questioning is implicit in social practices. In democracy, "no one has the answer to the questions that arise," and whatsoever "has been established never bears the seal of full legitimacy."[76] The current wielders of power, the people, even the concept of democracy itself: all are essentially contestable. Democracy is the social state principled upon the indeterminacy and uncertainty of conditions.

Recall Lefort's claim that to render intelligible one's regime even while inhabiting it, one must interpret its generative principle by returning to its founding moment and mode of institution. Democracy is unique in human history in that it is instituted via not incorporation but *dis*incorporation—via the dissolution of the embodiments of certainty. The founding representation of power is literally that of its beheading. Revolutionary opening—the contestation and potential overturning of all repositories of power, hierarchical or otherwise, personal and impersonal—is itself the mode of institution of the overall configuration of society. Paradoxically, democracy is constituted through revolution. And because democracy is born of revolution, revolution is inscribed in democracy's genetic code. The negative remains effective, to the point where democratic peoples experience what Keenan terms "ontological openness."

In Part III, I argue that Lefort's theory of democracy illuminates the constitutive nature of our restlessness—of our permanent passion for the phenomenon of revolutionary opening—which Tocqueville at times obscures in his singular focus on equality. If democracy is *for* equality, and *by* the rule of the people, it is *of* revolution. At the same time, I argue that the "fundamental indeterminacy" of our democratic existence is perhaps more determinate than Lefort recognizes. Indeed, the democratic regime comes to seem as immutable and ordained as the regime it overturned. Democratic society seems to us tailor-made for the mysterious movements of history (rather than for the divine hierarchy of Nature). I argue that the revolutionary *moment*—the historical event—rather than the *form* of the king stands as the mediating point of symbolic articulation between the universal and the particular. The architecture of openness replaces that of the body. In turn, restlessness and informality take on normative weight as ethical imperatives and standards of judgment: if one is not in motion, one is neither free nor "fully alive"; the concept of energy replaces that of harmony in our idea of health; the vitality of heart/body replaces the verticality of head/body; fraternity replaces paternity in our idea of community; quantum indeterminacy replaces orderliness and war replaces peace in our idea of nature; we come to define ourselves by the sum of our experiences, by our history rather than by our place in society; change is seen as both inevitable and good, as innovation rather than corruption; questioning supplants command. Born of the loss of any embodying figure or form, when all things symbolic are rendered abstract, democratic society is put into form precisely as the formless society—the open society, liberated from hierarchy's aristocratic, paternalistic, and absolutist representations. Regimented by its original vital principle of revolution, openness becomes the unquestionably proper form of society, and informality the proper form of social relations.

## III. Democracy as the Historical Society par Excellence

*The Democratic Adventure: Equality and Indeterminacy*

Lefort writes that we could not hope for a better description of the unique character of the democratic regime than the one provided by Tocqueville. In Lefort's view, Tocqueville's most profound theorizations of democratic society point to its dynamic vigor and vitality, to the superabundant force and energy at its heart. Democracy's "prime virtue," Lefort paraphrases Tocqueville, "is its characteristic agitation," its kinetic, dynamic quality of "all-pervading and restless activity" rather than "its potential ability . . . to improve the government's ability to conduct public affairs." Democracy is desirable as a form of government, to be sure, but above all it should be embraced as "an unprecedented historical adventure whose causes and effects cannot be localized within the sphere that is conventionally defined as that of government."[77] The social state of indeterminacy and uncertainty is, in turn, one of vital energy, restless activity, and adventure.

But even Tocqueville, Lefort argues, misinterprets the basic nature, and so shortchanges the extent, of this energy and activity. Tocqueville's misdiagnosis follows from his theorization of the equality of conditions rather than the dissolution of the markers of certainty as generative of our democratic adventure. However important this phenomenon may be, Lefort writes of equalization, it "leaves an essential mutation in the shadows."[78] Tocqueville "usually tries to uncover an inversion of meaning" in the rise of equality; "the new assertion of singularity fades in the face of the rule of anonymity; the assertion of difference (of belief, opinion or morals) fades in the face of the rule of uniformity," and so on. Consequently, his explorations are restricted to "the underside of the phenomena he believes to be characteristic of the new society"; he is "reluctant" to fully "confront the unknown element in democracy," and so he "does not pursue his explorations by examining the underside of the underside."[79] Indeed, Lefort argues that when considering this unknown element, we cannot even "limit our explorations to the underside of the underside": "On the contrary, we must recognize that, as long as the democratic adventure continues . . . the meaning of what is coming into being remains in suspense."[80] The indeterminacy of democratic society is ineradicably and irreducibly fundamental, with its openness manifest properly in this suspension of judgment. By his very attempt to decipher the ultimate meaning of the revolution, to predict the future of our democratic adventure (whether, via equality, toward freedom or despotism), Tocqueville necessarily misreads the revolution. He is blind to the ultimate blindness of our democratic condition—to its essentially open-ended and protean character.

For Lefort, then, the democratic revolution cannot be understood as giving rise to Tocqueville's notion of a *determinative* equality. Rather, as we have seen, democracy takes shape from the indetermination that issues from the loss of the substance of the body politic. The democratic revolution in the principle of authority gives birth to the unknown, which renders even the democratic equality of conditions provisional. In this sense, democracy's empty political form leads primarily to an open social form and only secondarily to equality. Democratic society, Lefort concludes, is "*instituted* through a new awareness of what *cannot* be known or mastered."[81] Consequently, "what is instituted is never established, the known remains undermined by the unknown, the present proves to be undefinable."[82] For Lefort, the meaning of the revolution is precisely that its course and meaning remain perpetually unknowable and uncontrollable; mastery goes the way of command. A sort of fecund and vitalizing uncertainty generates democratic modernity's intrinsically restless way of life. Lefort sums this state of affairs by theorizing democracy as "the historical society *par excellence*, a society which, in its very form, welcomes and preserves indeterminacy."[83] It is historical in that its destiny is to have no final destination, but only a sort of perpetual overturning natality: it is "destined to undergo a process of continuous institutional upheaval, destined to give birth to new social forms and explicitly to *experience the real as history.*"[84] The real and the right are simultaneously inscribed in our experience of linear time, and we are to welcome and preserve that which in any case we cannot deny. Truly a social state of becoming, democracy is a "historical adventure in the sense that *it can never end,* in that the *boundaries of the possible and the thinkable constantly recede.*"[85] The last impossibility left standing is the end of democracy's historical adventure.

For Lefort, it seems the democratic adventure comprises both the basic condition and the prime aspiration of modern times—our truth and our good. "Historical" subsumes both the immutable fact of our modern democratic situation (indeterminacy and uncertainty) and the central value of democratic society (freedom and the right to question). In turn, democracy's historical social form comes to seem inscribed in the historical time in which we inescapably live. Put differently, "history" is to the democratic order what "nature" was to the laissez-faire order: the venue of fact/value elision. Our democratic adventure stands as both that which we willingly affirm and that which we cannot deny.

*Historical Freedom*

Tocqueville argues that the social state of democracy harbors within it the potential for both new types of freedom and a new type of despotism, whether of the tutelary state or of public opinion. For Lefort, democracy is not such a mixed bag. As we have seen, Lefort argues that Tocqueville misinterprets the source of democracy's revolutionary abstraction and in turn underestimates how irreducibly fluid and in flux democratic society truly is. The implication of Lefort's argument is that the final form of democracy *cannot* be despotism, tutelary or otherwise, simply because democracy *has* no final form, only an endless series of provisional reformulations. That which has been opened can never be closed again: history never stops moving; the democratic revolution never relents; our historical society never settles down. Indeed, instituted through an awareness of what cannot be known or mastered, as Lefort puts it, democratic society is no less than destined to undergo a process of continuous institutional upheaval. Insofar as we understand freedom as the denaturing of any particular representation of power—as "the operation of negativity" wherein conventions are made to confront their mere particularity and conventionality—freedom itself must be an innate characteristic of our democratic condition. The king's head cannot be reattached to his body, and so we cannot but be free. We can never be truly certain again (although we might pretend otherwise), and so questioning remains, at least in principle, always possible. So long as we live in history, we ourselves cannot be known or mastered. We are, at bottom, restless and undomesticable. Liberty is woven into the vicissitudes of our historical adventure. We are inescapably free.

Recall Lefort's claim that the prime virtue of democratic society is its characteristic agitation. In his account, this agitation is equally characteristic of the condition into which we are born. In this sense, democracy's prime virtue seems inherent in its very condition of existence. The openness induced by the dissolution of the markers of certainty seems to stand as a description of the unpredictable world we find ourselves stuck in and as the normative principle of the social arrangements and relationships we affirm as good and right. Providentially, democratic society is open, and it is good. "Democratic" characterizes the reality of our existence (as revealed to us by the revolutionary rupture) and the proper free form of society. "Historical" signifies the *is* of indeterminacy and the *ought* of restless questioning. In the age of laissez-faire, the "survival of the fittest" was perhaps taken as both the defining fact of nature and the central value of the good and free society—society in accord with nature. For Lefort, democratic openness seems both the defining fact of history and the central value of the good and free society—society in accord with history.

This linkage of fact and value in freedom is apparent in Lefort's notions of both political freedom (against the domesticating tutelary state) and the freedom of the individual (against domesticating public opinion). Lefort writes, "The operation of negativity and the institution of political freedom are one and the same. And the fact is that political freedom survives so long as it is . . . deemed impossible to occupy the locus of power."[86] The survival of political freedom here is contingent only upon the perpetual emptiness of the place of power. Political freedom lasts as long as nothing established can bear the seal of full legitimacy. In turn, Lefort argues that we should temper our fears of the growth of a tutelary state within the political form of democracy. "What I have termed the operation of negativity," Lefort writes, "is no less constitutive of the democratic space than the erection of the state into a tutelary power. The system thrives on this contradiction and, so long as the system is perpetuated, neither of its terms can lose its efficacy."[87] At every turn, the gap between the state and what it is to represent proves obvious. Far from occupying the seat of power, the democratic state holds only the modicum of authority proper to the material realm of everyday politics. Thus the state can never possess the tutelary authority of the father figure; comprised of parties, the state is always subject to being challenged as merely particular. "It is often said that the power of the state is increasing as a result of . . . new demands" for welfare and rights guarantees, Lefort writes, "but the extent to which it is being challenged tends to be forgotten."[88] The state is expected to do everything, but everything it does is contested. Indeed, the politics of democracy is no less than a "theatre of . . . contestation."[89]

With a similar logic, Lefort argues that the denaturing, negating flow of history "counteracts the petrification of social life" that Tocqueville fears will follow from conformity to majority opinion. While "the legitimacy of the pole of opinion can be asserted to be unlimited," we should temper our fear because "opinion remains shapeless; it cannot be localized in a body and it cannot be reduced to a set of statements as it is constantly being created and re-created." And the moment opinion is localized and given shape, it loses much of its legitimacy. Public opinion must always be voiced by somebody (usually multiple and conflicting somebodies) and is thereby brought down to size as merely particular opinion. The power of majority opinion is limited by the fact that it is recognized as the opinion of some particular majority. The power of public opinion is thus undermined the moment it is polled—the moment it is given form in the here and now. Against social petrification, then, democracy inaugurates "the experience of an ungraspable, uncontrollable" social life that is "constantly . . . open to question."[90]

Ultimately, Lefort concludes, "[We] have to reject the alternative formulated by Tocqueville . . . [wherein] the individual either appears in the fullness of his self-affirmation, or disappears completely as a result of his weakness and isolation, and is swallowed up by opinion or by social power. . . . [The individual's] strength does not reside in his full positivity as a subject, and . . . any attempt, no matter how refined, to enslave him will fail because there is within him something that escapes objectification." His fears notwithstanding, and through no particular efforts of his own, the democratic individual cannot be domesticated. The individual escapes objectification when he "discovers that he is un-defined, and has no contours," that he is "constituted beneath the pole of a new indeterminacy."[91] For Lefort, the individual's own formless form assures his freedom. Democratic man cannot but be free precisely because he is a historical being, constitutively uncertain, abstract, opaque. Living in history, after the dissolution of the markers of cer-tainty, we cannot know or master, but then neither can we be known or mastered. We cannot be shaped by power because we are inherently ungraspable. Free because fugitive, we less question power than are a question to power. With the disappearance of the father figure, we can-not be domesticated because we cannot be named. Contrary to Lefort's assertion, we do find something like this notion of freedom in the writ-ings of Tocqueville, in his claim that democratic peoples easily elude power's grasp by their own mobility and insignificance.

Ultimately, we might say that Lefort inverts Tocqueville's terms (al-though without Tocqueville's critique) by theorizing a social state wherein freedom rather than equality is implicitly taken as given and final—a determinative feature of our protean social form. If not exactly a quality of nature, Lefort's freedom is inseparable from our postrevolutionary social-symbolic order, which governs our access to and experience of the real. Henceforth, as Lefort writes, we experience the real as history. If not quite "a truth inscribed in the real," democratic freedom is constitutive of our "new relation to the real."[92] Freedom-as-openness is affirmed as underwritten by history's endlessness. And in its bundle of associations with freedom and revolution and history, Lefort affirms the democratic order as both true and good. Born in revolution, the democratic regime seems warranted by the revolutionary nature of history—assured by and at home in the unpredictable flow of indeterminate time. Democ-racy is as inevitable as change itself. Tocqueville argues that authority can be displaced but never eradicated; it always settles somewhere. After the revolution, when no authority can be massively affirmed, the unsettling operation of negativity—freedom-as-revolutionary-opening—is itself mas-sively affirmed.

*Democratic Man as a Rights-Declaring Animal*

Democratic peoples enact the operation of negativity, Lefort explains, by declaring their rights. At times, rights have been formulated as an obstruction to democratic politics—whether as superpolitical "higher law" that closes off from debate certain untouchable absolutes or in fostering of a sense of privatism and possessive individualism. Whether by taking on the characteristics of a religion or by developing within us an economic consciousness, rights work against democracy. Against both of these notions, Lefort democratizes the idea of rights. For Lefort, rights are the generative principles of democracy: "The singular thing about the freedoms proclaimed at the end of the eighteenth century [specifically in the 1791 French Declaration of the Rights of Man] is that they are in effect indissociable from the birth of the democratic debate. Indeed, they generate it."[93] Like the liberty of contract in the laissez-fair order, the right to debate—to associate and argue—is the foundation of democratic civilization. With the democratic revolution, Lefort argues, right is severed from the figure of the monarchy and attaches to the abstraction of man and the multiple particularities of individual human beings. With a logic we have seen before, Lefort writes, "The rights of man reduce right to a basis which, despite its name, is without shape . . . and, for this reason, eludes all power which would claim to take hold of it—whether religious or mythical, monarchical or popular. Consequently, these rights go beyond any particular formulation which has been given of them, and this means that their *formulation* contains the demand for their *reformulation.* . . . From the moment when the rights of man are posited as the ultimate reference, established right is open to question."[94] The disembodiment of right leaves this ultimate standard of judgment open to constant and indeterminable reinterpretation, ensuring once again the movement of restless reformulation in the very form of democratic society. Representing rights as residing with man implies not so much the institutionalization of rights as the institutionalization of conflict over the meaning of rights. No establishment—not even of rights themselves—can be taken as fixed and final; the foundation and pinnacle of the political is itself left open to question.

There are a number of key points here. First, notice that the abstraction "man" parallels that of "the people" discussed earlier. We saw how the sovereign rule of the people is itself materially undermined by the indeterminacy and absence of the people—the condition of full legitimacy itself checks the effective use of the people's power. Here, the rights of man are similarly posited as an unconditional rule or "ultimate reference." But because this rule is seated in the indeterminable idea of man or humanity, it eludes the grasp of the holders of power. The rights of "man" are the rights of no-body—and as such never fall into a contemptible particularity. In turn, human rights less impose determinate limits on the exercise of legitimate power than render uncertain every claim by power to speak in the name of right. Honoring democracy, the hierarchy implied by the notion of higher rights is supplanted by the egalitarian negative of "who is to say?" Honoring democracy, settled borders and boundaries that constrain power are supplanted by a ceaseless revolutionary overturning of power.

Second, notice that the general principle of human right goes beyond any particular formulation. Just as the sovereignty of the people can never be fully represented, the rights of man can never be fully realized in the here and now. It would be misleading, Lefort writes, "to declare simply: here, in our societies, [that] rights exist"; one "must refrain from granting them a *reality*."[95] The principle of right does not reside in any political practice or institution, and indeed recognizing the principle implies recognizing the necessary gap between principle and practice. Put differently, we must acknowledge the tension between enumerated and conventionally established rights, which are multiple, settled, and determinate, and the singular, universal, and open-ended *"right to have rights,"* which gives "rise to an adventure whose outcome is unpredictable."[96] Lefort writes that the "symbolic dimension of right is manifested . . . in the irreducibility of the awareness of right to all legal objectification, which would signify its *petrification* in a *corpus* of laws." For Lefort, the principle of right cannot be put into legal words or conventional forms—it cannot be embodied even in the impersonal repository of laws. To give right form in the sphere of politics would be to debase it in the register of the political. The norm of restlessness is inscribed in the idea of rights: more verb than noun, rights "are not simply the object of a declaration"; rather, "it is their essence to be declared."[97]

The pole of right cannot be denied; it is compelling, but it cannot be made manifest in the here and now; its imminent presence in the regime is effective precisely in its final transcendence.

And third, Lefort goes further to write that "where right is in question, society—that is, the established order—is in question."[98] It is not only that we might acknowledge the positive law establishment of rights as inadequate to the principle upon which they stand. To invoke right is to call our particular rights into question, recognizing the universality of the principle that "reduces right to the questioning of right."[99] And to question our rights—to enact right—is to call the society principled upon rights into question. Rights consciousness enjoins an openness to revolution; the disembodiment of right enjoins an openness to the disestablishment of conventionalized society. In this sense, democracy signifies the subversion not only of hierarchical conventions but of the conventional as such. We enact democracy by dissolving the markers of certainty—displacing authority in every form becomes an ethical imperative. After the revolution, social order rests upon the right of question rather than the right of command (or the right to contract); abdicating the right to question in democracy would be akin to abdicating the right to command in aristocracy. In a world defined as without final answers, the good of questioning of every decision becomes self-evident. It is not that democracy is inherently anarchic or unruly, then, but that questioning itself stands as the ordering rule of our democratic way of life. The figure of the question stands sovereign.

Lefort claims that, to understand our social form, we must return to its generative mode of institution. Democracy was instituted by the revolutionary event; subversion is its original vital principle and defining gesture. The democratic pillars of human rights and popular sovereignty ensure the reoccurrence of this founding moment in the perennial beheading of the authority figure—the debasing of the father figure, as it were—and the perpetual return to a state of openness, a social state of nature without command or decree, where the question always has the last word. More than merely effective, the negative is determinate: practice is necessarily subverted by principle; the universality of the principle of right is necessarily a critical standard. Democratic right is the right to revolution. We arrive here at the full view of democracy in Lefort's account. Democracy is "the theatre of contestation" in which we, "on the basis of rights," "transgress . . . boundaries" in a "history that remains open."[100]

For Lefort, then, the democratic articulation of the universal and the particular is apparent in the moment one declares one's rights. And this event displaces the body of the king in giving form to society, in establishing a new norm of proper human association—the norm of public expression. "Far from having the function of masking a dissolution of social bonds which makes everyone a monad," Lefort argues, "[rights] both testify to the existence of a new network of human relations and bring it into existence." As opposed to atomism and privatism, the rights of the individual generate wide-open public spaces in which for the first time in history free and equal individuals may congregate and make contact with one another. The recognition of rights does "not imply that the individual withdraws into the sphere of his own activities" but rather "gives full recognition to the . . . *freedom of movement*" and "therefore facilitates the multiplication of human relations" that were previously "frozen in the relation of authority, or . . . confined in privileged spaces." Above all, it is the freedom of movement, with its ancillaries of free association and speech, that replaces the aristocratic obligations of place in shaping the order of human relations. Informal networks of communication supplant the formal chain of command, and free expression supplants aristocratic codes of etiquette as the means of recognition in association. And by this "relational freedom" of rights, society ensures the openness of democracy: "As everyone acquires the right to address others and to listen to them, a symbolic space is established; it has no definite frontiers, and no authority can claim to control it. . . . Speech as such and thought as such prove to exist independently of any given individual, and belong to no one."[101]

Thus far, we have seen how, for Lefort, democracy is not one element of freedom but its essence, and the good from which most others follow: rights; freedom of speech, thought, and association; a superabundant energy and activity in society. He goes on to conclude that, with the revolutionary declaration of rights, the human being does no less than declare himself democratic man. The extraordinary event of the revolution represents "a declaration which was in fact a *self-declaration*, that is, a declaration by which human beings . . . revealed themselves to be both the subject and the object of the utterance in which they named the human elements in one another."[102] In the absence of the father figure, the human being can—and must—name himself, signifying what he finds meaningful in himself. And what he finds meaningful is his democratic element—the self-naming and so essentially free element. Modern man comes to recognize himself as "the being whose essence it is to declare his rights."[103] Democratic man comes to be seen as man as such. Declaring his rights, he opens unto a democratic consciousness, understanding and evaluating himself as a free and equal member of the human race. In this context, the democratic expression of right itself "becomes *unconditional;* it is a human attribute, and it reveals the *vocation* of humanity."[104] Democracy is revealed as humanity's calling.

*Historical Nature*

Democracy seems to have taken on something of a religious status today. We hear that democracy is the end point of the providential progress of history or, conversely, that we have "lost faith" in democracy. Lefort, I argue, represents the democratic phenomenon as given and inevitable, but precisely because history has no end point. So long as we live in history, the operation of negativity endures and prevails. After the democratic revolution, the denaturing of authority itself seems in a sense natural—decreed by history. Put differently, when we experience the real as history, when our experience of nature is itself governed by the rule of history, by historical time's endless revolutionary movements, the open order of democracy seems imprinted in the open order of the real. Democracy is assured not as the end of history but by the endlessness of history.

In Lefort's account, the democratic revolution seems in a sense to democratize our experience of nature itself. The flip side of the denaturing of the social world is the desocializing of the natural world—removing the human fingerprints from nature. Through the revolution, we move from nature affirmed as higher Nature (as a hierarchical, eternal, and closed order within which the human world is embedded) to nature experienced as accessible only through the veil of history. Inescapably stuck in linear time, we cannot but perceive nature as Bergsonian, as it were—as unpredictable and open ended, fluid and in flux, overflowing with birth and death, mysterious and creative, rather than cyclical, tele-ological, mechanical, or millennial. Like freedom, nature (as we can know it) is rendered "historical." History becomes the master term un-der which nature is subsumed and by which it is conditioned.[105] And we live life necessarily *in* history, in a historical way. While the revolution-ary bursting forth of history liberates us from the *inhibiting* absolutes of closed Nature, we henceforth live with the *chastening* uncertainties of open history. Yet, this very uncertainty proves to be self-limiting: as the closed society comes to seem unnatural, the open society takes its place as apparently natural. We can no more question the conditions history imposes upon us—including our own freedom—than we could ques-tion Nature. In this sense, living in the course of history is analogous to-day to what living in accordance with nature once was: "The rule is different," as Tocqueville writes "but there is a rule."[106]

A leading description of this democratized, historical nature is put forth by William Connolly. Drawing on the Nobel Prize–winning chaos theory of Ilya Prigogine, author of *The End of Certainty: Time, Chaos and the New Laws of Nature,* Connolly writes of the insertion of "an irreversible historical trajectory into several (though not all) systems in nature," which thereby challenges "the regulative ideal of a closed system of ex-planation that traditionally informed the natural sciences, at least out-side of biology."[107] Connolly contends, "Nature itself is populated more by 'dissipative structures' than by the timeless systems of Newtonian mechanics. A dissipative structure, exemplified by cells, whirlpools, bio-logical evolution, aging, and the evolution of the universe, has self-productive capacities; it is marked by irreversible changes that give it a temporal or historical dimension; and it is susceptible to changes in the course of its development that are unpredictable."[108] In this account, the dissolution of the markers of certainty is no less a natural than a social phenomenon; nature itself works according to the operation of negativ-ity against closed systems and settled authorities. Our democratic third republic can still stand as inscribed in evolutionary nature, but with evolution a matter of "dissipative structures" rather than natural selec-tion. The natural order, just like the democratic social order, is marked by indeterminacy, unpredictable and irreversible changes, and even "self-productive" capacities. Revolution proves the original vital principle of historical nature, just as in the case of the democratic social state of nature. And insofar as nature challenges "the regulative ideal" of closed systems, it gratifies our democratic aspiration to openness.[109]

Connolly calls upon us to give up our tendency toward an "ontological narcissism" in which we "demand dispensations from within the world to replace the loss of a personal, willful, and powerful God located above it." We "domesticate" the "protean idea of contingency" by conceptualizing the world as either something "plastic" that can be "mastered" or as "providential" and "designed" for our "fulfillment"—insisting that the "world . . . must be for us in one way or another."[110] If our end is neither mastery nor harmony, though, but rather undomesticated freedom and the escape from authority, one wonders whether Connolly's description of nature's openness is any less narcissistic—whether the world we are born into is any less providentially designed for the fulfillment of our deepest purposes when those purposes are democratic.

Interestingly, this nature has even been reaffirmed as Nature by some. Take, for example, the Open Theism movement. As a challenge to the regulative ideal of God as sovereign, all-knowing, and unchanging, this "free-will theology" democratizes God as temporal. As one proponent puts it, "God, at least since Creation, experiences duration. God is everlasting through time rather than timelessly eternal." In this view, "God decided to create beings with indeterministic freedom, which implies that God chose to create a universe in which the future is not entirely knowable, even for God." Living under a chastening uncertainty, God "takes risks" and "makes mistakes" just like us.[111]

Lefort argues along similar lines that the democratic revolution set nature free, just as it liberated society and the individual. Prior to the revolution, nature was made to serve human purposes. It was assigned order in response to the needs and fears, the expectations and aspirations, of man. The unruliness of the world as it was actually experienced was repressed by the fictive, superimposed identity of an orderly and meaningful "cosmos" or supernatural design. The world was reduced to black and white so as to better accommodate us, morally and intellectually. But with the severing of the king's head from his body (the severing of Nature from nature), there burst forth the recognition of the actual fluidity and spontaneity of corporeal space and time—of the unfathomable *depth* of nature in the ungraspable *flow* of history. Of course, Lefort notes, even today we often dehistoricize the world in order "to assure ourselves of a truth which is already given and which will not betray us, in order to *conjure away*, in sum, the indeterminacy which constantly re-emerges in the history that we live."[112] Nonetheless, with the revolution we at least in principle leave behind the comforting but confining illusion of certainty and security (the idea of nature as our home) and live life in the open and untamed wilds of historical nature.

The revolution thus disentangles the social world and the natural world, liberating each from the other by revealing both to be open; both are ultimately undomesticable, unknowable, and unmasterable. Henceforth we have two distinct worlds following a single indeterminate orbit, two separate worlds represented as "historical." If not exactly decreed by nature, then, the modern democratic social form stands in Lefort's theory as uniquely suited to accommodate and function in accordance with our historical nature. Democracy alone abides by the rule of history. Democratic openness is the response, both necessary and proper, to our democratic condition of uncertainty (just as competition was the necessary and proper response to the market condition of "the survival of the fittest"). If not exactly standing under a cosmic seal of approval, democracy does seem self-evident—simply obvious, without viable alternatives, in little need of argument. Indeed, as we shall see, denying the decisive political and social relevance of our historical condition is for Lefort a matter of willful ignorance or wishful thinking. Not accommodating oneself to the dissolution of the markers of certainty in one's social arrangements and relationships is at best a sort of childishness and possible much worse.

Despite his critique of Tocqueville's theory of democracy and the revolution, then, we can take Lefort's theory as implicitly confirming one of Tocqueville's central insights. Tocqueville writes that democracy, for better and for worse, is experienced by its inhabitants as coming naturally, as in line with the plain truth and justice of equality, and so as a spontaneous, unmannered manner of being in society. Democracy is the social state of nature into which we feel ourselves born without labor and so in which we can live informally and without artifice. Democracy is the regime wherein the need for regimentation, for education or habituation into its form, is denied; taken as normal, the democratic way of life does not require normalization. Lefort offers just such a picture of democracy. As the social form that does not stand under the pressures of a prohibited and repressed uncertainty, democracy does indeed appear in Lefort's work as spontaneous and self-evident—that which springs up when obstructions and usurpations have been cleared away. To live in historical society, with its historical freedom, is to live in the social state of historical nature.

### The Totalitarian Illusion: A Society without History?

Tocqueville argues that liberal democracy might be just a middle stage between aristocracy and despotic socialism. His work can be read as an effort to alloy democracy with certain vestigial elements of aristocracy to prevent democracy's slide into socialism. Lefort too represents democracy as a middle point, between the premodern society of embodiment and the totalitarian society of oneness. While Tocqueville fears the permanent loss of freedom in the extreme equality of socialism, though, I argue that, for Lefort, democratic freedom—the freedom that comes from living in history—cannot be permanently lost to totalitarianism. In time, the repressed always returns. Totalitarianism is an illusion and so ultimately passing, rendering democracy thereby inevitable.

For Lefort, totalitarianism like democracy is made possible by the dissolution of the markers of certainty—by the collapse of Christian embodiment as the mode of representing the theologico-political matrix of society. But while totalitarianism "is engendered in 'historical society,' " its "phantasy is to abolish the historical in History; . . . to identify the instituting moment with the instituted; to deny the unpredictable, the unknowable."[113] Born of the revolution, totalitarianism seeks the end of revolution—its culmination and its cessation—by finally designating itself "as *a society without history.*"[114]

To understand this quest to abolish history, we must recognize the downside of the freedom of the social state of openness—the experience of openness less as freedom than as insecurity. Modern peoples might experience their historical condition of uncertainty as a sort of Edvard Munchian "vertigo in the face of the void created by an indeterminate society."[115] When society can no longer be publicly staged and made sense of by means of its unproblematic representation in the present figure of the father, its inhabitants are thrust into a tormenting uncertainty regarding the meaning of things and are in turn "haunted by the idea of the break-up of the social."[116] Disembodied, society itself might drift apart. The democratic social state of history ends up threatened by resistance to its very open-ended possibility and fluidity—to the oceanic sense of being without determinate forms and solid foundations. With the consequent temptation to "surrender to the attractions of a renewed certainty"—a return to a black-and-white world, a place called home— the appeal of totalitarianism lies precisely in "a nostalgia for the image of society which is at one with itself and which has mastered its history."[117] This temptation is strongest when society is experienced as having sunk into pure individualism and materialism—when "the reference to an empty place gives way to the unbearable image of a real vacuum."[118] The constitutive fear of democratic society is the collapse of authority that might follow from the beheading of authority. With this absolute dissolution of the concept of hierarchy, society would be freed of the constraints of meaning and purpose. It would descend entirely into the economics of "realism"—the final return to Hobbes's state of nature in all its absurdity. Here, the "symbolic efficacy of the democratic system is destroyed," and "power appears to have sunk to the level of reality . . . [as] no more than an instrument for the promotion of . . . interests."[119] Lefort writes, "The authority of those who make public decisions . . . vanishes, leaving only the spectacle of individuals or clans whose one concern is to satisfy their appetite for power."[120]

Reacting to the possibility of a world of power without any recognized principle of authority, modern peoples might give themselves over to the desire for a renewed "religious" certainty and unity of meaning. With society "put to the test of the collapse of legitimacy . . . by all the signs of the fragmentation of the social space, . . . representations which can supply an index of social unity and identity become invested with a fantastic power, and the totalitarian adventure is under way."[121] But crucially, this religious longing is itself radically transformed by the revolution. Totalitarianism, like democracy, is a modern rearticulation of the particular and the universal, but it is carried forth in denial of the transcendence of the religious universal. In its quest for the mystical union of society, totalitarianism disavows religion insofar as religion "indicates an *other* place."[122] Totalitarianism is the attempt to fully *realize* the primal unity of society while wholly rejecting the primal division between universal principle and particular practice.[123] It is the society not of imminent transcendence but of immediate transcendence realized in the world—not of openness but of the closed circle.

The body is reincorporated as the symbol of the social whole, but this symbol no longer represents the point of mediation between mortal and immortal, mundane and divine. Rather, indicating the difference between absolutism and totalitarianism, the body is said to signify the eradication of the need for mediation in the collapse of all divisions—including the instituting division—into a complete, self-sufficient, self-founding, self-ruling singularity. With totalitarianism, an "impossible swallowing up of the body in the head begins to take place, as does an impossible swallowing up of the head in the body."[124] The totalitarian adventure is not a return to the logic of the Capital Letter but a radicalization of democracy's self-circularity. But in its antidemocratic logic of oneness, totalitarianism strives to eradicate pluralism at every level—between state and society, individual and society, public and private, particular and universal.[125] In a sense, then, totalitarianism inverts the meaning of democracy in the name of democracy itself. Totalitarianism is a reaction against history carried out in terms of the realization of democracy. Totalitarianism "overturns the democratic transformation . . . while at the same time taking over some of its features and extending them at the level of phantasy."[126] It is "a response to the questions raised by democracy, . . . an attempt to resolve its paradoxes, . . . [and] to banish the indetermination that haunts the democratic experience. But this attempt . . . itself draws on a democratic source."[127] Rather than living with a constant displacement of the answer to democracy's questions and the solution to its paradoxes, totalitarianism strives to actualize the democratic universal of the people. The inherently latent and open quality of the sovereign people is effaced in "the fantasy of the People-as-One, . . . [with] a substantial identity, . . . free from division," and in turn power "ceases to designate an empty place: it is materialized in an organ (or, in extreme cases, an individual) which is supposed to be capable of concentrating in itself all the forces of society."[128] To exit the social state of openness, totalitarianism imposes a Leviathan unlike the world has ever seen.

Against the vertigo of uncertainty, then, a sense of potency is supported by the image of a fixed history, a history both known and mastered. There is a "prodigious refusal of any innovation that might transgress the limit of an already known future, a reality that in principle is already mastered."[129] In this "phantasmagoria of the Plan," the unknown, unpredictable, and indeterminable are categorized not as the opportunity for freedom but as "avatars of the enemy," whether barbaric or parasitic.[130] And where democracy navigates uncertainty by means of people's questioning and arguing together, totalitarianism represents a "retreat towards a point of certainty where the necessity to speak is cancelled out."[131] The negation of the democratic adventure's characteristic restlessness and agitation, totalitarianism's final solution proceeds in silence, with a "certainty that *can do without words*."[132]

Lefort leaves us with the picture of democracy as potentially too demanding and so as perpetually threatened by the collective temptation to surrender to a renewed sense of certainty and peace, identity, and purpose. Far from inevitable, democracy would seem perpetually under siege by modern man's longing for home. Implicit in his analysis, however, are three ways in which totalitarianism actually demonstrates democracy's hegemonic and unquestionable status.

First, totalitarianism is an illusion. "More than any other system," Lefort argues, totalitarianism "is contradicted by experience."[133] The validity of the democratic representation of our situation as unpredictable and indeterminate is constantly reaffirmed by our experience of the events of the world. The antidemocratic counterrevolution cannot ultimately succeed, given our experience of the real as history. Thus we "would be victims of the *phantasy* which inhabits [the totalitarian] system . . . if we imagined that it actually realized itself, *that it could ever succeed in realizing itself*, even in the heyday of Stalinism."[134] Totalitarianism is truly a politics of the impossible, "the *impossibility* of . . . materializing power in the persons of those vested with it, of representing society as a body without supplying it with an external guarantor of its organization and limits, and of abolishing social division."[135] Like a repressed Freudian desire, democracy always returns, indeed bursts forth; totalitarianism is always subject to "the threat of a violent return of all the signs of division and otherness."[136] Whether experienced as liberation or as an ordeal, the revolutionary flow of history eventually undermines every ordering assertion imposed upon society and the world. Totalitarianism cannot, over time, sustain the "fantastic attempt to compress space and time into the limits of the social body," and so it eventually collapses in the "return of democratic aspirations."[137] We simply cannot, in the long run, deny the fact of or aspiration to democratic openness. Even when democracy is momentarily obstructed, even when we occasionally strain and struggle against the uncertainty of our democratic condition, the return of our historical social form is inevitable. History is on the side of democracy.

There is already in Tocqueville the sense that, with the advent of openness, we have reached a sort of end of history—a condition taken as universal, endless, and characterized by the absence of great revolutions (if not of disturbances and violence). Democracy is the final regime, and the democratic revolution the final great event. At the same time, Tocqueville fears democracy might descend into the extreme and oppressive egalitarianism of socialism. The passion for equality might destroy freedom. For Lefort, there seems no such threat to freedom. The longing for certainty cannot destroy freedom, understood as the historical operation of negativity, the denaturing of authority, and the return of a state of openness. Freedom is inevitable; certainty is a lie. Outside of the realm of illusion—or, better, delusion—there is no sustainable alternative to the democratic theologico-political matrix.

Second, against totalitarianism, democracy stands as singularly civilizational. Recall William Graham Sumner's view that an attack upon capitalism was an attack upon the foundations of civilization. For Lefort, democracy enjoys a similar standing. The fundamental opposition running throughout his work is "between a totalitarian model of society . . . and a model which implies the recognition of rights."[138] There is a borderline, black-and-white, all-or-nothing logic to these modern alternatives. The opposition is between democracy, with its characteristic vitality and restless activity, and totalitarianism, which amounts in its final solution to the silence and stillness of death. Tocqueville's formulation of democracy, aristocracy, and socialism dictates a sort of Aristotelian approach to striking a mean between the excesses and defects of democratic equality. When democracy is formulated in terms of openness, there can be no sense of balancing or moderating the democratic principle, only the logic of threat and self-preservation. And even if the historical outcome in democracy's favor is in a sense predetermined, the apparent stakes could not be higher in the existential struggle between democratic freedom and totalitarian antifreedom—the great enemy or other of democracy. With such a dichotomous worldview, the internal indeterminacy and uncertainty of our democratic way of life stand sharply in contrast to the unconditional good of our democratic way of life. What would it mean to question democratic values and beliefs in this context? What are the alternatives? Moreover (and again we can make the comparison to Tocqueville's analysis of the modern usefulness of certain aristocratic norms and forms), the logic of Lefort's dichotomy dictates that all possible social and political goods simply must fall within the infinitely complex form of democracy. There is no good that is not at the same time democratic, nothing democratic that is not at the same time good. Principled upon freedom-as-openness, democracy seems unquestionably true and unquestionably good.

And third, even while we cannot deny the often tormenting uncertainty inherent in our democratic situation (any more than we could competition in a market situation), the capacity to cope with uncertainty (as with the capacity to cope with competition) constitutes an ethical measure of self and society, below which we sink into our totalitarian longings. Lefort depicts totalitarianism as a sort of childishness, a wishful surrender to the illusion of security and certainty. Against this nostalgic self-abdication, the ability to live life in history—unblinking in the face of uncertainty, tolerating a world of questions with no answers—constitutes a norm of democratic maturity. Rather than obstinately standing with arms crossed and eyes shut against the true complexity and unpredictability of life after the revolution, we are challenged to bear up under the anxiety, vertigo, and frustration of our existential insecurity—to struggle through our self-reliant but not self-sufficient existence. Without father figure or fatherland, democracy demands of us the psychological and emotional strength and flexibility to take responsibility for, rather than repress, the ordeal of freedom. We are measured and judged here by our capacity to affirm the freedom we in any case cannot deny.

### Conclusion: A Democratic Religious Articulation, between Capitalism and Christianity

Lefort's analysis of modern society supports the notion that it is rendered more fully intelligible as democratic rather than market in nature.

To reduce the social world to economic concepts and categories is to succumb to an illusory realism, no less a fantasy than the totalitarian Plan. The modern social form is not publicly staged as a market; it is not made sense of and meaning is not assigned in terms of economic values. The corporation is not at all like the church before it; CEOs are not at all our high priests. Such an interpretation confuses power in the symbolic register of "the political" with the empirical exercise of power. In Lefort's account, we in democratic society are prone to succumb to just this confusion. The collapse into materialism is the original fear of democratic society (thus the totalitarian temptation). At the same time, the democratic revolution marks the collapse of the Christian mode of mediating the universal and the particular and so of giving definite form to society. We do not live in a capitalist society, nor do we live in a Christian society. Our lives are not without meaning, nor is the meaning of our lives settled and assured.

In our "historical society," the normative dimension of universality persists but takes on a purely critical function: the rule of the people as the rule of no-body; freedom as the denaturing operation of negativity; the declaration of rights as an expression of revolutionary mobility. Revolution, to paraphrase Pierre Manent, is the revelation of democracy.[139] The democratic way of life is given form and animated less by its end of equality, Lefort argues, than by its original vital principle of revolution. It is in the unsettling performance of questioning—in the restless movement away from home—that we put the democratic principle into practice. In this social-symbolic milieu, freedom takes shape against domestication: in Lefort's terms, we are free because no present power has the authority to name us—we escape from every attempt to master or know us into ontological openness. Equality takes shape not as dull uniformity but as formlessness, as the absence of hierarchical regimentation, and so as coextensive with freedom. Openness describes the conjoined equality and freedom of life without a father figure—a radicalization of the antipaternalism of laissez-faire competition and social contract liberalism. And life is lived from moment to moment, in the unpredictable, eventful, dramatic free flow of history. A life well lived becomes a life fully lived, full of vital energy and restless activity.

Surely we recognize ourselves—usually with regret—as materialistic consumers, pleasure seekers, self-interested choosers, and the like. In democratic society, this is one aspect of our public self-representation. But insofar as we are to speak of "existential badges of identity," it would seem we more fully recognize ourselves in historical rather than economic terms. In public as in private life, we identify ourselves by our experience of events—births and deaths and being born again, the moment of leaving home, epochal innovations, the coming of what's next, our being present at the creation or the collapse, on the day everything changed.[140] These are what "define" us. We are not what we consume but rather the sum of our experiences, only one of which (and far from the most significant) is the experience of consumption. Life is experienced as meaningful insofar as it is dramatic, a narrative of life-altering events—or events that are said to be life altering. Where once people were their social status, today we are our history—democratic man as a story-living animal. Thus, for instance, trans-formative rupture effaces continuity in the identity of the American polity, which is defined by the conversion narrative of being born again out of the laissez-faire second republic. Indeed, every day comes to seem the day that everything changed: every scientific discovery announces an imminent utopian or dystopian future; every election is imagined a watershed event of radical reconstruction, a breaking down of old barriers, or a wave of tsunamic proportions; every political, technological, or business alteration of the status quo is celebrated as a "game changer."[141] We saw previously how democratic society is one of impatience; here it seems one of exaggeration—of hype. If the media overdramatizes most every story, perhaps it is because such representations makes sense to us—pandering "infotainment" performed not through reducing the news to pleasing trivializations but through the stark depiction of what we experience as meaningful, through the generation of newsworthy content for our historical condition. In its very absurdity, the following example illuminates the extent to which we imagine revolution everywhere and elevate even trivial things properly consigned to the sphere of consumption to the status of revolutionary rupture onto an ever more open and colorful historical adventure. "The iPod arrived in October 2001, . . . to a world in transformation from its *comforting* analog roots to a *disruptive* digital future," and so today we must contemplate "the ways that the iPod changed the world" into "Planet iPod."[142] How could such audacious nonsense be considered intelligible outside of the historical society par excellence? And to what extent does this familiar narrative itself actually prove "comforting" by reinforcing the conventional wisdom regarding our modern situation and by gratifying us in its depiction of our ability to cope with the revolutionary trials of modernity?

To extend this sketch of what it would mean to live in a democratic society, we might say that far from inaugurating a "bourgeois" celebration of the here and now, the democratic revolution degrades the status of the present, material world. The death of the Christ figure signifies not the demise of meaning but its displacement to whatsoever is taken to be wholly immaterial, unconventional, and transcendent—the all natural or purely spiritual.[143] The dissolution of Christian embodiment leads not to the experience of something like Heidegger's flat and empty existence, characterized by the cold ascendancy of the will and a debased self and society subject to economic calculation and scientific prediction. Democratic existence is not reduced to calculation but opened to uncertainty, rendered not predictable but questionable. With our opening onto history, we experience the world as neither occult nor transparent, but as opaque.[144] The previously *mystical* religious dimensionality of society is not lost to *mechanical* materialism, but neither does it remain enclosed in the symbol of the body. Instead it is rendered *mysterious*, displaced to the register of the phenomenal—of revolutionary/creative becoming. The religious dimension of democratic society—of the democratic theologico-political form of society—is the depth of history. History—between economic shallowness and religious foundationalism—is characterized by neither an adrift weightlessness, wherein all that is solid melts into air, nor by a secure groundedness or sense of place, but by their amalgam in an oceanic sense of depth and fluidity—the openness of the fecund ocean rather than the barren desert, of the wilderness rather than the wasteland.

A further consequence implicit in this historical situation is the debasement of conventional norms and forms. In times past, human convention was represented as an establishment (if an imperfect, partial, and diminished one) of a higher nature or Nature. Insofar as legitimate, the world of human artifice instituted the natural world, positive law instituted natural law, the terrestrial kingdom instituted the divine kingdom, and so forth. Temporal authority was both warranted and limited by one or another notion of transcendent authority. With democracy's revolutionary rupture, the hierarchical chain is broken: temporal representations of authority are subverted by the felt absence of transcendent authority. Meaning and authority settle exclusively with those vast abstractions that seem to escape embodiment in particular conventional or institutional form: humanity, human rights, the biological/economic market, history, unmediated modes of experience and expression that cannot be captured in ordinary language. If totalitarianism is the attempt to *do without words,* democracy is the search for something that *cannot be put into words.*

The authority of the divine, we might say, can no longer be made manifest in the world, but then that which cannot be made manifest gains a sort of divine authority. Take, for instance, the history of religious practices in America, with its ongoing cycle of more secular and liberal "mainline" religions—as they "compromise their 'errand in the wilderness' "—being replaced by "less worldly," more radical and demanding "outsider" or "upstart sects."[145] The purity of spirituality that seizes the democratic imagination is experienced as devitalized and domesticated (rather than realized, if only partially) by being housed in institutional form. The rejection of mainstream institutions itself becomes mainstream as democracy's original rupture is perennially reenacted. Along these lines, democratic society takes shape in the restless, self-radicalizing striving for a world before or beyond conventional form.

And just as conventionalized religion is undermined by the democratic movement, so too is conventionalized politics. The sphere of democratic "politics" is devalued within "the political" form of modern democracy. And insofar as democracy, through the normative/descriptive bundle of associations contained in the idea of democratic openness (revolution/history/freedom), comes to seem natural or ontologically axiomatic—inscribed not in the eternal order of Nature but in the immortal movement of history—the institutions and conventions of democratic politics come to seem devoid of principle and meaning. The operation of negativity is always effective; precisely as democratic politics takes on some actual shape, it thereby reveals itself to be merely particular, representative not of the universal people but of some particular body—a special interest. Tocqueville writes that it is "impossible to eliminate the existence of dogmatic beliefs,"—the "opinions that men accept on faith without discussion."[146] As the truth and good of openness is accepted on faith without discussion—as we understand ourselves to live inescapably in a revolutionary state of openness, and at the same time embrace this openness as constitutive of freedom—the sphere of politics is either elevated to the status of the impossible or consigned to the merely economic.

# CHAPTER 4

# Political Phoenix

*Sheldon Wolin on the Limits and Limitlessness of Democracy*

Nothing is more repugnant to the human mind in ages of
equality than the idea of submitting to forms.

—Tocqueville, *Democracy in America*

## I. The Economic Polity

*The Separation of Democracy and Politics*

Tocqueville famously warns of "the danger that religion courts when it
joins forces with power." As long as "a religion rests solely on sentiments
that console man in his misery, it can win the affection of the human
race. But when it embraces the bitter passions of this world," or when it
"joins forces with political powers of any kind," religion itself descends
into bitterness and particularity. The unequal exchange is one of transcendent moral authority for temporal political power. Tocqueville thus
offers the paradox that "diminishing religion's apparent strength could
actually make it more powerful." The separation of church and state is
above all to the benefit of church (one wonders how well state comes out
in the bargain). American religion, Tocqueville writes, enjoys the enduring advantages of this separation. Realizing that religion "cannot
share the material might of those who govern without incurring some
of the hatred they inspire"—that it cannot command "respect . . . in the
midst of partisan conflict"—Americans fortuitously "created *a place apart*
for religion." And from this immaterial preserve, religion can exert its
proper power over politics in America, leaving the clergy free to "blast
ambition and bad faith in men of all political stripes" by "zealously"
marking their distance from petty partisanship.[1]

175

In what follows, I suggest that we have come to think of democracy's place in the world in precisely analogous terms. We have created a place apart for democracy, from the standpoint of which we can blast ambition and bad faith in men of all political stripes. Democracy's hegemonic moral authority is contingent upon its washing its hands of material power. Democracy consoles us in our misery and wins the affections of the human race by remaining above the fray of bitter passions, partisan conflict, and the hatred of those who govern. Democracy's diminishing strength has made it infinitely more powerful.

To think through this separation of democracy and politics, I turn to its most explicit and forthright formulation in the democratic theory of Sheldon Wolin, particularly his theory of "fugitive democracy." Theorizing democracy as fugitive—with all that term connotes—is, I argue, Wolin's attempt to incorporate the modern democratic principle of openness into the practice of politics. Fugitive democracy is democracy-as-revolution and, as such, is the ideal political moment after what Lefort terms the dissolution of the markers of certainty. I conclude that this association of authentic democracy with the revolutionary phenomenon of opening is itself a primary source of our contemporary political cynicism.

We have seen how the master term of modernity is equality for Tocqueville, and uncertainty for Lefort. For Wolin, in much less a mixed bag, it is economy. Modern times are characterized not by the leveling of authority, nor by the questioning of authority, but by the compulsive organization of existence per the requirements of the efficient generation and projection of power. At its core Hobbesian, modern life comes to be ordered and animated by "a perpetuall and restless desire of Power after power, that ceaseth onely in Death."[2] In this world, authentic democracy is all but impossible. As we shall see, given the inefficient and disorganized character of the people's power, democracy simply cannot compete with what Wolin terms the "Superpower" of economy. In the "contemporary world democracy is not hegemonic but beleaguered and permanently in opposition to structures it cannot command"; it is "perennially outspent and overmatched."[3] Relative to "too big to fail," democracy is too small to matter. We are consequently "entering a moment in our history when it will become extremely difficult to find the terms for limiting power or for holding it politically accountable, much less for sharing it."[4]

As opposed to Tocqueville's explicit statements and Lefort's implicit logic, Wolin's prognosis for democracy is bleak, with its prospects few and fleeting. Of course, Wolin recognizes the "near-universal acclaim accorded democracy," and its current status as a "transhistorical and universal value."[5] Far from demonstrating the vitality of democracy, though, this empty rhetoric effects the cover-up of democracy's near demise, concealing the extent to which "democracy" is perverted to serve other, antidemocratic and antipolitical, ends. The language of democracy has been systematically co-opted and managed by the powers that be to pacify the people. Like a Freudian dream, the promise of democracy functions as a harmless vent for the people's forbidden democratic passions. Moral mask and sales-pitch image, "democracy" is today's opiate of the masses, a virtual-simulation seduction, the distracting spectacle of shadows on the wall. Thus the "fact that democracy continues to be invoked in American political rhetoric and the popular media may be a tribute, not to its vibrancy, but to its utility in supporting a myth that legitimates the very formations of power which have enfeebled it."[6] The fantasy of democracy is used to domesticate the demos.

Wolin describes three notions of democracy that take shape in our economic times, which I explore in the subsequent three parts of this chapter. The first is liberal democracy. Meant to service the needs of economic power, this political system functions according to the logic of efficiency, organization, and expansion. It is a politics rendered as economical as possible by the near-total exclusion of the people from any sort of meaningful participation in their administration. In the American context, it is the "constitutionalized democracy" proselytized by the proponents of the Constitution. Throughout the 1980s and again more recently, Wolin offered what he called "archaic" democracy as the primary authentic and oppositional mode of democracy. An expressly Anti-Federalist mode of politics, this is a conservative, decentralized, culturally and historically situated, and robustly participatory practice of democracy. It exists today largely as a remnant of the past, a memory (not unlike aristocracy for Tocqueville). Preserving the plurality of local political experiences and practices makes possible the retreat from economic power and also serves as sand in the gears of its systematizing machinery. It is quite literally an anomalous place apart from liberal politics and state power. By the early 1990s and in his 2004 expanded edition of *Politics and Vision,* Wolin reformulated democracy as "fugitive," at once on the run from and prepared to confront Superpower. Fugitive democracy is less an anomalous place than an anomalous time apart and seeks less to evade than to wield power.

Taken together, these two genuine iterations of democracy form a sort of Jeffersonian admixture, uncomfortably straddling educative township ward and declarative revolution, historical continuity and historical disruption, the common and the exceptional. The archaic is a place of settlement; the fugitive is a moment of openness. Archaic democracy is rooted in the prosaic; fugitive democracy is the epic poetry of struggle. Archaic democracy is obstinately ordinary and uneventful; revolutionary action, when popular power finally bursts forth, is truly an extraordinary event. Archaic democracy is a matter of the people's escape from economy; fugitive democracy represents the people's (inevitably short-lived) striving for mastery. Wolin writes that Tocqueville was perpetually confronted in his theorization of democracy by "the conflicts between action and culture"; this formulation applies equally well to Wolin's own theory.[7] A the same time, Wolin's two democracies do come full circle, together in their shared hostility to the present world of conventional norms and forms. Archaic democracy is reaction; fugitive democracy is revolution.

Taken on its own, fugitive democracy can be understood as Wolin's attempt to formulate the conjunction of material political power and democracy's moral authority without degrading the latter—without democracy's incurring the hatred of all repositories of power or descending into particularity and partisan conflict. The key is that the people's solidarity, their coalescing as a collective actor—a demos—capable of exercising political power, is intrinsically impermanent and without need of mediating conventions. The people's power is limited because its preconditions are fleeting; indeed, its very successes are self-subverting. But for that pristine moment between its coming into being and its passing, this power is audacious and righteous, vital and undomesticated—an exercise of material power that cannot sink into materialism or settle down into economic routinization. Material power and moral authority come together, but on condition that it is only for an instant. Here, democracy is a moment apart from the fallen present.

We have previously seen how the democratic way of life is principled upon openness. I argue here that Wolin's democracy-as-revolution is the putting into practice of this principle. It is democracy as event rather than institution, moment rather than form. As the act of "rational disorganization" (similar to Lefort's "operation of negativity"), fugitive democracy occurs as the overcoming and overturning of the world of conventional representations, which cannot but be constituted according to the imperatives of economy. It is the savage response to the domesticating advance of economy. Along these lines, Wolin's theory of democracy harbors the same dialectic of idealization and devaluation we have seen before. Everyday democracy—participation in the liberal system of voting and elections, even Wolin's earlier formulation of local action and association—comes to seem co-opted and inauthentic, more banal process than spontaneous movement. The democracy that rebels against the machinery of the material world, the democracy that is itself reborn with each new revolutionary rupture, never settles down or compromises or grows corrupt. The dialectic becomes one of political cynicism and a sort of democratic heroism.

## Modern Power and Postmodern Power

Wolin writes that, far from Tocqueville's democratic social state, we live today in an "economic polity."[8] The modern way of life issues not from the rise of the political principle of equality but from the spread of the economic imperative of power production. What Tocqueville would call the mores of our social state—those points at which fact and value are taken to coincide at the generative center of a society's characteristic habits and faiths—are formed and imposed by the economical ways and means of power. The human world is reduced to an economy. "The economic rules all domains of existence," Wolin writes, and we (as premodern man before nature) are "hammered into resignation, into fearful acceptance of the economy as the basic reality of [our] existence, so huge, so sensitive, so ramifying in its consequences that no group, party, or political actor dare alter its fundamental structure."[9] The irony, of course, is that so successful have been the techniques of economy in liberating us from fearful resignation to nature's basic reality that we have come to experience the economy as a sort of second nature. Economy comes to stand as unmoved mover, an "autonomous entity independent of history, religious values, moral constraints, and political regulations . . . [and] determinative of all other social and political relationships."[10] Society is "absorbed" into economy, which operates as the "first principle of a comprehensive scheme of social hermeneutics" and "an interpretive category of virtually universal application." Wolin writes, the principle of economy is "used to understand personal life and public life, to make judgments about them, and to define the nature of their problems. It supplies categories of analysis and decision by which public policies are formulated, and it is applied to cultural domains such as education, the arts, and scientific research."[11]

We end up with equality as competitive opportunity, freedom as rational choice and purchasing power in consumption, justice as distributive, civic virtue as shopping, action as behavior, realism as capitalism, man as a power-seeking animal, judgment as price valuation, prosperity as profit, progress as technological innovation, law as a matter of supply and demand, nature as a market, education as a means to the end of competing in the global economy, governance as administration, elections as advertising, and politics reduced to "it's the economy, stupid."

Wolin explains the rise of the economic polity in two distinct phases—modern and postmodern—with the second half of the twentieth century as the turning point. He characterizes the modern phase in largely Weberian terms, as the fabrication of the world as a stable and orderly mechanism for the production of power. Modernization is simply the process of rationalizing, routinizing, and homogenizing existence to ensure that the machine runs smoothly. The engine of this rendering process is the unholy trinity of the centralized and bureaucratic state, the capitalistic business corporation, and Baconian science. For all of the supposed differences between the commanding heights of the state and the invisible hand of the free market, the institution of the monopolistic corporation within the market demonstrates the synergy between modern politics and modern economics. While it may be "unplanned," the market doesn't like uncertainty, as they say, any more than does the state. The concentration of economic power in the corporation is an attempt to suppress the conditions that create uncertainty. The state administers and polices; the corporation manages. The state imposes rules and regulations; the corporation imposes organization. Both seek the efficient panoptic control facilitated by monopoly. The modern methods of science, in turn, lend a sheen of impersonal objectivity (the selfless virtue of the moderns) and even transcendence (quantification) to the pursuit of a predictable (secure, profitable) universe—of an orderly, systematized, law-abiding self, society, and reality. The idea of science enables a "vision of power with no inherent limits," because it is "absorbed into reason" and so is "etherealized" and "pure."[12] Taken as a whole, this modern power mechanism runs at peak performance when left to operate according to its own internal dynamic, unfettered by the slow motion of popular power. The common feature of capitalism, science, and state "is that by nature each functioned best under conditions of autonomy: the capitalist was most efficient when least regulated, the bureaucrat most expert when least trammeled by public opinion or self-serving legislators, and the scientist most productive when allowed the maximum freedom of research."[13] All three seek subjects, not citizens.

The second phase in the rise of the economic polity is postmodernization. Modernization is a matter of imposing mechanistic form upon the world so as to facilitate the production of power. While power's raw material—the natural and human worlds—is made to suffer perpetual change and dislocation, the operation of modern power requires a settled location. It is autonomous and impersonal but still incorporated. Encapsulated in the "Hobbesian vision" of the leviathan "megastate," power's "embodiment was the administrative or bureaucratic state; its instrument was the government regulation." For all of its size, though, the state can still be seen and resisted through cultural and political counterformations. One can march in protest out in front of the megastate. Postmodern power, in contrast, is fluid and unfettered by the heavy machinery of political forms. Leaving behind modern power's factories, postmodern power becomes what Wolin terms the "formless form" of power. Postmodernization "signifies the concerted attempt to replace cumbersome bureaucracies with 'lighter' structures [with the capacity to] adapt quickly to changing conditions, whether those be in the marketplace, in party politics, or in military operations." Wolin continues, "Government bureaucracies are encouraged to become 'leaner,' to delegate more authority to sub-units, to 'privatize' their services and functions, and to govern as much as possible by executive orders rather than by the time-honored but time-consuming and unpredictable legislative process." Where "modern power was heavy, settled in location, and hence tending to identify with national power and its fixed boundaries, postmodern power is agile, restless, contemptuous of national boundaries." Like Tocqueville's social power of opinion, postmodern power's reach is radically extended by virtue of its disincorporation; it becomes at once ephemeral and pervasive. It is fully "abstract" and "nonphysical"— disembodied in a way that accords "with a 'virtual' way of being in the world."[14]

We might think of modern power as the mechanized infantry and heavy armored division of the Second World War—awesome in its immensity but, even in blitzkrieg mode, slow by today's technologically empowered aspiration to light, quick-strike, covert operations conducted largely without "boots on the ground." With postmodernity, power is about speed and stealth and precision rather than size and brute force— a transition from the "B-52 Stratofortress Bomber" to the "B-2 Spirit Stealth Bomber."[15]

### *Superpower and Inverted Totalitarianism*

Postmodern power culminates in what Wolin terms "Superpower." This is "the postmodern contribution to the Aristotelian taxonomy of possible constitutional forms." It is the regime of limitlessness, its characteristic virtue a "dynamic . . . ceaseless reaching out" to extend "the limits of the possible." With the "distinctive capability for generating power virtually at will," Superpower expansively "strains at limits as it projects power around the world."[16] The excellence of the regime, we might say, is its immoderation—its hubristic, globalizing ambition.[17] Where modern power imposes its laws upon reality, then, postmodern Superpower is utterly lawless, operating, in a sense, outside experienced reality. Where modern power ordered the particular facts of the world, Superpower operates independent of facticity. It pursues in earnest the imaginary of infinite, revolutionary possibility that Tocqueville analyzes as democratic in origin. And it reaches not only out but down and in and throughout. Superpower overcomes all constraints and boundaries not only in the universal projection of power but also in the microreach of its power through a perversion of the notion of privatization. Drawing on the indifference to human and natural borders inscribed in capitalism and the scientific method, Superpower has gone global. At the same time, power is downsized to become more efficient and invasive. It is privatized, but only so as to become clandestine: "Privatization is not the elimination of power but the elimination of . . . public discussion and argument over how power is to be used, for what ends, and who is responsible."[18] Power is "simultaneously concentrated and disaggregated" and "decentered without being decentralized," working through the purportedly impersonal forces of the market even as it retains its centered power in the state.[19] In postmodernity, power seems both everywhere and nowhere at once.

In its nascent mode of modern power, Superpower strove to standardize the world in order to render it a predictable system. All the multifaceted differences of lived experience were either absorbed or eliminated "in the yearning for totality of which systems-talk is the ideological expression."[20] All the human world was processed as a cost or a benefit, as the "rationalizing mentality" imposed "uniform rules" according to the demands of its "efficiency calculus."[21] In its mature mode of postmodern power, Superpower renders the world less a predictable form than a frictionless vacuum. The "emptying" of the world's diverse and dispersed sites of significance becomes one of power's preconditions.[22] With the economic abstraction mirroring the democratic abstraction described by Tocqueville, the process is one of generalizing from all things particular—a movement from cultural place to open space, from historical time to clock time. In a world depopulated via abstraction, all those aspects of experienced reality and meaning that might obstruct the free flow of power are defined as descriptively or normatively inessential—as, at most, quaint.[23] It is within this smoothed-out and streamlined, empty and abstract world that we find it difficult to find the terms for limiting power.

The human consequences of this restless striving for limitlessness are profound: "dislocation and deculturation," and "the destruction of established practices, institutions, ways of life, and values."[24] In the postmodern world economy, we are left in effect homeless and amnesiac, stripped of place and memory, and exposed before the vicissitudes of power. Wolin calls our attention here to what he considers a transformation of our way of life no less profound and sweeping than the one Tocqueville perceived, a transformation "as thoroughgoing as any experience of religious conversion."[25] The economic revolution operates like a religion, as did the democratic revolution before it. But where the democratic revolution destroyed the established practices, institutions, ways of life, and values of aristocratic hierarchy, the economic revolution destroys democratic political power, freedom, and pluralism. Equality is maintained only in our vulnerability and powerlessness. The Superpower social state leaves us with all of the discontents that modernity brings but with no democratic, political ways to cope—only the hope that power will somehow providentially provide for us. It is, at bottom, an antihuman social state.

Tocqueville argues that the democratic revolution might culminate in an unprecedented type of oppression, beyond traditional understandings of despotism or tyranny. Wolin similarly concludes that the hegemony of economy has come very near to constituting a new type of totalitarianism, one he describes as inverted. Here, all becomes not war but economics by other means. This is a primarily economic (and only secondarily political) totalitarianism in that the attempt to realize a conception of "society as a systematically ordered whole" in which all the parts of the social body are made to serve the singular purpose of the regime is coordinated from the center out rather than from the top down. Without coercion or charismatic leadership—in Lefort's architecture of bodies, with no head—all the parts of society fall into orbit as if of their own volition. The totality of economy is implemented by a sort of invisible hand, by "power-holders and citizens who often seem unaware of the deeper consequences of their actions or inactions." Wolin writes that "There is a certain heedlessness, an inability to take seriously the extent to which a pattern of consequences may take shape without having been preconceived." Every "apathetic citizen" becomes a "silent enlistee in the cause of inverted totalitarianism," routinely serving the unplanned but nonetheless totalizing economic order. Disseminated by private media rather than any state organ, the ideology of inverted totalitarianism is not the triumph of the will but the "triumph of contemporaneity"—of a condition of inescapable change so ceaseless and merciless, so impersonal and meaningless that only the retreat into political apathy and privatism seems to make any sense. It takes shape not as militarism but as fashionism, and it seeks of its citizens not perpetual mass mobilization to the cause but a causeless mobility in the space emptied of culture and history—a world of flux wherein the only logical response is resignation and consumerism. Wolin writes, "Unlike classical totalitarianism, which boasted of the unanimity of its citizens, inverted totalitarianism thrives on ambivalence and the uncertainty it breeds."[26] It mirrors the democratic social state described by Tocqueville (particularly in the West) in that a compulsive restlessness amid uncertainty belies the lockstep uniformity of movement—in that we are like travelers dispersed in a great forest in which all the paths lead to the same point.

It is in this context, against the postmodern economy of power's expansion toward limitlessness and totality, that authentic democracy is rendered archaic and fugitive and that "democracy" is used "as a brand name for a product manageable at home and marketable abroad"—as the "smiley face of inverted totalitarianism."[27] Emptied of substance and divorced from practice, "democracy" becomes a myth to legitimize the formless regime-form of Superpower. But what does it suggest that totality requires such external legitimation and that democracy is in fact usable to this end? What is it about democracy that permits the "inversion" of its meaning to antidemocratic, antipolitical ends?

## II. Liberal Democracy: The Abstract "We"

*The Expansion of Democracy*

Liberal democracy, Wolin writes, "is almost universally held to be the best form of government for the contemporary world": "Its basic elements are formal provisions for equal civil liberties of all citizens; freely contested and periodic elections; mass political parties competing for the support of voters; elected officials who are accountable and removable by the electorate; a politics largely financed by powerful economic interests; and a constitution that specifies the authority and the powers of the main governmental organs and stipulates the rules controlling politics and policy-making. To this list should be added the 'free market.' "[28] In symbiotic relationship with the market's dynamic of competition and its mass demographic organization of rationally self-interested individuals, liberal democracy "is widely considered . . . indispensable . . . to a market economy" (which is almost universally held to be the best form of economy for the contemporary world).[29]

Wolin argues that we would be mistaken, though, to take the universal appeal of democracy in liberal form as evidence that democracy has won the day against all alternatives. What is "actually being measured by the claim of democratic legitimacy is not the vitality of democracy . . . but the degree to which democracy is attenuated so as to serve other ends."[30] The unquestioned universality of liberal democracy follows from its own abstractness and formalism—its talk of human rights and the individual, its routinizing procedural mechanisms—and so from its ability to service economy. The end-of-history hegemony of liberal democracy is largely a result of its assimilation into, and use to, the global hegemony of market capitalism. The unlimited legitimacy of liberal democracy is simply a function of the unlimited efficiency of capitalism. Liberal democracy has ridden capitalism's coattails to the top.

When power was personified by kings and priests, the liberal attempt to render power impersonal and subject to the rule of law made sense as an oppositional movement. But when power is disembodied, when absolutism is less a matter of arbitrary power than of abstract and systematic power—less of decree than administration, less of tyranny than of totality—the liberal form of democracy only reinforces the economy of power. Defined down to "a system in which parties lose elections," liberal democracy shares perhaps more than an elective affinity with market economics. Liberalized democracy thus becomes part of the problem, organizing democracy and ensuring its predictability and "management" according to the techniques and imperatives of power's economy, against genuinely democratic notions of shared power, common concerns, and engaged citizenship. Some of the staunchest advocates of liberal democracy apparently subscribe to Wolin's analysis without reservation. Stephen Holmes, for instance, writes, "It now seems obvious that liberalism can occasionally eclipse authoritarianism as a technique for accumulating political power. . . . Liberalism is not allergic to political power. . . . [It] is one of the most effective philosophies of state building ever contrived."[31]

### Constitutionalized Democracy

Wolin argues that to understand how democracy is made useful to economy, we must first recognize the "paradox at the center of the American

Constitution and perhaps of modern constitutionalism generally." Constitutionalism emphasizes the restraint and division of power but at the same time "makes possible the generation of power on a regular and assured basis."[32] Constitutional "constraints can be enabling," as Holmes puts it.[33] Power is harnessed by a constitution, meaning both contained *by* and contained *in* the constitutional mechanism. Constitutions limit, authorize, and organize the generation of power. The question becomes, what types of power are restrained and what types authorized and realized?

The constitutionalized form of democratic power is expansive in time and space, made to govern both perpetually and nationally. It is a democracy normalized and fitted to the modern nation state (with its dispersed, diverse, and otherwise-occupied populace) through the organizing devices of representation, routine elections, legal procedures, formal institutions, and so forth. For Wolin, however, this constitutionalization of democracy—rendering democracy formal and systematic—turns the democratic principle against itself. The "demos" is prohibited from ruling as a condition of a system structured purportedly so that the higher abstraction of "the people" may reign. Constitutionalism is a matter of "enclosing the dynamics of politics within a determinate structure and designated political space . . . , conceptualizing various institutions . . . , *norm*alizing their operation . . . , and projecting them over time. The purpose . . . [is] the establishment of stability through the containment of the demos." Democracy is disciplined and "domesticated"—made "stable, orderly, just," and largely undemocratic.[34] Such constraints thus "enable" democracy by making it something it is not, indeed by turning it against itself. Institutionalization, for instance, cannot but mark "the attenuation of democracy: leaders begin to appear; hierarchies develop . . . ; order, procedure, and precedent displace a more *spontaneous* politics: in retrospect the latter appears as disorganized, inefficient"—in other words, uneconomical.[35] Fitting the free flow of democracy to the ossified and predictable routines of conventional politics "has the effect of reducing democracy to a system while taming its politics by *process*. . . . Then it becomes the stuff of manipulation: of periodic elections that are managed and controlled, of public opinion that is shaped, cajoled, misled, and then polled."[36] It becomes a politics of the televised advertising "image" rather than of the "substance" of "immediate . . . experience."[37] Such a taming, inhibiting, artificial political system enables the semipublic administration of the populace rather than the popular politics of a citizenry, solving the so-called problem of scale by literally economizing democracy. Wolin concludes that a "political constitution is not the fulfillment of democracy but its transfiguration into a 'regime' and hence a stultified and partial reification"; properly understood, democracy is "a *phenomenon* that can be housed, but may not be realized, within a form."[38] Like Superpower, democracy demonstrates a constitutive formlessness that bridles at the domesticating effects of its own housing. Liberal democracy is not democracy made practical but democracy compromised—which are perhaps one and the same thing.

Wolin concludes that to distinguish between the authentic practice of democracy and the liberal democratic form of government, we must distinguish between "politics" and "the political." Similar to Lefort, Wolin writes that politics "refers to the legitimized and public contestation, primarily by organized and unequal social powers, over access to the resources available to the public authorities of the collectivity."[39] Politics simply is economics by other means. The political is the central idea of the entirety of Wolin's political thought, and it is the norm by which democracy itself is to be judged. While the relationship between democracy and the political is elusive in Wolin's writings, we might say that participatory democracy is the sole remaining practice of the political still possible in (post)modern times but that democratic participation alone is not sufficient to achieve the political, which requires participation above the level of interest politics and toward the end of the care and well-being of the commons. In his most explicit description (and this is quite different than Lefort's use of the term), Wolin writes that the political is "an expression of the idea that a free society composed of diversities can nonetheless enjoy *moments of commonality* when, through public deliberation, collective power is used to promote or protect the well-being of the collectivity."[40] To practice the political, then, "is not identical with being a part of government or being associated with a political party. These are structured roles, and typically they are highly bureaucratized. For these reasons, they are opposed to the authentically political."[41]

Wolin does not shy away from the radical implications of this separation of democracy and state. On a conceptual level, no form of state or government can be considered democratic. Wolin argues that the "idea of a democratic state is a contradiction in terms"; "democracy needs to be reconceived as something other than a form of government . . . [or a] political system."[42] From ancient times, political theorists "have made a category mistake by treating democracy as a possible constitutional form for an entire society."[43] The very notions of regimenting form, state power, governmental rule, and political system are antithetical to the values and experiences of the democratic political. Democracy is no longer democratic when it becomes affiliated with the economy of power that a governing state requires, just as religion is thought no longer properly sacred and spiritual when it becomes involved in the material power of the temporal world, whether of state or church. Again like Superpower, to be true to itself, democracy must transcend its institutional mechanisms.

## Liberal Theory: Rights, Law, Order

The domestication of democracy by constitutional form is, for Wolin, the evident aspiration of liberal theories of democracy. Prioritizing liberal legality over democratic vitality, liberal theory works to depoliticize democracy by rendering it abstract and systematic. Wolin argues that John Rawls, particularly in *Political Liberalism*, offers the paradigmatic attempt to circumscribe democracy. Specifically, by "assigning a mechanism, 'constructivism,' precedence over politics," he attempts to impose an apolitical/prepolitical settlement of the political, thereby confining democracy to an objective normative form. For the sake of legitimacy and stability, Rawls theorizes "agreement" as prior to deliberation and contestation; a sort of abstract consensus becomes the foundational prerequisite of democratic political talk. For Rawls, "the meaning and scope of politics is to be 'settled' beforehand, that is, before conflict and controversy among social groups and the alignment of classes is recognized"; politics is settled "into constitutional arrangements of representative government, periodic elections, a bill of rights, and judicial review . . . lest it unsettle broader social concerns." And this settlement is itself abstracted from the historical and cultural context of political existence and "made to appear to take place in a pure 'political' realm outside politics." Democracy here is emptied of all but its most abstract normative content: "Democracy is [thus] not a distinctive presence in *Liberalism*. . . . Its supreme political value is not dispersed power but individual liberty; its pivotal institution . . . is the supreme court; and it locates the true expression of political identity not in the vitality of local institutions but in the constitution." According to Wolin's reading of Rawls, "democracy is invoked only to be subaltern," denying certain political "possibilities, realities, and . . . memories." Conceptualizing a democracy without the demos as a political actor, Rawls's "politics of reason" is a "neutralizing" rather than a "neutral" principle, resulting in the notion of democracy as a "hermetically sealed condition of deliberation that allows rationality to rule." Against such an ideal of conflict suppression through abstraction, through forgetfulness and dislocation, Wolin argues that in an "age of vast concentrations of corporate and governmental power, the desperate problem of democracy is not to develop better ways of cooperation but to develop a fairer system of contestation."[44]

This depoliticization of democracy, Wolin argues, takes shape today primarily in the reduction of democratic equality to the abstraction of equal rights—in the "liberal formula" of "Equal Rights + Freedom = Democracy." Authentic equality is lost in the "idealizing blur" of the "ready-to-wear categories of equal rights for everyone." Rawls is again exemplary, elevating concerns of abstract and formal authority above issues of actual power. The equality of rights opposes the hierarchical right of commands but permits and even to an extent authorizes material inequalities: "The fundamental primacy accorded individual rights justifies unequal persons and powers, but because every citizen can claim them formally, the norm of equal rights gains priority over the fact of inequality. Thus liberal inequality is democratized and democratic equality is liberalized." Just how equal rights justify inequality "is illustrated when Rawls, apparently without sensing its antidemocratic character, insists on equal opportunity for all to positions of political and social power, that is, to positions in hierarchical organizations where they can exert unequal power and influence while receiving disproportionate compensation and protection."[45]

Citizenship, conversely, is diminished to a matter of being able to claim rights that derive from some higher realm outside and above politics and in relation to which political passions and conflicts are understood as a threat. We have come to assume that the extension of rights is an advance toward the realization of democracy. In actuality, Wolin writes, the ideal of rights is "usurping the place of civic activity" within a "liberal civic culture [that] never supplied any content . . . [or] guidance to the exercise of rights."[46]

As traditionally conceived, then, liberal constitutionalism is naturally amenable to the dictates of economy: to the primacy of law and so to the domestication of democracy by form; to the reductive elimination of difference through abstraction; to the paving over of historical experience and cultural existence in the quest for objective reason and systematic order; to the reduction of equality to equal rights. Constraining popular power while enabling state power, what a constitution permits is not a more moral but a more economic politics.

### The Imperial Citizen

With its domestication by liberal constitutionalism, Wolin writes, our democracy has become "a democracy without the demos as actor."[47] At a basic level, this is because we no longer think of ourselves as political people. The citizenry no longer recognizes itself in political terms; it is not conscious of itself collectively, as a public, but instead sees the political role of the individual limited to that of a voter, job holder, taxpayer, and consumer. We have come to accept "a collective identity in which the collectivity—'We the People,' in the brave words of the Constitution—becomes the passive object of power rather than the active political subject."[48] The result is "the anomalous presence of the powerless many in a democracy"—a "ventriloquous democracy" conceived in terms "that allowed the American political animal to evolve into the domesticated creature of media politics."[49] We abandon ourselves to being "periodically courted, warned, and confused but otherwise kept at a distance from actual decision-making," happily trading the responsibilities of democratic citizenship for purchasing power, market choice, and consumer sovereignty.[50] Worse yet, we are tending toward active complicity, toward the eager willingness to trade the democratic exercise of power, with its inherently small scale and limited potential, for vicarious association in and identification with much more spectacular and effective power systems. As fervently patriotic as we are apolitical, we are becoming what Wolin terms imperial citizens, embracing the shock-

and-awe grasping of Superpower and even the purging actions and pan-optic exactions of inverted totalitarianism. We love the power and its repositories.

Today, Wolin writes, we are in desperate need of a genuine alternative. We need to develop "a politics that cannot be co-opted, which is precisely what has happened to the original democratic dream of basing democracy upon voting, elections, and popular political parties." Wolin argues, "Democracy needs a non-cooptable politics, that is, a politics that renders useless the forms of power developed by the modern state and business corporations."[51]

What, then, is to be done? When we are confronted by the postmodern Leviathan of Superpower, what is to be done? Superpower's totalitarian economy of power is antidemocratic, even antihuman, yet we the imperial citizenry embrace the world it has wrought as second nature. Liberal democracy—democracy at once expanded and domesticated by constitutional form—is no solution. It is just the economy of power imposed upon politics, the rhetoric of democracy inverted to serve its own subversion. Liberal democracy is the abstract and systematized politics—the streamlined simulation of democracy—proper to the economic polity.[52]

In this context, Wolin argues that authentic democracy is rendered either "archaic" or "fugitive." It perseveres either as vestigial remnant or as revolutionary moment. As we shall see, Wolin himself comes to question the former as any sort of effective solution to the problems of the day. Such a limited, powerless practice of democracy offers a means of escape from domestication, a port in the storm, but it cannot meaningfully oppose twenty-first-century totalitarianism. In turn, Wolin turns to the idea of democracy as an event wherein the demos transgresses the laws and orders of economy. This is a form-breaking democracy, undomesticated and wild, that, if only for an instant, generates the power to stand up to Superpower. In living fast, though, it dies young, not lasting long enough to be corrupted and co-opted. The spirit enters the body, but for only a moment.

I argue in what follows that fugitive democracy comes to share certain elective affinities with its adversary, affinities which are in opposition to archaism. Superpower is the economic practice of limitlessness; fugitive democracy is the political practice of democratic openness. In his attempt to theorize a power-wielding democracy, Wolin offers an imperial demos that is as eager as Superpower to transgress limits and laws, if for diametrically opposed ends. He offers a revolutionary democracy that celebrates rupture from constitutional and conventional norms and forms as much as postmodern power encourages rupture from archaic cultural settlements. Where the pace of archaic democracy is that of historical-cultural accretion, the tempos of fugitive democracy and Superpower are those of revolutionary action. Moreover, Wolin offers a notion of collective action motivated if not by economic efficiency, then by economic necessity—we come together as a demos largely to oppose our material oppression. This mode of human association is depicted as in a sense natural, spontaneous and unspoken, outside the need for mediating words and argument. Where the archaic is a venue for civic education and democratic habituation, fugitive democracy does without such character formation—it is instigated rather than cultivated. And conceptualizing the unity and energy of the demos as being produced by external crisis and as opposing the enemy of Superpower, Wolin offers a sort of executive-action or emergency-power mode of democratic action and association. Where archaic democracy is rooted in culture, fugitive democracy is caused by crisis.

## III. Archaic Democracy: The Communal "We"

*Domesticity versus Domestication*

We have seen how postmodern power strives to simplify reality, eliminating through abstraction and systematization all those particularities that muck up the perpetual motion machine of power generation. Against this theoretical depopulation of existence, democratic archaism stands for the preservation of local cultures and histories—the conservation of the democratic many and their places in the world. And against ceaseless dislocating and disorienting change, the revolutions and innovations imposed by the economy of power, archaism stands for the conservation of settled places in which human beings locate themselves as at home in the world.

To say democracy is archaic is a statement of fact for Wolin: authentic democracy has been "excluded, forgotten, passed by." At the same time, he conceptualizes this very obsolescence as a normative resource because it offers an oppositional pluralism to monolithic Superpower. The archaic is significant precisely because it could not be assimilated and so was left behind (as we shall see, even the nondemocratic archaic is therefore worth preserving). Archaism introduces a countervailing cultural complexity to the reductive, totalizing inclination of postmodern power. It counters the economy of power with a sort of primitivism, and the globalizing reach of Superpower with what Wolin calls "democratic feudalism" and "democratic fundamentalism." It frustrates conglomeration through dissonance, like the difference of language that stymied power at Babel. It constitutes, Wolin writes, "the domestication of power by an unplotted conspiracy of difference." While Tocqueville's archaic aristocracy was to "teach democracy the importance of providing counter principles at the center of its system," the "anomalous" and "anachronistic" element of archaic democracy serves as a "counterprinciple to a new, postmodern regime."[53]

Archaic democracy's radicalism thus lies in its conservatism.[54] It represents continuity in the service of disorganization—remembrance as resistance. Wolin writes that the "central challenge at this moment is not about reconciliation but about dissonance, not about democracy's supplying legitimacy to totality but about nurturing a discordant democracy— . . . discordant because, in being *rooted in the ordinary*, it affirms *the value of limits*."[55] Precisely in its domesticity, archaic democracy resists domestication. For its manifesto, Wolin offers: "The crucial challenge to radical democracy is to be as zealous in preventing things of great value to democracy from passing into oblivion as in bringing into the world new political forms of action, participation, and being together in the world. Radicals need to cultivate a remembrance of things past, for in the capitalist civilization . . . of 'creative destruction,' memory is a subversive weapon. . . . What is at stake simultaneously is the past *and* the future. Radicals cannot leave the past to conservatives. . . . [The] highest aim [is] renewal and radical change."[56]

*Memory and Place*

Against power's streamlining of existence, Wolin identifies Montesquieu as the leading defender of the cultural places in which we live our lives—of the particular against the general: "[His] ideal might be [stated] as power moderated by the complexities of political culture or, more briefly, as acculturated power." Wolin juxtaposes Montesquieu's culturally oriented thought with Cartesian reason, which is "stripped of myth, superstition, and religious fable, . . . custom and tradition" and reduced to "scientific and mathematical modes of analysis." Cartesian reason, striving for total harmony, constructs a monological reality abstracted from social context—a reality that obeys the necessary truths of universal law. Based upon the "uncontested power of reason," law "appears 'irresistible' and 'self-evident' because the self has nothing to resist with": "Selves, so to speak, have been severed from their 'evidence,' which has been left behind in the context from which they have been abstracted." Stripped of situation, the self stands naked and powerless before the necessity of reason and law. Conversely, positing a "social whole" that has not been "assembled by theoretical reason but deposited by historical actions and inactions," Montesquieu offers no such idealization of totality. Society here is not "the artifact of [a] single founder" or a " 'system' of rationally arranged and interconnected institutions" but rather a " 'labyrinth' [characterized by] tortuous . . . , undesigned, unpremeditated qualities . . . that time and custom have smoothed into a working arrangement." Its laws are a matter of accretion rather than of imposition and should be understood not "as "commands but as reciprocal relationships expressive of the natures of those to whom the laws apply." In this sense, Montesquieu theorizes the multiplicity and complexity inherent in the ad hoc "accommodations" of practices to places—to "climate, geography, religion, morals, manners, and political understandings."[57] Against the empty space of Cartesianism, Montesquieu's world is cluttered and textured by all those variations and particularities of local places.

In addition to the conservation of a sense of place, Wolin theorizes the preservation of memory in opposition to power. The central antagonist here is not Descartes but Hobbes and more generally the art of forgetting that enables the social contract. For Hobbes, the central demand of the move from nature to civil society—formulated as "complaesance" in his fifth law of nature—is that "every man strive to accommodate himself to the rest." Accommodation requires the mutual absolution of past wrongs and resentments. Peace is a matter of forgetting, of not allowing oneself to be buried by the past. The prospect of socialization hinges on leaving behind historical baggage, wiping the slate clean, and starting over again: "In the act of reconstituting the self into a civic self, forgetting becomes a rite of passage and as such a condition of membership." Hobbes's covenant is thus "a device to incorporate social amnesia into the foundation of society." The result is a society built upon the abstraction of the free and equal individual, or, in other words, "blank individuals who fake their nature by denying historically acquired and multiple identities." Any perceived threat of faction or conflict or unruliness is to trigger the reversion to the peace-producing moment of contract, when everyone puts aside their differences for the sake of becoming one. And the abstraction from identity and difference by which society is founded enables the absolute sovereignty by which society is enforced. "A lack of traditions and customary institutions allows the will to extend itself almost without limit," and so it is "made to order for despotism or for centralized bureaucracy."[58] The rule can be without exception, and the order without anomaly; the expansion of power finds itself without horizons or obstructions.

Wolin goes on to argue that the economy of power, with its ceaseless creative destruction, actually accomplishes the sense of dislocating mobility that the seventeenth-century contractualists could only imagine. The acceleration of time and frequency of flux so characteristic of the postmodern celebration of innovation (whether scientific or economic) has left us amnesiac and homeless, disoriented and defenseless before the relentless workings of power, and necessarily willing to move for work. In this context, the conservation of memories and places stands not for "an atavistic urge to return to a simpler age" but for "the creation of conditions which encourage complexities that live by different laws and defy Cartesian solutions" and Hobbesian accommodations.[59]

For Wolin, the founding debates of the current American regime were precisely between a politics of the ordinary and the local, versus an abstract and distant politics seated in a single national government. The choice was between "a *constitution* of government on one hand and a political *culture* on the other." The Revolution of 1776, Wolin writes, was "a protest of the periphery against the center," of "local liberties and institutions against . . . remote and hence abstract imperial authority."

The ratification of the Constitution signified the suppression of this pluralism—*e pluribus unum*. Pluralism was represented as primal chaos, while unity was represented as elevated to "a different political plane, abstract rather than immediate, intellective rather than sentimental, administrative or executive in its outlook rather than participatory or suffrage-oriented." It was a revolution in its own right, of reason against passion and centralizing power against local practices. The counter-revolution of 1787 thus marked the beginning of a return to empire and the uniformity that the economy of power prefers. It was a rebellion not against the "arbitrary power" of an "unjust and illegal" British Crown but against the "inefficiency" and "weakness" associated with local differences, inefficiencies, and peculiarities. The "politics of particularism" represented by the thirteen states was depicted as irrational, "inherited and regressive," something that must be replaced by "rational foundations" and "rational administration." And the discourse developed by *The Federalist* centered on the basic terms of political economy against local liberty: " 'system,' 'efficiency,' 'energy,' 'power,' and 'administration.' " Combining "Old Testament conceptions of monotheistic power" with "eighteenth-century conceptions of a rational science of politics," Publius justified the constitutional counterrevolution against the Declaration of Independence and the Articles of Confederation as "an exodus from a condition of political polytheism." It was an exodus from the "disunity, even dismemberment, weakness, and division . . . of a nonsystem without a center."[60] The avowed goal was to found a commercial republic, with a concomitant political economy, conducive to the concentration and generation of power.

Yet, in one crucial respect, this rhetoric of constitution was misleading. Given the existence of the diverse political cultures of the thirteen states, along with "state governments, various institutions of local government, jury systems, and a vast array of spontaneous ad hoc life forms," the Federalist science and economy of power cannot be understood as the solution to a political vacuum. Instead, it must be seen as "the superimposition of a new . . . national form of politics."[61] Constitutional ratification was as much an act of destruction as it was of creation, not bringing order out of anarchy but reordering (depopulating) what was already in existence. The problem of a political vacuum had to be rhetorically invented before it could be solved.

Ultimately, American constitutionalism effaced the very idea of difference. The key document is *Federalist* 10. Wanting to protect the diversity associated with the inequality of faculties and acquisitions yet "expressing the fear of being overwhelmed by difference," Madison made the pivotal move of representing difference as faction.[62] The American people were to forget or forsake their deep regional and religious differences in their economic factionalism, which, despite its cacophonous quality, is actually based upon the homogeneity of identities and interests. Madison domesticates difference, rendering it in terms of negotiable interests that can be accommodated (compromised) so long as they are "compelled to appeal to a center of authority to mediate" disputes.[63]

In significant ways, Wolin argues, "We the People" can consider ourselves the creatures rather than creators of the constitutional order. We have been regimented to our constitutional form and our commercial republic. In this context, Wolin writes, any counterrevolution to the constitutional counterrevolution—any return to the centrifugal principles of the Declaration of Independence and the Articles of Confederation—will be dismissed as reactionary. With the present hegemony of economy—when, for instance, the centralization and extension of power is taken as definitional of progress—the archaism of the Anti-Federalists appears extreme and fanatical. For Wolin, antifederalism is the beating heart of radicalism today. In a passage that would seem to characterize his own position perfectly, Wolin writes that "the contemporary inheritors of the antifederalist tradition have seen themselves as radicals fighting against the centralization of power and the overproduction of it." Their conservative vision is "driven to radicalism because there is no way for [their] conception of life forms to be maintained without opposing a system of power in which change has become routinized."[64]

### Democratic Feudalism and Democratic Fundamentalism

Tocqueville famously argued that in many respects democracy in France was never more robust than during feudalism, prior to the centralization and bureaucratization of power inaugurated under the Old Regime monarchy and accelerated by the French Revolution. While this was not a period of equality, power was never more dispersed and limited, and so freedom was never more extensive, than during the rule of the feudal aristocracy. It was an era of pure particularism and of the ingrained "landedness" of traditional and customary social orders. Wolin theorizes feudalism along similarly democratic lines. Feudalism signifies a society in which "inheritance, with its implicit historicity, is the master notion." It is a disposition of preservation rather than innovation—of "tending to" and "cultivating" one's own cultural place, understood as "a complex of shared beliefs, values, habits, practices, and experiences that define the particularity of a place and envelop its politics." It thus centers politics around "habits of competence or skill that are routinely required . . . in the intimate political experience . . . of everyday existence." Because it was "a conception that depicted and explained political society as a concatenation of differences . . . it could be said to pit political culture against political rationality, the centrifugal tendencies of the one against the centripetal impulses of the other."[65]

Like authentic democracy, then, feudalism stands against abstraction and systematization and for the entirely uneconomical dispersal of power to the small scale of firsthand localism. Like authentic democracy, feudalism is cluttered with what Tocqueville calls "intermediate bodies" that serve as speed bumps in the generation of power. Feudalism and authentic democracy both subordinate the needs of the economy of power to the nonmalleable, nonnegotiable "identity" of "historical and biographical beings" and to the "biography of a place." Both ways of being are less concerned with "straining toward the future" and "acting effectively" than with "the preservation of pastness . . . [as] an important element in the narrative structure of identity."[66] Democratic feudalism, we might say, represents the premodern antithesis to postmodern power's tendency toward totalitarianism.

The homogenization of "feudal" differences as a means of greasing the wheels of power is, for Wolin, the singular trait of American political development. As opposed to the famous so-called Tocqueville/Louis Hartz thesis that America had no feudal tradition to overcome, Wolin argues that such a tradition is precisely what has been paved over, beginning with the ratification of the Constitution and accelerating with most every so-called turning point in American history. The high point of this tradition of affirming difference and particularity was the "feudal revolt" of the American Revolution.[67] The slow erosion (punctuated by a few periods of rapid retreat) of this democratic and antistatist line—extending from the Anti-Federalists "to the Virginia-Kentucky resolutions (1798–99), to the Hartford Convention, the nullification controversy, and the Civil War"—is the actual political history of America. While the Civil War destroyed "the last serious defense of feudal politics," the New Deal marked the beginning of the consequent "triumph of the state."[68] Like feudalism before it, "participatory politics [that is] centered around small towns, villages, cities, and state governments" has come to seem anachronistic, obsolete, and even bizarre.[69] We are left today with a reversal in the status of democracy, from being modern to being archaic.

As odd as the association of democracy and feudalism might seem, Wolin goes further, to formulate what he terms "democratic fundamentalism." In today's ubiquitous dichotomy of fundamentalism and globalization— "Jihad vs. McWorld," as Benjamin Barber famously phrases it—Wolin suggests that authentic democracy has more in common with fundamentalism, or at least that the common enemy of both democracy and fundamentalism is globalization.

At times, Wolin suggests that democracy is forced to fundamentalist extremes by current conditions, forced to fight a rear-guard action against totalizing economy. Fundamentalist democracy is the notion of democracy "dictated by the inherently anti-democratic structures and norms characteristic of the . . . the contemporary corporation and the Superpower state."[70] At other times, Wolin suggest that there is a more intrinsic connection between democracy and fundamentalism: "Religious fundamentalism, 'moralism,' and racial, religious, and ethnic prejudices belong to the same historical culture as traditions of local self-government, decentralized politics, participatory democracy, and sentiments of egalitarianism. . . . All are suspicious of distant authorities, centralized power, and new moral fashions. [The] prejudices [of fundamentalism] appear as anachronisms. But then, so does democracy itself."[71]

In either case, fundamentalism is allied to authentic democracy insofar as fundamentalism is the expression of irreconcilable, nonnegotiable difference that simply cannot be homogenized, abstracted from, or reduced to economic factionalism. In this sense, both hold out against the centralizing, depopulating thrust of (post)modernity. Archaism, Wolin writes, has found its defenders in many brands of antimodern centrifugalism: "the Klan, militiamen and -women, neo-Nazis, Protestant fundamentalists, would-be censors of public and school libraries, champions of an 'original Constitution.' " While not always appealing, such nonaccomodationism serves (like Tocqueville's aristocracy) to introduce countervailing dissonance into the process of uni-forming. The political value of such groups lies not in their truth or justice, but in their role as "provocateurs whose passionate commitments can arouse self-consciousness in the public." Wolin writes, "The resulting controversies are crucial to the cause of anti-totality and its vitality."[72]

Fundamentalism is thus allied to democracy insofar as it is the "religion" of those "threatened . . . by a relentlessly modernizing society that exposes their most cherished beliefs as archaic." Protestant fundamentalism was shaped as a direct response to "efforts at modifying religious teachings to harmonize them with the findings of modern science"; fundamentalism therefore hungered "for nothing so much as a return to . . . original principles."[73] In its archaism, democracy too is shaped as a direct response to efforts at harmonizing democracy to science and economy; democracy hungers for nothing so much as the preservation of our original slow-motion, small-scale democratic mode of being.

## The Powerlessness of Archaic Democracy

Wolin himself has argued that theorizing democracy in terms of archaism—of feudal decentralization/fundamental difference—is inadequate to the challenges of the day. The political action open to archaism amounts to quietism, to escape rather than struggle: "While it is of the utmost importance that democrats support and encourage political activity at the grassroots level, it is equally necessary that the political limitations of such activity be recognized. It is politically incomplete. This is because the localism that is the strength of grassroots organizations is also their limitation. There are major problems in our society that are general in nature and necessitate modes of vision and action that are comprehensive rather than parochial."[74] General problems require, beyond holding fast to particularism, democratic modes of action that can operate at a general level. A politics rooted in the ordinary cannot respond to the extraordinary power generated today. The very limitations that archaism introduces into the economy of power rebound to limit the democratic generation of power. The uncompromising difference at the heart of archaism is so pronounced—whether feudal or fundamental—that democratic association is disorganized right along with economic systematization. Tending toward the logic of secession from any mode of association not based on the quasi-familial ties of memory and place, archaic democracy is excessively self-limiting.

The dilemma follows of how to envision a mode of "organization" and power generation wherein democracy rather than economy, with its greater efficiency, serves as the integrating agent. The difficulty lies in formulating a mode of association that does not efface difference, and that does not follow from economic abstraction and liberal formalism and institutionalization. To be effective, democracy needs to realize its power; to be authentic, this mode of realization must not fall into the material politics of parties, institutions, elections, and interest group pluralism or be co-opted into the economic language of organization, systematization, and so forth.

To this end, Wolin theorizes democracy as fugitive. He writes, "A range of problems and atrocities exists that a locally confined democracy cannot resolve. Like pluralism, interest group politics, and multicultural politics, localism cannot surmount its limitations except by seeking out the evanescent homogeneity of a broader political."[75] The solution to the problem of envisioning a powerful but essentially noneconomical collective actor is to render its homogeneity evanescent. Expansive in space but constricted in time, democratic association and action are effective but incorruptible because they come into material existence for only a moment. The fugitive demos rides into town to challenge "the democratic credentials of a system that legitimates the economic oppression and culturally stunted lives of millions of citizens while, for all practical purposes excluding them from political power," but it doesn't stick around to govern.[76]

Far from encouraging or empowering political activity at the grassroots level, I argue that fugitive democracy undermines such activity. Indeed, in many respects fugitive democracy seems more in accord with postmodern power than with archaism. The radicalism of fugitive democracy takes shape not as conservation but as revolution, as rupture with the patterns of everyday existence. It is a matter not of preserving cultural counterformations against constitutional formalism but of transgressive form-breaking. A wholly *extraordinary* politics, its momentary quality stands in sharp contrast to the continuity of memory and the biography of place so central to archaism. Revolution replaces cultivation as the "master notion" of democracy; the metaphor of "overflowing" supplants that of "grass rootedness." Ultimately, fugitive democracy seems to amount not to an imposition of limits upon power, but to a sort of counterlimitlessness. As we shall see, where archaic democracy is allied with feudalism and fundamentalism, fugitive democracy is allied to imperialism—the demos' squandering passion for empire.[77]

There is one central way in which archaic and fugitive democracy will be seen to intersect. Both are born of an abiding contempt for the present moment and the longing to return to a sort of nature, social or otherwise. Whether in reaction or revolution, authentic democracy stands against the present world of conventional forms and institutions. Nonetheless, there is a disconnect between the archaic and the fugitive at what Wolin considers a fundamental level. He writes that we should always consider politics from an educative perspective. The "fundamental question" is always, "what kind of citizen or political being would [a mode] of politics encourage?"[78] One wonders whether Wolin's two democracies—torn between continuity and disturbance, between cultural time and revolutionary action—might not encourage diametrically opposed dispositions. Is the good citizen of democracy most closely related to the citizens of 1830s America or the France of 1789? Is the practitioner of democratic politics one who storms barricades or one who attends town meetings, one who wields power or one who shares power, one who strives or one who tends, or both from one moment to the next?[79]

I conclude by suggesting that all three forms of democracy that Wolin identifies—liberal, archaic, and fugitive—do have one basic similarity: they are incapable of envisioning political associations that take shape despite differences. Liberal democracy abstracts from deep difference in formulating "association" as mere aggregation; for the system to work, individuals need to function similarly but not necessarily collectively. Archaic democracy formulates association as the community of memory and place, as a sort of tribalism. Fugitive democracy takes shape not as the community of memory and place but as the fleeting community of victims; the demos coalesces briefly around the shared experience of oppression. The options seem to be individualism or communalism (whether continuous or momentary), with nothing in between—association via abstraction or authenticity, with nothing in between. Collective action is either tallied by a third party in terms of demographic and behavioral statistics, or it comes about through a sort of spontaneous affiliation with (in one way or another) identical others. All three modes of association are thus in effect unspoken, with no need for mediating words and arguments.

## IV. Fugitive Democracy: The Revolutionary "We"

*Democracy as Revolution*

Democracy, Wolin writes in a key passage, contains within it "two diametrically opposed notions that symbolize two equally opposed states of affairs": "One is the settled structure of politics and governmental authority typically called a constitution, and the other is the unsettling political movement typically called revolution. Stated somewhat starkly: constitution signifies the suppression of revolution; revolution the destruction of constitution." Wolin urges us to recognize that authentic democracy takes shape exclusively around the latter pole. We should embrace "the familiar charges that democracy is inherently unstable, inclined toward anarchy, and identified with revolution." Instead of assuming that "the problem is to adapt democracy to the requirements of organization, we might think of democracy as resistant to the rationalizing conceptions of power and its organization. This democracy might be summed up as the idea and practice of rational disorganization."[80]

Historically, democracy has been associated with the revolt of the many against the few or the one. The "democratic agon" is "performed," as Wolin puts it, in "revolution or popular uprising, collective disobedience, and mass protest."[81] In turn, democracy is metaphorically represented as passion over reason, energy over order, movement over settlement, flux over form, openness over closure, anarchy over tyranny, and so forth. Conceptualized along these lines, democracy necessarily comes to a crossroad when it is time to transition from the revolt of the many to the rule of the many—from questioning to decision making. Democracy can stay true to itself, to its original vital impulse, and remain in the street, or be housed in attenuated conventional form. During revolution, the "demos as autonomous agent . . . gathers its power from outside the system"; the "political challenge of the demos inevitably overflows . . . customary and institutional boundaries."[82] When the revolt ends and the permanent institutionalization of politics begins, the "democracy carried along by revolution comes to appear as surplus."[83] In ordinary times democracy's dynamic thus appears undisciplined, excessive, irregular, and spasmodic. Similar to Superpower, democracy's characteristic virtue is its own overflowing excess, which is deemed out of order after the revolutionary movement.

Liberal constitutionalism is precisely that mechanism whereby democracy is disciplined. The avowed ambition is to tame "continuous struggle" by means of "reified law."[84] With its discourse of objective reason (impersonal, impartial, higher) as vulgar passion's harness, constitutionalism has always been as opposed to democracy as to absolutism. Constitutionalism amounts to an "attack upon the vitality and energy displayed by a demos": "The aim was not simply to check democracy but to discourage it by making it difficult for those who, historically, had almost no leisure time for politics, to achieve political goals."[85] Archaism too would seem to constrain democratic excesses. In the dichotomy between "settled structures" and "unsettling movement," archaic democracy's discourse of complexity and local *tradition*, no less than liberal democracy's abstract and universal *reason*, frustrates revolutionary democracy's simplifying and overflowing *passions*: "The rhetoric of the desperate is likely to be a simplifying one, reflective of conditions reduced to essentials. A rhetoric of complexity, ever since Burke, has found favor with those whose expectations are secure."[86] Complexity obstructs democratic power just as complexity obstructs economic power; simplification—the reduction to oneness—remains above all a metaphor for power. Settled structures, whether constitutional or cultural, threaten authentic democratic action. Democracy's unsettling movement threatens archaic memory and place, just as such movement threatens liberal institutional forms. "Revolution might be defined," Wolin writes, as the "transgression of *inherited* forms": "It is the extreme antithesis to a settled constitution, whether that constitution is represented by documents ('basic laws') or by recognized systems or practice."[87] Indeed, revolution means "snapping the continuity between past and future" and inducing "the destruction of . . . prior identity."[88] Revolution "wants to begin history, not continue it."[89]

In Wolin's account, then, the inevitable course of fugitive democracy's life span is from a youthful and wild squandering to economization and domestication. He identifies the overthrow of communism in central and Eastern Europe as a leading example: "[During the revolt,] politics was primarily the affair of 'civil society,' not of conventional political parties or parliamentary processes. Various extralegal groups of . . . ordinary citizens energized and sustained revolutionary movements whose internal politics was remarkably participatory and egalitarian. After the success of those movements, a different politics began to take shape, a politics of organized parties, professional politicians, and economic interest groups. Above all, it was a politics in which the overriding problems were declared to be economic."[90] Paradoxically, democracy's success marks the beginning of its own attenuation. Democratic revolutions "seem to lose their dynamic once they succeed."[91] Like Superpower, fugitive democracy is essentially dynamic; unlike Superpower, it cannot sustain its own dynamic

## Momentary Democracy

With the association of democracy and revolution, it becomes unclear whether democracy's fugitive character precedes from the postmodern conditions of the economy of power or from democracy's own principle. Is democracy on the run from Superpower or of its own accord? Is democracy contingently rendered "rare" and "episodic," or is it intrinsically so?[92] In theorizing democracy as an overflowing but fleeting moment, is Wolin depicting its current limits or its essence, its shortcomings or its zenith?

At times Wolin suggests that democracy need not be merely episodic and that the democratic practice of politics might continue after the revolutionary moment. Democracy and revolution are not synonymous; revolution is just the negative first stage in the realization of democratic politics: "Revolutions activate the demos and destroy boundaries that bar access to political experience. . . . Thus revolutionary transgression is the means by which the demos makes itself political."[93] Once the barriers to the political have been overturned and the people have assumed their rightful political place, democracy's initial oppositional "dynamic" is no longer needed and so is less "lost" than superseded by some other democratic mode of politics. In our age of economy, unfortunately, democracy is seduced, overawed, and outspent at the very moment it attempts to organize its energies into political practices. Thus, democracy *"in the late modern world* cannot be a complete political system."[94] It is rendered fugitive, "doomed to succeed only temporarily."[95]

At other times, Wolin suggests that democracy simply is revolution and so by nature fugitive.[96] Sounding a Madisonian note, Wolin writes, "The fugitive character of democracy is no mystery": it is explained by the factional "heterogeneity [that] is *a consequence of liberty and equality,* the two values that since antiquity have been associated solely with democracy."[97] In its liberty and equality, democracy makes "unequal power" possible, which can be eliminated "only by betraying its own values."[98] Moreover (and here we might recall Alan Keenan's argument about the tension between inclusion and exclusion—legitimacy and effectiveness—at the center of democratic collective action), "common action is rendered more difficult" insofar as democratic "inclusion is expanded to legitimate new differences."[99] Liberty and equality produce unequal power; legitimate democratic agency requires both inclusion and exclusion: in either case democracy is destined to betray itself. Democracy is "doomed to succeed only temporarily" because of its own tragic internal tension between openness and collective action—between having no principled justification of exclusion, as Wolin argues, yet having a practical need to exclude in order to cohere.

This tension is resolved within the idea of democratic revolution, wherein the passion for rather than the products of liberty and equality dominate, and wherein differences are bracketed in the struggle for inclusion. The spirit of democracy coincides with material reality in that singular moment of revolt against antidemocratic norms and forms—in Lefort's "operation of negativity" or Wolin's "rational disorganization." Principle and practice, authority and power, legitimacy and effectiveness can be made to intersect episodically but not institutionally. Democracy can be kept from being co-opted and managed *and* from betraying its own principles by burning itself out. It is doomed to succeed only temporarily, but its temporality preserves its untouched and uncompromised purity. Each new moment is pristine and full of youthful vitality. Democracy remains authentic on condition that it is not enduring. The practice of democratic politics is thus reconciled with the principle of democratic openness by theorizing democratic politics as revolution. Appearing only long enough for the act of beheading, democracy's momentary nature guarantees its perennial return to a state of openness.

The question then becomes not whether democracy can be made "a complete political system" in the late modern world but whether democracy and politics are mutually exclusive. Wolin writes, "The true question is not whether democracy can govern in the traditional sense, but why it would *want* to. Governing means manning and accommodating to bureaucratized institutions that, *ipso facto*, are hierarchical in structure and elitist, permanent rather than fugitive—in short, anti-democratic."[100] Established democracy is oxymoronic, and insofar as politics has something to do with government, a schism opens up between democracy and politics. Authentic democracy amounts to the revolt of the people, while the rule of the people would seem to be consigned to the status of economized democracy. Robust democracy is therefore an "ephemeral phenomenon," "protean and amorphous," rather than a "settled system" or "institutionalized process."[101] Democracy is robust *because* it is ephemeral; diminishing democracy's apparent strength makes it more powerful. Protean and amorphous, democracy never falls from revolutionary openness into materiality; its unquestioned authority is premised on the impermanence of its power. While democracy can no longer be considered a form of government, or a way of life, it is a fleeting, elevating "moment of experience" against which government and society are judged.[102]

### Democracy and Necessity

Among the most basic of Wolin's philosophical presuppositions is that "commonality" is "fugitive and impermanent"—a matter of sharing "in a common *experience* rather than in a common *life*."[103] Commonality is not located in shared historical memory or cultural place; rather, it is something that comes into being and passes as quickly as an experience. There are historical moments of upheaval "when collective identity is collectively established or reconstituted," but no "pre-existent, continuous entity" of the people beyond, or perhaps even within, the local community.[104] As much descriptive as normative, commonality both cannot and should not be permanent—commonality is and should be uncommon. Since it is momentary, commonality is in accord with the fact and value of openness. It is a formless or informal sort of commonality, neither constitutional nor cultural.

Distancing his theory from the language of "organization," Wolin describes fugitive commonality as "spontaneous"—arising as if ex nihilo. This spontaneity translates into the notion of association not through deliberation, nor through socialization, but through the experience of necessity—and, in particular, material necessity. A phenomenon rather than a regime, democracy is founded/caused not by a law giver but by crisis—*e pluribus unum* via, in particular, oppression. "Corporate solidarity and self-consciousness," Wolin writes, "are responses to oppression": "Resistance brings with it a heightened sense of self-awareness, of distinctive identity."[105] The sameness required for collective action follows from "a common condition of oppression, of injustice, which is to say that sameness is created not by democracy when it is installed as a construction, but by a *predemocratic experience*. . . . Misery creates the basis for a . . . conception of the political based on community."[106]

Authentically democratic association is a function not of the abstract congregation of the market, nor of the solid community of settled tradition, but of periodically shared commiseration—a community of misery. The democratic "we" is revolutionary rather than economic or quasi-religious: "[Democratic commonality] begins with the demos constructing/collecting itself from scattered experiences and fusing these into a self-consciousness about common powerlessness and its causes. The demos is created from a shared realization [of] powerlessness."[107]

This raises two issues. First, representing democracy in terms Carl Schmitt would recognize, democratic association and action become contingent upon a common enemy.[108] Beyond Wolin's work, the idea that we come together and are roused to action only in response to some common problem or common evil seems ubiquitous today. In an inversion of Aristotle, it is precisely in an alliance of mutual defense rather than in pursuit of some common good (or in relations of exchange and commerce) that the demotic city identifies itself. The social bond is not a shared conception of justice but the simultaneous experience of injustice, which is partitioned off from questions of justice by being reduced to "objective" harm of one sort or another. The odd conclusion of premising democratic association and action upon the struggle with evil, as it were, rather than upon the pursuit of good is that evil and democracy would wax and wane in unison. Inherently responsive, democracy loses steam as it advances. Born of deprivation and oppression, the paradoxical prerequisite of democracy is the lack or loss of democracy. The less we are victimized, the less we are capable of democracy. If democracy is "created from a shared realization of powerlessness," then perhaps paradoxically the presence of the powerless many becomes the precondition of democracy. Along these lines, it seems Superpower actually empowers or motivate fugitive democratic association and action.

Second, in Wolin's account fugitive democracy seems largely like a radicalization of liberalism. The occasional quality of the "revolutionary we" mirrors that of the "electoral we" in both cause and effect. Wolin writes that the fugitive character of democracy is in part related to the fact that "democracy's politics is the creation of those who must work." It is the act of those without power and leisure, for whom sustained political participation and action is necessarily a sacrifice. Collective action is the "crystallized response to deeply felt grievances or needs on the part of those whose main preoccupation—demanding of time and energy—is to scratch out a decent existence." Wolin argues that, "given the material conditions of the demos," then, "the actuality of democracy is necessarily episodic and circumstantial."[109]

Material necessity is both the cause of democracy and the cause of its devitalization. We band together and take the public stage to protest or resist oppression; then we disband and return to making a living. Need explains why we become political beings and why we fail to remain political beings. Wolin thus seems to accept the idea of an ordinarily apolitical, economically oriented, disengaged populace. The assumption that democracy was to be "a form of government in which the people governed" on an ongoing basis was mistaken "in part because it assumed that the authority and power to govern was what a people would aspire to."[110] Reminiscent of Machiavelli's formulation, the demos, like a liberal citizenry, is "unable to rule yet unwilling to be ruled."[111]

In liberal democratic theory, the solution is an ordinary politics by proxy punctuated occasionally by the people speaking for themselves. Wolin rejects this notion for its failure to "promote participation" and in turn for its reliance on "the political forays of an occasional citizenry."[112]

Yet, fugitive democracy is itself based on such an occasional, momentary citizenry. The fugitive moment is the radicalization of the electoral moment, which "involves the taking back of one's power, not just the revocation of legitimacy."[113] Eventually, though, the people relinquish their power, and a new equilibrium sets in. Fugitive democracy amounts to a more forceful throwing out of the bums.

### Democracy as Instinct

We have seen how fugitive democracy is limited in duration and power, both by Superpower and by its own internal dynamic. Yet, in Wolin's account this ineffectiveness belies the ambitions of the fugitive demos. In its passion for revolution, in its striving to transgress all limits, Wolin's authentic demos (like Tocqueville's men of '89) displays a rapacity and audacity of epic proportions. The demos harbors Superpower's desire, if not its capacity, for creative/destructive limitlessness. Where archaic democracy mirrors the Athenian act of wall building, fugitive democracy mirrors the Athenian grasp for empire.[114]

"The demos exists as striving," Wolin writes, "but that drive may be directed not at assuring duration to its existence but at *challenging its own finitude.*" In a striking parallel to the metaphor used to characterize Superpower, Wolin describes the demotic return of the repressed at its most basic level as "a barely civilized, almost raw force—the demos as Id and crude Superego."[115] Where archaism was a means of escape, the demos of fugitive democracy seeks mastery. Where archaic democracy was cast in the language of loss, fugitive democracy is a matter of sublime struggle and suffering. Where archaism was in part a way of conceptualizing a type of civic education that was based in culture and history rather than in elite intervention (as in Jefferson's ward system), fugitive democracy does away with the educative entirely, relying instead purely on unreformed instinct. Where archaism cultivated and tended to domestic memory and place, fugitive democracy is undomesticated savagery. The fugitive demos is in accord with Superpower in seeing the world in the terms, if not the extremes, of Hobbes's state of nature. When peace is impossible, power becomes the only currency.

Wolin adopts a term from Spinoza—*conatus*—to theorize this overreaching, overflowing demos. The formula, Wolin writes, "of actor-action, with its clear-cut notion of agency, excludes the demos, always a somewhat shadowy, inchoate identity, always in need of the crystalliz-ing energy of a 'leader.' " Spinoza's notion of *conatus*—the striving inher-ent in any living thing for the power " 'to persist in its own being (and oppose anything) that would take away its existence' "—enables Wolin to envision a purely natural and democratic source of democratic action. The "continuing self-fashioning of the demos" is driven exclusively by its own *conatus*. The idea here is that the demos becomes self-aware and gains a distinctive sense of identity, not by means of leadership, but through the crystallizing effect of external events. More specifically, op-position to the event of its own negation imbues the demos with self-awareness. Democratic organization is spontaneous in that it is caused only by the impulse of collective self-preservation. Democratic action becomes instinctive. And this instinct becomes the great equalizer, pro-viding for the many what "wealth, status, education, and tradition" pro-vide for the few. The primal power of a demos is a consequence of its primal fear: backed into a corner, the people "threaten because their ex-istence is continuously threatened."[116]

Wolin explicitly sets out here to embrace a longstanding tendency to resort to "physical or animalistic imagery to describe the multitude"—the tendency to associate the demos with the passions and " 'things of the body' " and to identify "the Many with a natural power," a "raw power," and an "elemental force."[117] For Wolin, "the demos represents the existence and vitality of a natural entity."[118] We should "reconceive democracy as an elemental politics about the needs and the aspirations of the Many."[119] And we should think of the demos as "agonistic," "driven by the needs of its nature to strain at constitutional restraints."[120] Thus the "possibility of a popular sovereignty as a will to power on the part of an actor struggling to be both collective and autonomous" resides pre-cisely with the demos' savage nature.[121] The is the undomesticated poli-tics par excellence.

Not only is the demos driven by its instinctive nature, but its revolu-tionary actions deliver the many from the constraints of conventional forms back to the Lockean state of nature. In Locke's formulation, Wolin writes, nature "is a condition of commonality and 'equality . . . without Subordination or Subjection' ": "We might call Locke's construct a de-mocracy without form."[122] In its "suspension of heterogeneity," it is "a

metaphor of lost commonality, an exceptional moment that keeps returning in times of revolutionary crisis when power returns to 'the
Community and agency to 'the People.' "[123] This return to nature is "the
truly democratic moment."[124]

Detaching this conception of agonistic democracy from democracy's
contemporary confrontation with postmodern power, Wolin writes that
ancient Athenian democracy above all exemplified the *conatus*-driven
character of the demos: "Before its fourth-century institutionalization,
Athenian democracy was less a constitution in the Aristotelian sense of
a fixed form than a dynamic and developing political culture, a culture
not only of participation but of frequent rebellions."[125] This culture of rebellion took institutional form as rotation in office and selection by lot,
the function of which was to "limit the effects of institutionalization."
Such forms are, Wolin writes, "paradoxically institutions that subvert
institutionalization"—they are the institutionalization of rational disorganization. They ensured the continuous "disruption in continuity."[126]
Even as the "elemental, physical quality of democratic power" was "condensed and institutionalized," then, Athenian democracy did not lose its
transgressive character.[127] The beast, as Wolin puts it, was institutionalized without being domesticated: "The beast has become the citizen without losing its vitality, truly a *politikon zoion*."[128]

Theorizing democratic action and association in terms of "vitality"—
rooted in passion and instinct—thus leads Wolin away from the archaic
and toward a notion of democracy that actually mirrors many of the characteristics of the economy of power. Democracy comes to seem both natural and (at least in aspiration) limitless. Describing democratic action as
an instinct makes it seem given and spontaneous, not unlike capitalism
and liberalism in that it takes shape without need of any process of regimentation, socialization, or education. Capitalism is based on the assumption of the competitive and acquisitive individual, and liberalism on the
private and self-interested individual. Both are premised upon our supposedly native characteristics. We do not need to learn to be acquisitive or
self-interested but are assumed to be so. For Wolin, democracy is similarly
premised upon our native—one might say primitive—characteristics and
the assumption of the essentially power-asserting self. We arrive at the
democratic moment as already democratic, just as we arrive at the market

as acquisitive and at the voting booth as self-interested. Put differently, as a matter of unleashing our animal instincts in the face of fear and desperation, democratic action is as natural as fear and misery and suffering. And as long as a democracy rests solely on sentiments that console man in his misery, democracy is fundamentally inclusive—it can win the affection of the human race.

Further, Wolin readily acknowledges that the outcome of institutionalizing a power that by nature strives to challenge its own finitude is empire. Materially empowered, the barely civilized democratic Id turns from self-preservation to self-expansion. A "testimony to both the transgressive and aggressive impulses of the Many," empire is at once the negation of democracy as well as a manifestation of its original nature.[129] The only limits authentic democracy knows are those imposed upon it. At the same time, he attempts to distance this overflowing of all conventional forms and territorial boundaries from its potential for violence. The emphasis shifts from destruction to creation. "Democracy is a rebellious moment that may assume revolutionary, destructive proportions," yet the "fugitive character of democracy [does not] stand for a pent-up revolutionary fervor waiting for an opportunity to wreak havoc."[130] It is true that nothing "short of a long revolution . . . makes much sense today," but "a campaign of violent insurrection," while "politically and morally justified by democratic standards of legitimate authority, is neither possible nor prudent": "Revolutions of that nature are plainly pathological under contemporary conditions of interdependency."[131] While warranted in principle, violent revolution is simply not practical. "Democrats," in turn, "need a new conception of revolution"—one conceived in terms of "creativity rather than violence." The right to revolution is not "solely a right to overturn and destroy institutions but to fashion new ones"; it is a "right to create new forms."[132]

Of course, capitalism too is as creative as it is destructive. Given their shared challenge to finitude and lawfulness, one wonders whether the forms democracy and economy create (only to eventually destroy) will be very different. Superpower strives for the formless forms conducive to global monopoly; fugitive democracy strives for the formless forms conducive to empire. Both employ the rhetoric of oneness, which Wolin characterizes as the rhetoric of limitlessness—whether phrased in terms of economic "power" or democratic "energy." The rational systematization of economy is efficient, while the wild passion of democracy burns itself out and suffers set-backs, but the spirit seems the same. One wonders whether there is not a more human mode of politics and society in between the systems and mechanisms of economy and the animalistic nature of fugitive democracy. One wonders whether there is not a language of human association in between those of abstraction and authenticity.

## Conclusion: Heroism and Cynicism

"Although the desire to acquire the goods of this world is the dominant passion of Americans," Tocqueville writes, "there are brief intervals when their souls seem suddenly to cast off all material bonds and fly impetuously toward heaven."[133] This description of American's "impassioned, almost wild spiritualism" is perfectly analogous to Wolin's formulation of the fugitive democratic moment of revolution. The dynamic is one wherein ordinary material existence is punctuated by extraordinary events of transcendence. For Wolin, transgression is the mode of transcendence, revolution is the revelation—elevation as breaking out of domesticating conventional norms and forms. Ordinarily we are totally unfree, but we are able to transmute oppression and necessity into brief intervals of total freedom. Here again we see the dualism of idealization and devaluation characteristic of our democratic way of life.

Wolin's theory of democracy helps us identify the consequence of the radical critique of existing politics so prevalent in his work—and in American society. Extreme heroism—one might say superheroism—becomes the only possible solution to the conditions that have brought about extreme cynicism. Wolin equates the fugitive demos with the Nietzschean aristocrat. This demos is the collective version of the "vigorous warrior-type, a man who takes risks, provokes strife, overflows with vitality, in short, a natural transgressor of conventions." This "figure of primal energy and demonic will," according to Wolin, "delights in the images of 'smashing' restraints." And "spectacular types of action" are the product of the "agonistic impulse of heroic actors."[134] Given the extraordinary degradation of our economized material existence, this appeal to extraordinary action-movie heroism seems the only thing that makes sense. In a world mired in systematic dehumanization, the appeal of an agonistic demos is rendered more fully intelligible in terms of "vigilante democracy" rather than fugitive democracy—we need to step outside the systems of the world in order to set things right.

Wolin adapts the notion of aristocratic actor to democracy not only by rendering this idea collective but also by depicting aristocratic action as a function of victimization. Central to Wolin's theory of fugitive democracy, and it seems to American thought in general, is the idea of ordinary people forced to rise to the occasion. In the face of crisis or oppression, the victim/hero is called to service out of everyday, private life. Elevated less by his or her own virtues than by events, the ordinary person proves capable of extraordinary deeds. Coming from and returning to equality, the common man of democracy momentarily becomes an aristocratic actor. As the momentary response to events beyond our control, rather than as a product of superior character or virtue, aristocratic action is made safe for democracy. The hero did what any of us would have done under similar circumstances.

The consequences for the practice of democratic politics are two. First, the dialectic of ordinary/extraordinary leads to what we might call a two-tiered notion of citizenship. While the people retain the *authority* to rule at all times, only occasionally do they attain the *capacity* to rule. In liberal democratic theory, the occasion is routinized as periodic elections. Increasingly, though, the view is that ordinary elections do not sufficiently induce the elevation of the people, who just vote their wallets (if they vote at all). There are, however, certain extraordinary, epic elections wherein people come together as a demos in revolutionary action. Along these lines we might say that Bruce Ackerman, for instance, offers the liberal version of Wolin's fugitive democracy—the electoral moment radicalized. The key to both theories is that crisis and necessity do not reduce people to their base and conflictual natures but rather induce the overcoming of mundane limitations and self-interested preoccupations. But is the political practice of democracy the likely response to necessity and crisis? Or is democracy more likely to be sacrificed in times of trouble, in the quest for more efficient modes of power?

This two-tiered notion of democracy and citizenship is so appealing, I suggest, because it allows us to combine into one coherent picture both sides of democracy's dualism. Ordinary pettiness and degradation, individualism and materialism are punctuated by intervals of extraordinary elevation and freedom. For long stretches democratic society is characterized by banal neediness and bourgeois mediocrity, but it is never without indefinite revolutionary possibilities. Epic literary events burst forth from commercial society, and under the right circumstances the small man of business might become the artist—a fugitive creator. If only for a moment, the prosaic economy of existence gives way to the poetry of democracy.

Second, democratic association and action come to be represented as unity and energy in response to crisis, which is to say, in executive rather than legislative or judicial terms. Deliberation and judgment fall by the wayside as political agency is reduced to a Lockean sense of prerogative—democratic "vitality" as emergency power, whether of the elected leader or the demos itself. Indeed, in relation to heroic executive action, deliberation and the freedom to be found in endless meetings might well seem absurd and obstructive (or impossible, given fundamental difference—or dangerous, given our power-driven world). In any case, argument stands apart from or in opposition to decision and action. This is a democracy that has no need of mediating words.[135]

Wolin writes that despite the almost complete "evisceration of democracy" today, there "appears to be no widespread public recognition of crisis."[136] All of the "elements for radical protest appear to be present," and yet "there has been no general mobilization of outrage . . . [only an] astonishing passivity."[137] I suggest that thinking of the political along the lines Wolin lays out in his theory of fugitive democracy actually contributes to this astonishing passivity. Associating vital democracy with the phenomenon of revolution is itself a cause of the devitalization of the political practice of democracy today. The idealization of the revolutionary moment goes hand in hand with the devaluation of the everyday practice of democracy. The latter, whether archaic or liberal, cannot but seem absurd relative to the audacious politics of the impossible of the former. With the televised images of every recent popular uprising, from Eastern Europe to Egypt, we hear declared, "This is what democracy looks like!" One imagines that Wolin would agree. One also wonders what democracy looks like in more mundane, less romantic circumstances. Further, Wolin celebrates the radical democratic potential for disorganizing the liberal democratic constitution of government. But as we have seen, this spirit of disorganization would equally seem to subvert the culture of grassroots organization. Both in principle and in practice, the fugitive democratic moment of revolutionary opening cannot be institutionalized at the level of ordinary politics, whether cultural or constitutional, local or national.[138] Fugitive democracy, precisely in its idealized rhetoric of the extraordinary, undermines the ordinary practice of democracy—arguing and acting in association with equal others, within institutions and in the streets. Democratic politics becomes something that erupts, a phenomenon rather than a practice, a matter of natural instinct rather than civic education. As such, it seems less something we undertake, much less a way of life, than something we wait for. We await the hero, collective or otherwise, of the revolutionary moment. The world in which we live cannot be reformed from within; rupture and transcendence is the only possible way out. And so we bide our time until the next catastrophic, catalytic event occurs—until the spirit moves us.

# Conclusion

## *Despotism and Democratic Silence*

---

It is the political man that we must develop in ourselves.

—Tocqueville, Letter to Beaumont, October 25, 1829

### *To Love Our Oppression*

In his classic work of social commentary, *Amusing Ourselves to Death*, Neil Postman argues that we are living in—or fast approaching—something like Aldous Huxley's *Brave New World*. Postman famously juxtaposes the mode of domination characteristic of this dystopia to that of Orwell's *1984*: "Orwell warns that we will be overcome by an externally imposed oppression. But in Huxley's vision, no Big Brother is required to deprive people of their autonomy, maturity, and history. As [Huxley] saw it, people will come to love their oppression, to adore the technologies that undo their capacities to think." Such oppression is less overwhelming than undermining, operating through degradation rather than deprivation, aiming not to defeat people's strengths but to prey upon their weaknesses. It is based not primarily in prohibition but in permission; far from being constrained, the oppressed are immediately granted their every felt desire: "In *1984* . . . people are controlled by inflicting pain. In *Brave New World*, they are controlled by inflicting pleasure. In short, Orwell feared that what we hate will ruin us. Huxley feared that what we love will ruin us."[1]

So what do we love ruinously today? What do we adore without thinking and against our capacity for thought? In Postman's account, what we love above all and perhaps exclusively is the narcissistic, visceral pleasure derived from a certain form of entertainment most closely associated with music and images orchestrated in an immediately accessible, intellectually predigested, ego-massaging, emotion-stirring narrative.

We love television, in other words, along with any other screen-image, response-stimuli device. Television is our soul mate, perfectly and exclusively suited in its technological capabilities to present that which we at bottom most want, without compromise. We are oppressed, in turn, as were Pavlov's dogs by the dinner bell. Conditioning and control come to seem like freedom when freedom seems like desire fulfillment. The scale model of domination here is not the gray, walled-up city of Soviet-occupied East Germany but rather the excessively permissive, blindingly colorful dream cities out west: Las Vegas and Hollywood. "Today," Postman writes, "we must look to the city of Las Vegas, Nevada, as a metaphor of our national character and aspiration . . . [to live] entirely devoted to the idea of entertainment."[2] When Las Vegas becomes our defining aspiration, when we are devoted to the orthodoxy and orthopraxy of entertainment "in a society that worships TV," when our existence is so flattened and we have so sunk below the level of humanity, the circle is closed and our oppression becomes self-sufficient and self-perpetuating.[3] Beyond futile, resistance becomes incomprehensible. That which should be highest—our sources of devotion and worship—has been consumed by that which is lowest. Modernity's democratic promise of popular self-government has given way to modernity's democratic promise of popular self-gratification.

It is, of course, difficult to gauge our complicity in this process of salivating domestication. In one sense, unwilling to perform the hard work of leaving home, of laboring to produce autonomy out of paternalism, we seem in our dumb and soft hedonism the agents of our own domination, taking the road far more traveled by, from one sort of dependence to another. In another sense, such oppression involves a sort of conspiracy against us so insidious and creeping, so vast and abstract, so impersonal and in a sense accidental, that we are not even aware of our domination, much less responsible for it. Where in the first formulation we have given in to our lower nature, in the second we are lost in a second nature. Whatever the source of our addictive indulgence, though, the outcome is the same: oppression operates unseen, through seduction rather than repression—indeed, in part through the taboo against repression and inhibition. Censorship is unnecessary, as no one pays attention to or says anything worth being censored—indeed, the prohibition of censorship fits well with the Las Vegas brand of oppression. Books need not be burned, as no one cares to read—especially those books that would be unsettling enough to require burning. This notion of oppression through distraction, amusement, and trivialization is so pernicious because it proceeds without question, protest, or even much notice. It catches us sleeping, or celebrating: "America's consuming love-affair with television . . . appears benign, when it is not invisible altogether. . . . But it is an ideology nonetheless, for it imposes a way of life, a set of relations among people and ideas, about which there has been no consensus, no discussion, and no opposition. Only compliance."[4] The more television indoctrinates us to the ideology of the image, the less are we aware of its influence over us. So vast is its power that its power goes undetected. Our situation becomes quite apparently like Plato's cave, whose inhabitants grow so habituated to their shadowy and constrained condition that they affirm it as true and good; they literally cannot conceive of any other way of life, and so they embrace their oppression even once it is exposed.[5] No first-time reader of Plato's *Republic* fails to notice the similarity between the architecture of the cave and that of our living rooms.

Postman's powerful critique of television culture continues to resonate broadly and deeply today, if anything even more so with the technological revolutions that have, it seems, cast all in television's image. Cogent social commentary now sounds like chilling prophesy as the amusing image has gone viral, insinuating its way into our every waking hour—all the world's a screen, and all the men and women merely viewers. What better reflects the regrettable course of our culture back to us than the familiar images of the iPod zombie, the Internet junkie, the video game besotted, the creature with the body of a man and the head of a cell phone? Who hasn't heard parodied those monuments to narcissism that are YouTube and Facebook? We turn our private lives into advertisements for ourselves, to accumulate "friends" with whom we never converse but who will be informed as our audience of the news of ourselves. Human relations are reduced to social networking, lived literally on-screen, with communication performed via computer image, all in the society of privatism, passivity, and egoism par excellence. What in popular imagination has come to demonstrate our age of show business and its "descent into a vast triviality" better than (sur)reality TV—from Las Vegas to the Jersey Shore?[6] And if not in the sophisticated terms of Postman's analysis, who isn't amused by the gallows humor of the age of typography ending in Twitter—in with the Bible, out with a 140-character tweet?

When we criticize our culture, it is perhaps most often by reference to these screen idols. To point out their pervasive and stultifying influence is by now less an insight than a cliché. Reflexively scorning and ridiculing the mainstream of our multimedia habitat has itself become mainstream. Our public discourse—accessed almost exclusively through a screen, of course—constantly decries the cocoon of amusing distractions that for instance cut children off from meaningful relationships in the family and the community and from meaningful experiences in the classroom and the world. What could be more familiar than the satire of kids traveling on family vacation to some foreign land but never looking up from their armory of personal electronics? Americans more generally are accused of being reduced to softness by the endless stream of junk we consume—whether the junk food that softens our waistlines or the junk-food entertainment that softens our minds and wills. While Postman, as we shall see, is primarily concerned with the intellectually debilitating consequences of a culture that turns public discourse from argument centered to amusement centered, the primary concern today seems to be this culture's strength- and drive-sapping consequences. In either case, the difficult things of life—those things that require discipline, concentration, and fortitude—are abandoned for the entertaining things of life. We have become a "nation of wusses" and a "nation of whiners," so addicted to our pleasures and comforts, so dependent upon our luxuries, that we are unable to compete in the global market (the concern here focuses not on our declining capacity to argue together, as Postman writes, but rather on our declining math and science skills).[7] We have become a nation spellbound by the silliness, superficiality, and downright unreality of "celebrity culture" and its manifestations in such enormously popular TV shows as *American Idol* (the concern here is not that we are unwilling to do the hard work of exposition but that we are unwilling simply to work hard, struggle, and sacrifice—we wish to move from rags to riches through not daily labor but rather overnight fame, by simply having the camera turned upon us).[8] Even our most serious public business is represented as a game and performed as a public relations advertising campaign. Our experience of politics is as a game-show business, televised to audiences as ratings-driven "infotainment." In Postman's terms, we hear that the American Dream has departed Boston, New York, and Chicago, leaving behind all that those cities might have once stood for, to be buried somewhere in the desert outside Las Vegas and replaced by the American Fantasy.[9]

In all of these familiar elements of our contemporary cultural self-critique (and in many, many others), Postman's analysis resonates, leaving us to wonder whether Huxley didn't go far enough. A popular recent representation of our fears in this regard comes from the 2008 movie *Wall-E*. Here, the human being has been fully domesticated: being too overweight to move, lounging in a luxury-bed hovercraft at a pool under a fake sun, indulging every desire for food and drink, being catered to by robots that seem like servants but are actually masters, staring vacantly at huge television screens. But does the very fact that Postman's critique is so widely recognized today—to the point of being the moral of a children's movie—undermine its validity? Far from making it a best seller, translated into multiple languages and released in numerous printings, the inhabitants of the brave new world would not have been interested in or able to comprehend *Amusing Ourselves to Death*, or even *Wall-E*—barring John the Savage, of course. Postman's argument would not have resonated in the London of 632 A.F. As we have just seen, this is not to say that Postman's analysis doesn't cover a great deal of the terrain of our contemporary culture. But it does suggest that "America's consuming love-affair with television" is only part of the picture, that we need to detach his insights from the notion that our media environment functions as a sort of Platonic cave, and that we need to account for the perspective from which we join Postman in condemning our age of show business.[10] Only then would we arrive at an interpretation of the full spectrum of America's love-hate relationship with television and its progeny.

*Argument as Entertainment*

Postman actually pardons the junk-food programming one finds atop the ratings on television. The existence of trivial and distracting amusements isn't significant. The existence of nothing but trivial and distracting amusements, conversely, indicates "spiritual devastation."[11] When politics, journalism, religion, and education are all put through the television rendering plant, processed into the stuff of campaign commercials, infotainment, televangelism, and *Sesame Street*, "the machinery of thought-control" is operating at full capacity—prison culture by means of not censorship or surveillance but totalizing "burlesque."[12] When television has achieved "sovereignty over all of [society's] institutions" in such a manner, entertainment value becomes the sole standard of judgment, which is really no standard at all.[13]

Like the escape from nutrition in a fast-food culture, a certain "escape from meaning" that was exceedingly difficult to achieve in a word culture becomes possible in an image culture.[14] The "language-centered discourse" that was dominant prior to the advent of television was perfectly suited to conduct "content-laden and serious" arguments, as was the printed page, upon which such a discourse was modeled. Thinking in and communicating through the printed word potentially cultivates certain habits of mind—the "typographic mind"—that involve patient reasoning, analytic thought, sustained critical reflection upon claims to rationality and validity, the capacity to logically order assertions and comprehend lengthy and complex sentences, and so forth. Thinking in and communicating through the televised image lacks this potential. Put simply, the printed word primarily involves one's intellect; the televised image, one's emotions. Television might contain propositional content but presents it in such a way as to take effect as a feast for the senses—rapid-fire images, saturated in swirling colors, dynamic and strikingly beautiful, set to music. The image, in turn, less persuades than pleases—or stupefies. It performs an argument, in a sense, but without reference to previous knowledge, context, or continuity, without perplexity, and without exposition, evidence, discussion, and refutations. Persuasion, such as it is, occurs by reflex rather than reflection, by the giving off of appearances rather than the giving of reasons. The image manipulates rather than convinces.[15]

One need only view the presidential debates that are allowed by the medium of television to see Postman's point. Argument is made to take the form of advertisement, and so we judge the candidates by the standards of how they emote and what "impressions" they leave.[16] The spoken word is ancillary to the image, and intellectual weightiness is performed to the extent necessary to appear presidential. These show-business debates are to actual argument what the dinner bell was to actual meat, exciting but without substance and effortless to digest, leaving us with a politics of psychic secretions. On television, Postman concludes, "propositions are as scarce as unattractive people," and for much the same reason.[17]

Perhaps above all, then, what the television social state—the society not of equality or uncertainty or economy but of the image—eliminates from the human world is the possibility of arguing together. All that argument represents, all the capacities and dispositions that the practice of argument fosters in and requires of people, is undermined when the screen becomes our gateway to encountering each other and the world. As beautiful as it is simplistic, the screen image seduces and stultifies; as ugly as it is complicated, argument either submits to the power of the image and abides by the standard of entertainment, or it is expelled as indigestible from the body politic. Argument, like all else in television society, becomes intelligible exclusively as a sort of game—at best a vigorous contest to score points, at worst juvenile name calling. Politics, the venue of argument and practical judgment in their most serious forms, becomes something to be played—at best a sport, at worst a petty and silly children's game. Culture's descent into meaninglessness is the end point of this degradation of the social conversation: "When a population becomes distracted by trivia, when a cultural life is redefined as a perpetual round of entertainments, when serious public conversation becomes a form of baby-talk, when, in short, a people becomes an audience and their public business a vaudeville act, then a nation finds itself at risk; culture-death is a clear possibility."[18] The dissolution of the place of the word in society signifies that society's collapse into absurdity.

## Image and Openness: The Dimensionality of Democratic Society

In a number of ways, then, Postman and I arrive at similar interpretations of modern American society. There seems no place for the politics of arguing together in the prevailing culture and consciousness. But we identify very different pathologies. In Postman's account, we no longer take arguments seriously because we no longer take much of anything seriously. As in *Brave New World,* there is a sort of bottomless absurdity to the society that takes shape around television technology. This is not a condition that is critiqued as absurd, mind you, but an absurd condition that eliminates the possibility of its critique. The cultural crisis that follows is all the more tragic for its not being recognized as such; the real crisis is that there is no crisis. I have raised the prospect—both more and less troubling—that our condition is based not in meaninglessness but rather in that which we find meaningful. Postman writes of our consuming love affair with television, suggesting that the life of the image reduces love to desire and then flattens desire to pleasure. We end up in the terrible state of loving our meaninglessness. We are devoted to and worship our amusements in a truly one-dimensional way of life, a flat-screen society. My analysis is less troubling in maintaining that a society of such totalizing absurdity—wherein its inhabitants do not suffer a sense of meaning's loss but instead enjoy an unsensed meaninglessness, unaware of anything having been lost—is most likely impossible and, in any case, very far from our current predicament. My analysis is perhaps more troubling, though, in diagnosing the emaciation of our politics and of the practice of argument more generally, as a symptom of precisely that which we affirm as deeply meaningful—that which we love not as entertaining but as authoritative.

I have argued that the democratic principle of authority is itself the source of our political discontent. This is the principle of equality, born of the revolutionary destruction of the counterprinciple of hierarchy. Not the advent of a technology or a mode of power or even a form of communication, but the principle of proper and conceivable relations between people gives shape to a society. The political, as Tocqueville and Lefort argue, is primary. We thus more fully make sense of our time as the age of democracy rather than as the age of show business—as taking shape in the wake of the democratic revolution more so than in the wake of television, the photograph, the printing press, or the industrial revolution. Postman recalls the cultural changes that the automobile brought, changes that would "tell us" how we were to "conduct our social and sexual lives" and that created "new ways of expressing our personal identity and social standing."[19] I suggest that we reverse the causal arrow between culture and technology and consider the social-symbolic milieu in which social standing persists only feebly and narcissistically as the product of work and wealth (car ownership), a milieu in which personal identity becomes both paramount and open to question and so in *need* of expression, one in which back-seat sex-objectification becomes interesting, and above all one in which mobility comes to equal freedom. Only then can we make sense of the automobile as a significant social artifact, one which seemingly can tell us how to live. The automobile is of interest as more than a mere instrument—like a coffee table or indoor plumbing—primarily because it can be interpreted as an agent of a democratic freedom, equality, and ontology (of auto-mobility) and as a threat to democratic community.

Building primarily upon Tocqueville, I have attempted to trace the multifaceted logical consequences of equality's rise and hierarchy's fall in our norms of *freedom* (mastery and escape against domestication, totalizing independence and totalizing liberation against totalizing paternalism); in our norms of *association* (informality against etiquette, both in the intimacy of communal resemblance, from the familial to the human, and in the competition of the market); in our norms of *elevation and degradation* (limitless possibility and indefinite perfectibility toward imminent transcendence, and against the collapse of the human into stultifying mediocrity and meaningless materialism); in our conception of *the human being* (a rights-declaring animal, who interprets himself as primarily self-interested and self-expressive); and in our understanding and embrace of revolution as that which situates us in *time and space* (a compulsive restlessness born of living within indeterminate and eventful history after the dissolution of settled absolutes, always leaving home on pilgrimage into the wilds of New World primitivism and future opportunity, a state of nature always before or beyond the conventionalized present). I summed up these sometimes contradictory, sometimes reinforcing elements of democratic society as its characteristic openness— the open society, the regime of revolution, the social state of nature.[20]

In my analysis, the perceived absurdity of the politics of persuasion is relative, not absolute. For Postman, meaning deeper than amusement cannot find purchase in the image society. I argue that, in the open society, the experience of significance is not trivialized but rather in a sense radicalized. With democracy's revolutionary abstraction—what

Lefort terms the dissolution of the markers of certainty—the authority of democratic openness coincides with that which never falls to the level of mere material power or partisan particularity, that which cannot be enclosed in representative or embodying form, that which rises above or drops below the shallow surface of the conventional world. A schism between principle and practice takes shape not contingently but essentially at the center of democratic society, across the spheres of politics, religion, economics, and so forth. Democracy is a society of separations between its sources of authority and its repositories of power—whether between church and state or economics and state, whether between faith and organized religion or democracy and organized politics.[21] In the open society, the only permissible walls are those that ensure these separations. Authority, the precondition of any experience of meaningfulness, is thus not desiccated into amusement but expanded into openness; it is not lost, but it is absent—located not yet in this world or, eventually, in the next. And relative to this standard of judgment, the politics of arguing together, the politics of partisanship and small measures, the political art of the possible, cannot but seem petty and absurd. Democratic politics goes the way of aristocratic dueling, and for much the same reason. Like the practice of dueling outside the context of aristocratic codes of honor and etiquette, the politics of arguing together ceases to signify.[22] Democracy, ultimately, lies not in the argument but in the dreaming—in faith and imagination. In this sense, not the shallowness but the capaciousness of the democratic way of life dissolves the political element of human association. The consequence is not the boundless stupidity of the age of show business but the conjoined, irreducible and irreconcilable, cynicism and idealism of the age of democracy.

One benefit of this interpretation is that it enables us to account for the phenomena Postman identifies, as well as the equally prevalent critique of those phenomena. A full three-dimensional mapping of a social state, free of generalization and speculation, is of course impossible. But initiating an analysis from the presumption that a society of whatever form—even a formless form—takes shape around certain principles of human relations provides at least a two-dimensional theorization wherein the norms invoked to critique society can be understood as internal to that society. One can critique aspects of society while still speaking as part of that society (rather than necessarily taking up the position of the Platonic guide out of the cave), and one can offer a critique that does not inevitably tend—impelled as if of its own accord—toward grossly reductive exaggeration (that we are, for instance, approaching a brave new world, or any other version of consumer society). One can account for one's own interpretation and one's audience, offering a critique that might plausibly begin with "we." Focusing on the openness of democratic society allows us to make sense of the experiences, both elevating and degrading, of equality, uncertainty, economy, consumerism, the television image, and so forth. We can account for the standard of judgment by which we come to both love and hate television—TV as a pleasure, but a guilty one. Indeed, we can explain why the loss of meaning described by Postman, along with couch-potato docility, boob-tube infantilism, and seduction by advertisers into wanton materialism and neediness are some of the constitutive insecurities of democratic society.[23] The dissolution of settled absolutes and the absence of the father figure imbues the open society with the sense that something eventful is always just about to happen, and the collapse of hierarchy makes it seem as if that something will be the swallowing up of head and heart by gut and groin—consumer society. Revolutionary liberation means that autonomy has become possible but also that we might henceforth be enslaved by way of our needs and desires—from paternalism to maturity or to permissiveness. The inhabitants of democracy experience it as a society always on the verge, whether of transcendence or trivialization.

### Democratic Despotism? The Politics of Personality and the Impersonal

At the outset of *Democracy in America*, Tocqueville writes that he looked to America to see "democracy itself," in its natural state, so that he might "find out what we had to hope from it, or to fear."[24] Regarding the latter, Tocqueville concludes his considerations by formulating what he calls tutelary power. This is the power that domesticates. It looms in the sense of extreme degradation inherent in democratic equality. It is a perversion of "paternal authority" in that it seeks not to "prepare men for manhood" but rather to "keep them in childhood irrevocably": "It likes citizens to rejoice, provided they think only of rejoicing. It works willingly for their happiness but wants to be the sole agent and only arbiter of that happiness. It provides for their security, foresees and takes care of their needs, facilitates their pleasures, manages their most important affairs, directs their industry. . . . Why not relieve them entirely of the trouble of thinking and the difficulty of living?"[25] Whatever its medium—the state, the market, television culture—tutelary power offers the oppression that we love. As such, it becomes our most pernicious fear—the fear that we will betray ourselves and lose ourselves. We invoke *1984* when we want to congratulate ourselves for our strength, and *Brave New World* when we want to expose ourselves in our weakness.

I have argued that if something approximating democratic despotism is possible today, it is by way of the depth rather than the shallowness of democratic society. Our situation is not one wherein society-wide meaninglessness, decadence, laziness, cowardice, shallowness, or stupidity is leading toward a modern form of paternalism—or maternalism. Rather, the door is opened to despotic power with the migration of meaning from public to private life, and the consequent colonization of the public by the private. It advances, in other words, with what Richard Sennett cast as the "fall of public man." In his 1974 work of that name—perhaps the finest of works in the Tocquevillian tradition—Sennett analyzes the "tyrannies of intimacy" over contemporary public life. "Intimacy," Sennett writes, "is a field of vision and an expectation of human relations. It is the localizing of human experience, so that what is close to the immediate circumstances of life is paramount. The more this localizing rules, the more people seek out or put pressure on each other to strip away the barriers of custom, manners, and gesture which stand in the way of frankness and mutual openness." Intimacy turns despotic when it is embraced as the sole principle of human association. And it is oppressive in that, in its very depth, it flattens other possible experiences of significance. Communication, for instance, is reduced to self-expression, the self to be expressed is reduced to a personality, and the standard of judgment in the act of mutual personality expression is reduced to authenticity: all the world's a confessional, and all the men and women merely voyeurs. It is forgotten, for instance, that displaying manners in accordance with a formal code of etiquette—that "disguise and self-repression"—may be "morally expressive." Instead, "self-disclosure becomes a universal measure of believability and truth," and "intimate feeling" becomes "an all-purpose standard of reality."[26] Self-expression and intimate feeling become to the social state of nature what self-preservation and rational interest were to the state of nature; recognition becomes to intimate society what honor was to aristocratic society.

"Intimacy," Sennett writes, "is an attempt to solve the public problem by denying that the public exists."[27] Largely over the course of the nineteenth century, Sennett explains in a nuanced and wide-ranging historical and sociological account, public life came to be understood as morally deficient, meaningless, and threatening; every stranger came to represent compromise, confusion, and potential narcissistic injury. The solution to the trauma of leaving home was to reimagine public space as an extension of private life. The emotional immediacy and intimate unions once thought possible only in the small republic of family life were to be superimposed onto the "dead public space" of repressive formalities, cold competition, and the mystifying operations of the mass and the industrial machine.[28] Where private life had once been deemed an alternative to and shield from public life, it had now become the model for public life. As a way of being together in public, familiarity was to replace formality, nature's informality was to replace the realm of conventional settlements, authenticity was to replace civility, and the embrace was to replace the argument. The modern community—the unmediated association with those like oneself that Tocqueville described as collective individualism—becomes the building block of public life.[29] Beyond one's communities, public space is passed through in the role of the tourist, as a fleeting encounter with strangeness, an encounter intended as an adjunct of self-development.

Sennett's intimacy is thus no less destructive of public life—particularly *political* public life—than Postman's image. Like the image, intimacy can do without mediating words.[30] Both thereby discredit what today can only seem a matter of "public relations" or "mere rhetoric." But where Postman's analysis depicts us as too shallow to argue together, Sennett interprets us as believing we are too deep for argument. The display of personality is central for both, but for Sennett it's in terms of an expansive passion for intimacy rather than as just a source of amusement, which affords Sennett's subjects a range of emotions and feelings beyond the simple desire for pleasure. In turn, the fall of public man, as opposed to the rise of show business, helps us understand the *felt* absurdity, and so the reflexive cynicism, so characteristic of our political public sphere. Sennett suggests that " 'Intimacy' connotes warmth, trust, and open expression of feeling. But precisely because we have come to expect these psychological benefits through the range of our experiences, and precisely because so much social life which does have a meaning cannot yield these psychological rewards, the world outside, the impersonal world, seems to fail us, seems to be stale and empty."[31] Insofar as public life conveys this sense of intimacy—insofar as the public abides by the norms of the private—it will be experienced as deeply meaningful. As Sennett puts it, we "care about institutions and events" when we can "discern personalities at work in them."[32] Insofar as public life falls short of warmth, trust, and the open expression of feeling— insofar as it is formal, power laden, contentious, scripted, and unfeeling— it will be experienced as contemptible and absurd, and we will either cease to care or engage to reform it, that is, to make it more intimate and personable.

Much is made today of the devaluation of privacy in our Internet age, when it seems every detail of one's personal life is publicly revealed or displayed. But what could better demonstrate the demise of the public as a distinct sphere of thought and action than its colonization by such exhibitions of confessional intimacy? And much is made of the incessantly shrill and bitter arguments that wrack our political life. But what else beside the incivility of clashing authenticities would one expect when communities (or cultures) come into intimate contact in the absence of political mediation? This is exactly the sort of exchange conducted by private individuals in public space when partisanship and persuasion are no longer taken seriously, when communication cannot be both open and ongoing, when natural sympathy is not supplemented by an artificial politeness, when self-interested and self-expressive individuals are not spontaneously mediated by, as Pierre Manent puts it, the "immediate presence of humanity beyond all forms."[33] This is the postpolitics of collective individualism.

It is by a paradoxical consequence of this tyranny of the personal over the political that something like a tutelary power might arise in democratic society. Sennett extensively chronicles the ways in which "intimate vision" involves people in the active participation in their own degradation, and the damage this causes to their public *and* private lives, leaving postpolitical man self-centered but lacking sufficient resources to generate self-respect. As in Tocqueville's account, nothing less than human dignity is threatened by the collapse of political public life.[34] Even as the intimate society may well prove to be a hospitable environment for tutelary power, though, we should recognize that such a society cannot deliver its inhabitants over to a material manifestation of that power, lest the intimate society contradict its own principle. We grasp the full appeal of intimacy in democratic times when we see it as a strategy for coping with power: the soul-mate union enables democratic people to come together without compromising their ideas of equality and freedom by rendering power *unconditional* and therefore *immaterial*—a general will.[35] The moment this power is embodied and operationalized in material form, it abdicates its sovereignty. Precisely by so debasing the power of the word, intimacy breaks up the moment it is spoken. We cease to love our oppression the moment we see or hear our oppressor, whether coercive or seductive, represented back to us.

But intimacy is only one aspect of democracy's constitutive informality (thus can it be criticized from the alternate mode of informal power relations, competition, as weak and naive foolishness). The vehicle of tutelary power cannot be *personified* informality, which might well convey a certain intimacy but which is eventually exposed as ridiculous. We are all too familiar with, for instance, the politician seeking power by acting authentic: seeming down to earth with a folksy warmth and a populist heat, making a connection with overwrought sympathy and confessional emotions, speaking in anecdotes and scorning a teleprompter (the political equivalent of reality television's unscripted appeal). Such strategies are effective (and so both troubling and dispiriting) to a point but are ultimately too conventional and recognizable—to the point of being clichés. They are too obvious, the stuff of beheading-by-parody. To honor democratic freedom and equality, to proceed under cover of that which we find meaningful, oppression would have to take shape as formless, as an *impersonal* informality.[36] In the company of equals, the aspiration will be to sustain (and expand) openness and intimacy not by confining power to the political sphere of society, which was once thought uniquely constituted for the purpose of managing power effectively and legitimately, but by locating power outside of society altogether. In this context, democratic despotism would have to be a stealth power, not personable but the perfectly selfless power of nobody—of some superhumanistic abstraction. Were paternalism to reemerge in the society founded against the paternal principle, it would have to be as the authority of the absent father.

This, of course, is just how Tocqueville thought the state would be understood in democratic times. But the state is not nearly stealthy enough to approach tutelary omnicompetence and omnipresence. While citizens might want the government to do and provide everything for them, it will be, as the most obvious of repositories of power, despised at every turn, for each use and nonuse of its power. Insofar as government itself seems a postpolitical system of administration—being perfectly expert and perfectly impartial, operating like a business and a science—it approaches the possibility of practical authority. Yet, as Lefort argues, every representation (above all, every election) exposes the system's connections to particular people, special interests, and institutional machinery—shunting Wolin's postmodern power back into its modern housing. Far from achieving a closed-circuit power system, it seems the state must increasingly rely upon secrecy and ad hoc justifications for its actions, such as prerogative in times of crisis. The use of power must be declared the exception, as opposed to operating as the rule, silently and routinely, in tutelary rather than emergency mode. Along these lines, perhaps the continuous invocation of crisis today attests to (along with the democratic fascination with, and expectation of, the transformative event) the fragility rather than the hegemony of the state's authority.

More so than the state, the quiet peer pressure of public opinion might accumulate into a sort of tutelary power, but only until someone speaks in its name. Religious authority cannot be made manifest in the here and now without degrading itself, nor be fused to politics without suffering the cynicism politics generates. The free market—insofar as it is perceived as a spontaneous, unplanned, and objective natural order—is a more likely vehicle of tutelary power: encouraging consumerism's fantasy of eternal youth and the discipline of nonstop play, taking care of our needs and facilitating our pleasures, managing our most important affairs. The invisible hand is the ideal informal, impersonal Leviathan.

But again, every representation of the particular actors and institutions that populate the market exposes the dirty fingerprints of the invisible hand; "market forces" translate into Big Corporation's profits and the rich getting richer, for instance. The distance between the authority of the market and the political power of corporations is the distance between market society and mere plutocracy. Perhaps the real threat of tutelary power today would lie not in the Platonic cave but in a Platonic guardianship of embodied virtue, were such a thing remotely believable today. Manent writes that "when *no one* governs, the desire grows to *identify* those who govern the society that no one governs." In democratic times, the persistence of freedom *and* the anticipation of despotism issue from in this insistence on identifying "the phantasm of invisible power"—perpetually reimagining the king who is to be beheaded.[37]

Tocqueville writes that he concluded his journey and departed America still full of hopes and fears: "I see great dangers that can be warded off and great evils that can be avoided or held in check, and I feel ever more assured in my belief that in order to be virtuous and prosperous, democratic nations have only to want to be so."[38] His fears ultimately seem to converge on the fatalism of democratic times, that democratic peoples will take themselves to be "necessarily obedient to I know not what insurmountable and unthinking force born of previous events or race or soil or climate."[39] The most free people in human history, who need only to want to be so, might imagine themselves the most obedient. Tocqueville's logic of the tutelary state plays out here on a far vaster—but for that reason immaterial—scale. Perhaps to open society, to transcend our political condition, we seek out and cede power not to the state, or even to the market, but to such wholly impersonal informalities as history and nature. Fearing domestication, whether by coercion or seduction, we renounce the practice of managing power through politics and readily explain power away as belonging to these purely selfless, objective, efficient stealth authorities. We abdicate the place of political argument, persuasion, practical judgment, and collective action—and so of mediating partisan divisions, of mediating particular and general goods, of mediating principle and practice, of mediating individuals who understand themselves as primarily self-interested and self-expressive. Absent politics, the center cannot hold. Absent these mediating opportunities and obligations, with the atrophy of political life, the imagination, "that ambiguous blessing of modern democracy," tends toward unmediated extremes, losing itself at once in utopian idealism and faux realism.[40] The open society proves to be the cynical society. In the absence of politics, we imagine ourselves equally free and powerless.

# Notes

## Abbreviations

DA    Alexis de Tocqueville, *Democracy in America,* trans. Arthur Gold-hammer (New York: Library of America, 2004).

DI    Sheldon S. Wolin, *Democracy Incorporated: Managed Democracy and the Specter of Inverted Totalitarianism,* (Princeton, N.J.: Princeton University Press, 2008).

DPT    Claude Lefort, *Democracy and Political Theory,* trans. David Macey (Minneapolis: University of Minnesota Press, 1988).

Letters    Alexis de Tocqueville, *Selected Letters on Politics and Society,* ed. Roger Boesche, trans. James Toupin and Roger Boesche (Berkeley: University of California Press, 1985).

NF    Sheldon S. Wolin, "Norm and Form: The Constitutionalizing of Democracy," in *Athenian Political Thought and the Reconstruction of American Democracy,* ed. J. Peter Euben, John R. Wallach, and Josiah Ober (Ithaca, N.Y.: Cornell University Press, 1994): 29–58.

OR I    Alexis de Tocqueville, *The Old Regime and the Revolution,* vol. 1: *The Complete Text,* trans. Alan S. Kahan (Chicago: University of Chicago Press, 1998).

OR II    Alexis de Tocqueville, *The Old Regime and the Revolution,* vol. 2: *Notes on the French Revolution and Napoleon,* trans. Alan S. Kahan (Chicago: University of Chicago Press, 2001).

PFMS    Claude Lefort, *The Political Forms of Modern Society,* ed. John B. Thompson (Cambridge, Mass.: MIT Press, 1986).

PP    Sheldon S. Wolin, *Presence of the Past: Essays on the State and the Constitution* (Baltimore: Johns Hopkins University Press, 1989).

PV    Sheldon S. Wolin, *Politics and Vision: Continuity and Innovation in Western Political Thought,* expanded ed. (Princeton, N.J.: Princeton University Press, 2004).

TBTW    Sheldon S. Wolin, *Tocqueville between Two Worlds: The Making of a Political and Theoretical Life* (Princeton, N.J.: Princeton University Press, 2001).

## Introduction

1. James Allan Davis and Tom W. Smith, "General Social Surveys, 1972–2008," machine-readable data file (Chicago: National Opinion Research Center, 2009) accessible by searching "confidence" at http://www.norc.uchicago.edu/GSS+Website/Browse+GSS+Variables/Subject+Index/.

2. Despite some optimistic predictions, the recent election of Barack Obama to the presidency has thus far not significantly altered these perceptions. Down from the startling peak of 91 percent in October of 2008 but continuing its decades-long upward trend, around 70 percent of respondents consider themselves "dissatisfied" with "the way things are going in the United States at this time." Gallup Poll, August 31–September 2, 2009, www.gallup.com. A 2009 Gallup Poll found that "trust in the 'men and women in political life in this country who either hold or are running for public office' . . . dropped to an all-time low of 49%." Gallup Poll, August 31–September 2, 2009, www.gallup.com. Further "dissatisfaction with government" came in second only to "healthcare" as "the most important [non-economic] problem facing this country today." Gallup Poll, August 31–September 2, www.gallup.com. At 51 percent, President Obama's approval rating is the lowest of any president in the past half century at this point of his presidency. Gallup Poll, December 21–27, 2009, www.gallup.com.

3. The following are just a few recent instances of this truly inescapable strategy of persuasion. (Notice that the subtext is the same in most of these instances: "these are times of crisis"; "the common good"; "obvious to all of good faith"; "necessitates immediate action above stalling argumentation"; and "partisan self-interest disguised as arguments"; "politicians, like generals with no experience of the front," are "clueless and out of touch.") In February of 2009, for example, former secretary of labor and current UC Berkeley professor Robert Reich dismissed Senate Republicans' opposition to President Obama's proposed stimulus package as "playing politics when the economy burns." Reich, "Senate Republicans and the Stimulus: Playing Politics When the Economy Burns," Robert Reich's Blog, February 5, 2009, http://robertreich.blogspot.com. President Obama expressed a similarly low view of politics, saying of health-care reform, "This shouldn't be a political issue, this is an issue for the American people." Barack Obama, interview by Michael Smerconish, *The Michael Smerconish Program*, WPHT, August 20, 2009. In September of the same year, USA.com reported, "Rep. Joe Wilson, who faces a disciplinary vote in the House today for yelling 'You lie' at President Obama last week, posted a Twitvid in which he says the Democrats are 'playing politics' and should get back to health care." Eugene Kiely, "Rep. Wilson: Dems 'Play-

ing Politics,' " *USAToday.com*, September 15, 2009, http://content.usatoday .com. An "open forum" letter in the *Salt Lake Tribune* adds, "So Sen. Orrin Hatch accuses Democrats of playing politics with health care reform . . . Talk about the pot calling the kettle black. As a Republican, I am disgusted with how my party has played politics with this vital issue." Public Forum Letter, "Playing Politics," *Salt Lake Tribune*, September 28, 2009, www.sltrib.com. Of course this language isn't reserved for the debate, such as it is, surrounding health-care reform. In September of 2009, Fox News personality Glenn Beck demanded that Democrats "stop playing politics" and "fight to win in Afghanistan." Beck, "Stop Playing Politics: Fight to Win in Afghanistan," *FoxNews.com*, September 24, 2009, www .foxnews.com. In the same month, Jena Baker McNeill of the Heritage Foundation made her case by asserting, "Congress should stop playing politics with E-Verify." McNeill, "Congress Should Stop Playing Politics with E-verify," Heritage Foundation, September 22, 2009, www.heritage .org. Again in September, San Francisco Assemblywoman Fiona Ma rejected a bill that proposed early prisoner release as a cost-saving measure by claiming, "We should not play politics with public safety." Quoted in Tim Redmond, "Prison Report: Playing Politics," *San Francisco Bay Guardian online*, September 3, 2009, www.sfbg.com. In August of 2009, an editorial in *Nature* called for the U.S. House of Representatives to "stop playing politics with the peer-review process" by halting funding for three NIH studies that looked at substance abuse and HIV risk behavior. Maxine Clarke, "Stop Playing Politics with the Peer Review Process, *Nature* 460 (2009): 667. In May of 2009, Missouri Senator Kit Bond (R) commented on the Obama administration's selective release of information regarding the interrogation of terrorist detainees: "It's really distressing to see politics being played like this." Bond, press conference, May 14, 2009, www.c-span.org. In 2008, the *Boston Globe* accused vice presidential candidate Sarah Palin of "playing politics with family values." Barney Frank, "Playing Politics with Family Values," September 7, 2008, www .boston.com. And again in September of 2009, the mayor of Crown Point, Indiana, accused the sheriff of "playing political games" with the pot bust of a precinct official allied with the mayor. Susan Brown, "Pot Charges Dropped, Political Charges Still Run High," *nwi.com*, February 2, 2010, www.nwitimes.com.

4. Apparently, silliness isn't confined to the electoral season any longer. Presidential spokesman Robert Gibbs, for instance, recently dismissed critics of President Obama's plan to deliver a televised back-to-school speech to the nation's students by stating, "I think we've reached a little bit of the silly season when the president of the United States can't tell kids in school to study hard and stay in school." Quoted in Marcus Frank-

lin, "Gibbs: Furor over School Speech Is 'Silly Season,' " *Washington Times,*
September 4, 2009, www.washingtontimes.com.

5. Again taking the debate over health-care reform as our example, the
following passage from an editorial in the *Colorado Springs Gazette* perfectly
captures the view of ordinary politics as akin to school-yard antics: "The
health care debate has regrettably, tragically sunk into the painful Washington routine of partisan sniping, irresponsible scare tactics and name
calling by politicians on both sides of the aisle. Inject a record sum of
advertising and orchestrated demonstrations from competing interest
groups and you get volatile town hall meetings that deteriorate into
meaningless shouting matches. . . . This is that singular moment in history
when Congress must lead on the real issues and not lock down in party
ideology and politics as usual." Jeffrey A. Moody, "We Can't Allow Politics-
As-Usual to Derail Health Care Reform," *Colorado Springs Gazette,* September 15, 2009, http://findarticles.com. And it is apparently not too soon to
declare the failure of the 2008 presidential election to deliver the hoped-
for transcendence of ordinary politics. David Ignatius writes, "For all the
legislative commotion surrounding the economic crisis, we are still living
in the equivalent of 'the phony war' of 1939 and 1940. War has been
declared on the Great Recession, but it's basically politics as usual. The
bickering and mismanagement that helped create the crisis are continuing,
even though we elected a president who promised a new start." Ignatius,
"Despite Crisis, It's Still Politics as Usual," *Real Clear Politics,* March 12,
2009, www.realclearpolitics.com.

6. Karl Rove formulated the new identity politics of "core convictions" perfectly in his advice to Republican candidates during the 2008 primary
campaign: "Say in authentic terms what you believe. The GOP nominee
must highlight his core convictions to help people understand who he is
and to set up a natural contrast with [Hillary] Clinton, both on style and
substance. . . . The American people want their president to be authentic.
And against a Democrat who calculates almost everything, including her
accent and laugh, being seen as someone who says what he believes in a
direct way will help." Rove, "How to Beat Hillary (Next) November,"
*Newsweek.com,* November 17, 2007, www.theleftcoaster.com.

7. In the wake of the devastatingly effective "attack ad" featuring John Kerry
windsurfing—with the tagline "John Kerry. Whichever way the wind
blows"—during the 2004 general election, many described the 2008 campaign as a "flip-flop war." Listing the "waffling" accusations aimed at both
Barack Obama and John McCain, *Newsweek* summed up the situation: "So
it has already come to this. At the end of its first month, the great and noble
general-election campaign of 2008 has been defined by a single question:
who is the biggest flip-flopper? . . . True believers in both men are glum: if

Mr. Maverick and Mr. New Politics won't stick to their principles, who on earth will?" The account continues, "Too many candidates have offered conversion narratives that track too perfectly with the course of political expediency. The nation has lost its faith." Jonathan Darman, "Candidates Should Never Flip-Flop," *Newsweek.com*, June 28, 2008, www.newsweek .com. This framing dichotomy of the economic and the religious— "expediency" versus "conversion narratives" and "faith"—is, I shall suggest, revealing.

8. In August of 2007, Gallup found that "Congress' approval rating was 18%—matching the lowest Gallup had measured since it first asked the question in 1974. To gain more insight as to why Americans are so displeased with Congress, . . . [a] Gallup Panel survey asked Americans to explain in their own words why they hold the view they do about Congress. . . . All told, 67% of those who disapprove of Congress mention some type of congressional inaction as a reason why they disapprove of Congress." Gallup Poll, August 23–26, 2007, www.gallup.com. In January of 2008, a Gallup Poll found similarly that 80 percent of those surveyed thought it either a "crisis" or "major problem" that the government had failed "to solve the major challenges facing the country in the last few years." The same poll found that 82 percent thought "powerful special interests having too much control over what the government does" constituted either a crisis or a major problem. Gallup Poll, January, 10–13, 2008, www.gallup.com.

9. On "conceptual metaphor" and "framing rhetoric" see, respectively, George Lakoff and Mark Johnson, *Metaphors We Live By* (Chicago: University of Chicago Press, 1980), and George Lakoff, *Moral Politics: How Liberals and Conservatives Think* (Chicago: University of Chicago Press, 2002).

10. The 2009 Effie Award–winning ad "Stop Talking, Start Doing," television advertisement for IBM Corporation, Ogilvy and Mather, www.effie.org.

11. For an illuminating exploration of Western political thought's tradition of antirhetorical rhetoric, see Bryan Garsten, *Saving Persuasion: A Defense of Rhetoric and Judgment* (Cambridge, Mass.: Harvard University Press, 2006). Garsten traces the attack upon the classical humanist tradition of rhetoric to the sixteenth century's "crisis of confidence about citizens' capacity to exercise practical judgment in public deliberations." In reaction to the discord caused by "the dogmatism of private judgment as it displayed itself in the Puritan rhetoric of conscience," Hobbes, for instance, formulated a "rhetoric of representation" intended to persuade "citizens to distance themselves from their private judgment and to judge from a sovereign, unitary, public standpoint." In different ways, Garsten argues, Rousseau and Kant followed suit in offering a "rhetoric against rhetoric"—a sort of argument to end all arguments. Garsten, *Saving Persuasion*, 4, 10–11.

12. Alan S. Blinder puts this view succinctly: "The real source of the current estrangement between Americans and their politicians is the feeling that . . . elected officials are playing games rather than solving problems." Blinder, "Is Government Too Political?" *Foreign Affairs* 76 (1997): 115.

13. As Dana Villa puts it, "The most striking feature of the contemporary public realm is how uniformly the attitudes of manipulation and opportunism characterize all who enter it. . . . By universally taking up an exploitative, instrumental, and fundamentally strategic approach to politics and political action, we have rendered the public sphere an unfit place for human habitation." Villa, *Public Freedom* (Princeton, N.J.: Princeton University Press, 2008), 5–6.

14. As should be apparent, my approach to the study of political cynicism differs from most in that I draw upon patterns of speech more so than of behavior, to understand the beliefs that orient prevailing attitudes and opinions. In other words, the primary artifact analyzed in this work is our political rhetorical culture rather than the more familiar measures of voting behavior citizen compliance, the indices of social capital and political trust and confidence, and so on. The contours of this rhetorical culture, I shall suggest, are more telling of precisely how and why we both disengage from and engage in politics. Democracy is in large measure about speaking, and so I attend to what is said. For the most comprehensive compilation of data regarding political participation and alienation, see John Paul Robinson, Philip S. Shaver, and Lawrence S. Wrightsman, eds., *Measures of Political Attitudes* (San Diego, Calif.: Academic Press, 1999).

15. On the weakness in America and beyond of the link between levels of "trust in" or "satisfaction with" government and prevailing conditions (particularly economic conditions), see Robert D. Putnam and Susan J. Pharr, eds., *Disaffected Democracies* (Princeton, N.J.: Princeton University Press, 2000), chaps. 1, 2, 8, 9, and Russell J. Dalton, *Democratic Challenges, Democratic Choices: The Erosion of Political Support in Advanced Industrial Democracies* (Oxford: Oxford University Press, 2004). Interestingly, Dalton concludes that rising expectations of government rather than either the perceived poor performance of government or political scandals goes furthest in explaining the ongoing collapse of support for political institutions.

16. For the classic account of "rational ignorance," see Anthony Downs, *An Economic Theory of Democracy* (New York: HarperCollins Publishers, 1957). For a fine survey of the various strands of minimalist (elitist, economic, pluralist) democracy, see James Bohman and William Rehg, "Introduction," in *Deliberative Democracy: Essays on Reason and Politics*, eds. Bohman and Rehg (Cambridge, Mass.: MIT Press, 1997). For a seminal critique of

democratic minimalist, see Carol Pateman, *Participation and Democratic Theory* (Cambridge: Cambridge University Press, 1976).

17. Bruce Ackerman, for instance, advances the first line of reasoning in what he describes as the Madisonian project of enabling an "economy of virtue" by means of a constitutional system designed to ordinarily make only minimal demands of people's attention and public spiritedness. Ackerman, *We the People: Foundations* (Cambridge, Mass: Belknap Press of Harvard University Press, 1991), 198. Sheldon Wolin is perhaps today's leading theorist of the second line of reasoning. Whereas Ackerman sees the economization of virtue, Wolin (in a view deeply resonant with Madison's antifederalist interlocutors) sees "managed democracy"—a rationalized political economy so inegalitarian and opaque as to render people's attention and public-spiritedness simply irrelevant but which nonetheless advertises itself as democratic. We should question the "democratic credentials," Wolin writes, "of a system that legitimates the economic oppression and culturally stunted lives of millions of citizens while, for all practical purposes, excluding them from political power." Wolin, *DI*, 23–24.

18. John R. Hibbing and Elizabeth Theiss-Morse, *Stealth Democracy: Americans' Beliefs about How Government Should Work* (Cambridge: Cambridge University Press, 2002), 1–2. For works that reach similar conclusions, see Thomas Cronin, *Direct Democracy* (Cambridge, Mass.: Harvard University Press, 1989), and Morris P. Fiorina, "The Dark Side of Civic Engagement," *Civic Engagement in American Democracy*, ed. Theda Skocpol and Morris P. Fiorina (Washington, D.C.: Brookings Institution Press, 1999). Jane J. Mansbridge's classic study of local, participatory democracy in the context of even minimal diversity can also be read as in line with this finding. Mansbridge, *Beyond Adversary Democracy* (Chicago: University of Chicago Press, 1983).

19. Hibbing and Theiss-Morse, *Stealth Democracy*. Hibbing and Theiss-Morse write that indicators of political cynicism—trust, confidence, perceptions of being taken advantage of, and so on—rise and fall independently for the most part of both "policy-outcomes" (whether the economy is prospering, for instance) and "policy-outputs" (whether government decisions are seen to correspond with one's own preferences and ideology). Ibid., *130, 62–65*.

20. Hibbing and Theiss-Morse comment, "People are amazingly attuned, hypersensitive even, to the possibility that decision makers will attempt to improve themselves at the expense of everyone else." Ibid., 85.

21. Ibid., 44.

22. Hibbing and Theiss-Morse write, "People are not at all certain that the 'country would be better off if the American people rather than politicians

decided important political matters.' In fact, just as many people disagree with this statement as agree. . . . People themselves believe that people aren't very bright, . . . [that] they are selfish, . . . and [that] they don't want to be informed." Ibid., 126–127.

23. Invoking Rousseau, Hibbing and Theiss-Morse write that the existence of a "general will" remains "a popular myth among both academics and the populace." Ibid., 156, 9, 141.

24. Ibid., 7, 33.

25. Ibid., 135–137.

26. Hibbing and Theiss-Morse report that "the people would most prefer decisions to be made by what we call empathetic, non-self-interested decision makers. Elites are not what the people fear; self-serving elites are." Ibid., 3, 157, 85–86, 137–143.

27. Ibid., 9.

28. Ibid., 143.

29. A June 2009 Gallup Poll finds that, among American institutions, "the military" receives by far the highest grade, with 82 percent of those polled expressing "a great deal" or "quite a lot" of confidence. "Small business" comes in second at 67 percent (interestingly, "big business" comes in last, with only 16 percent). While "the police" receives the third-highest vote of confidence (59 percent), "the criminal justice system" enters in at just 28 percent. Other "systems" ("the public school system," "the medical system")—along with "banks," the "media," and "organized labor"—rank along with Congress at below 25 percent. The Supreme Court comes in at 67 percent. Gallup Poll, June, 14–17, 2009, www.gallup.com.

30. That people apparently have such a low opinion of themselves as citizens calls into question the explanation of Americans' alienation from politics put forward most notably by E.J. Dionne Jr. and Morris P. Fiorina. Their respective analyses point to the systematic disconnect between a pragmatic electorate and partisan elites who, in their ideological extremism, manufacture a rhetoric of false choices and a culture war polarization misrepresentative of the centrist positions of the electorate and resistant to commonsense solutions. Even granting the problematic claim that the electorate holds definable positions, which can then be classified as centrist or not, this characterization goes astray insofar as it implies either that people desire a greater role in government or that people believe government would work better if it better represented "average Americans." The average American apparently has little respect for the political capacities, whether intellectual or moral, of the average American. We might wonder, in turn, if this helps explain why in our democracy the government that responds to—or is even caught listening to—public opinion is derided as feckless and pandering. Whether in fact centrist and pragmatic or not, the electorate would seem to not want itself represented.

Dionne, *Why Americans Hate Politics* (New York: Simon and Schuster, 1991), and Fiorina, *Culture War? The Myth of a Polarized America* (New York: Pearson Longman, 2005).

31. In an exemplary iteration of this claim, we hear "Economics, as channeled by its popular avatars in the media and politics, is the cosmology and the theodicy of our contemporary culture. More than religion itself . . . it is economics that offers the dominant creation narrative of our society, depicting the relation of each of us to the universe we inhabit [and] the relationship of human beings to God. . . . This understanding . . . now serves as the unquestioned foundation of nearly all political and social debate." Gordon Bigelow, "Let There Be Markets: The Evangelical Roots of Economics," *Harper's Magazine* 310, no. 1860 (2005): 33.

32. For a wide-ranging and penetrating analysis of the two theorizations of political disengagement described here—those of abdicating and of being locked out of political power—see Tom DeLuca, *The Two Faces of Political Apathy* (Philadelphia: Temple University Press, 1995). DeLuca writes, "Where the first face of apathy indicates individual responsibility for nonparticipation, the second shifts responsibility . . . to other sources, perhaps elites, institutional practices, social structures, or even the organizing principles of a society . . . over which one has little or no control, and perhaps little knowledge." DeLuca, *The Two Faces of Political Apathy,* 11.

33. *Measuring Up 2006: The National Report Card on Higher Education* (a report commissioned by the National Center for Public Policy and Higher Education) points to a "looming crisis" in American higher education, demonstrated by lagging "performance" and "falling rankings" relative to those of other countries: "Other nations' gains in college participation and degree attainment reflect their recent recognition of the enormous advantages that a college-educated population represents in the context of a knowledge-based economy and growing global competition. . . . We can and must mobilize our nation, our states, and our colleges for success in this external competition—as we did in the mid-20th century when the G.I.'s returned from Europe and Asia, and when the baby boomers came of college age. . . . The current level of performance will fall short in a world being reshaped by the knowledge-based global economy." National Center for Public Policy and Higher Education, *Measuring Up 2006: The National Report Card on Higher Education,* available at www.pewcenter onthestates.org/uploadedFiles/Measuring%20Up%202006.pdf.

34. The critique of capitalism's totalizing tendencies has, of course, a very long lineage on both the Left and the Right. For one recent example, available at most any bookstore, see Benjamin R. Barber, *Con$umed: How Markets Corrupt Children, Infantilize Adults, and Swallow Citizens Whole* (New York: W.W. Norton, 2006).

35. Roger Rosenblatt identifies the following as the central trend of American life over the past quarter-century: "Now, one cannot think of a single area of American life that does not define itself proudly and brazenly by the bottom line. Books are judged on sales; movies by the first weekend's gross." But is this accurate? Do we "proudly judge" books and movies by how much money they make? Or do we, in fact, just assume that bestsellers and the latest Hollywood blockbusters are garbage—guilty pleasures we shamefacedly enjoy? Roger Rosenblatt, "Essay: The Bottom Line," *Newshour*, PBS, July 10, 2006.

36. In a nuanced and comprehensive analysis of the causes and effects of the consumer way of life, David Ricci at times recognizes this dimensionality in what he terms the "uneasy dialectic between consumerism and republicanism" in contemporary America. Nonetheless, there is a sort of tone deafness to his characterization of the American view of happiness, and ultimately republicanism ends up playing a rather insignificant role in the dialectic: "Consumerism did not reject the Declaration and its republican sentiments." But the pursuit of happiness was linked "to the phenomenal outpouring of commodities which modern industry and agriculture could produce. Thus in countless advertisements and eventually in countless political speeches, Americans described happiness to each other as making money, or, more technically, as the opportunity to earn the means to consume an endless supply of new commodities." For instance, Ricci points out, Calvin Coolidge "sanctified the pursuit of wealth when he announced that 'the man who builds a factory builds a temple . . . [and] the man who works there worships there.' " Ricci, *Good Citizenship in America* (Cambridge: Cambridge University Press, 2004), 292, 147. But do we still abide by Coolidge's sanctification? Do we equate the value of opportunity, even financial opportunity, to mere money-making and consumption (or rather to, say, the means of declaring our independence or providing for our children)? Do we describe money as being able to buy happiness?

37. Joseph N. Cappella and Kathleen Hall Jamieson define political cynicism as "mistrust generalized from particular leaders or political groups to the political process as a whole—a process perceived to corrupt the persons who participate in it and [to draw] corrupt persons as participants." In thinking about political cynicism, political and social trust (along with confidence in the fidelity and capacity of political institutions and actors, and satisfaction with the performance of government) are surely significant. My work, however, addresses something a bit different: the perceived absurdity of politics that seems to precede judgments of trust, confidence, and satisfaction. To the fine definition above, I would thus add the sense of contempt, disrespect, alienation, or disaffection generalized all the way to the practice of democratic politics as a whole. In this expanded definition, we might

expect the disposition of cynicism to actually generate very high levels of
trust in particular leaders, groups, or institutions acting *in* politics but perceived as not being *of* politics—as somehow not political in nature. More
generally, Capella and Jamieson cite the media's coverage of politics—
hyping conflict in the metaphors of sports and war, ignoring consensus
and civility, giving sound-bite simplifications and decontextualizations of
arguments, reducing "leaders to their presumed motives and substance to
its strategic intent," and so forth—as having "the power to activate cynical
reactions in the public." The question, which they themselves raise, briefly,
is whether the media manipulates or panders—creating the perceptions
and expectations that come to pass for reality or serving up the stories that
satisfy our taste for the dramatic and for knowing the "truth" behind the
words of those in power, including those in the media (thereby leveling the
power disparity between us and them). Have we arrived at the explanatory
bottom when we identify news framing that directs and organizes the way
people think, or is the media itself in effect organized and directed by the
broader social state in which it operates? Is the media primarily the creature or the creator of the narrative it depicts? Cappella and Jamieson, *Spiral
of Cynicism: The Press and the Public Good* (Oxford: Oxford University Press,
1997), 166, 4–10, 27–29.

38. For the leading contemporary analysis of modern cynicism as such, see
Peter Sloterdijk, *Critique of Cynical Reason*, trans. Michael Eldred (Minneapolis: University of Minnesota Press, 1987). Sloterdijk identifies cynicism
as the hallmark product of modernity's world-weary malaise of enlightenment reason, mass society, and the spirit of capitalism. Our cynicism is a
dead-end condition of "enlightened false consciousness" wherein we
jadedly live and work as faithless actors, as if we still believed in what we
now know to be illusion. The promises of modernity have been broken
and its faiths lost, yet still we persist in our modern ways and routines.
Against this melancholic condition, Sloterdijk calls for a return to the
ancient cynicism (kynicism) of Diogenes and his followers. Kynicism is a
counter-cultural rebellion from below via the subversive and emancipa-
tory "cheekiness" of disorderly, sensual, bodily antics, along with self-
inured powerlessness and exile from mainstream concerns. In its defining
act of laughing in the face of claims to authority and power (as did
Diogenes before both Plato and Alexander), kynicism would seem to
honor the equality and freedom of what I go on to describe as democratic
openness. Cynicism is itself judged good when it is in the service of democracy. On political cynicism more specifically, see William Chaloupka,
*Everybody Knows: Cynicism in America* (Minneapolis: University of Minnesota Press, 1999); and Alan Keenan, "Twilight of the Political? A Contribution to the Democratic Critique of Cynicism," *Theory and Event* 2, no. 1
(1998).

39. Which is more telling today: the number of people who feel compelled to undergo cosmetic surgery or the society-wide scorn heaped upon those who undergo cosmetic surgery, to the point where recipients must keep hidden any such procedure?

40. The phrases come, respectively, from the 1984 and 1980 campaigns of the "Reagan Revolution." Interestingly, the latter phrase (from Reagan's July 17 presidential nomination acceptance speech) is quoted from Tom Paine's *Common Sense.*

41. The speech continues, "It's the answer that led those who've been told for so long by so many to be cynical and fearful and doubtful about what we can achieve to put their hands on the arc of history and bend it once more toward the hope of a better day." Barack Obama, speech at Grant Park rally, November 4, 2008, www.news.com.au/adelaidenow/ story/0,,24607123–5006301,00.html.

42. Patrick J. Deneen addresses such questions with great subtlety and insight in his recent work *Democratic Faith.* Deneen's work is largely devoted to demonstrating the often unseen inversion from democracy's purported antiutopianism, antifoundationalist embrace of fallibilism and pragmatism, and rejection of faith (religious or otherwise) as a central element of political association, on one hand, to democracy's own utopianism, foundational embrace of the human capacity for self-transformation and perfectibility (whether via rational deliberation or agonistic engagement of otherness), and at times fanatical affirmation of democracy as itself an unquestioned faith. Exposing the attendant contradictions, paradoxes, and dangers of this simultaneous desacralization of human organization and sacralization of democracy as the principle of human organization, Deneen goes on to argue that there is "a dynamic by which 'democratic faith' contributes ironically to forms of democratic cynicism and even despair" because the actual "conditions of democracy fail to live up to that faith"—an "exaggerated and unrealizable vision of democracy leads to disillusionment; a response that dismisses 'faith' is the result, leading to a cynical democratic theory premised upon the inescapability of interest and manipulation; in turn, idealists resort to more fervent calls for democratic faith." Deneen, *Democratic Faith* (Princeton, N.J.: Princeton University Press, 2005), 36, 20, 8. While certainly significant, this "reinforcing cycle" view misses, I think, some of the fine contours of our situation. I suggest that our cynicism is best understood not as the alternate of our faith but as its instantiation. Faith and cynicism are opposite expressions of our affirmation of democratic openness, of the concept of perfectibility rendered indefinite. As such, they proceed not cyclically but in tandem. It is not that we lose faith and grow disillusioned but rather that our faith requires the disposition of cynicism toward conventionality. In turn, we should expect our belief in the democratic ideal to be as

unwavering as our discontent with the practices and institutions of democracy.

43. In this interpretation, we would expect not exactly Samuel P. Huntington's "creedal passion periods"—wherein dissatisfaction with the radical gap between democratic ideals and institutions boils over into "revolutionary situations" (characterized by "a pervasive unhappiness with things as they were" and "widespread and intense moral indignation" that are "manifested in the questioning and rejection" of "existing structures of authority")—which ultimately lead to a closer alignment of American institutions and practices with "American values." Huntington, *American Politics: The Promise of Disharmony* (Cambridge, Mass.: Harvard University Press, 1981), 91–92. More precisely, we would expect the constancy of creedal passion, occasioned not by dissatisfaction with things as they are but rather by democratic society's constitutive passion for revolution as such, with this passion leading to a radicalization of the gap between ideal and present reality.

44. Boutros Boutros-Ghali, "The Interaction between Democracy and Development" (Paris: United Nations Educational, Scientific, and Cultural Organization, 2002), 10, available at http://unesdoc.unesco.org/images/0012/0 01282/128283e.pdf.

45. Thus far I have written that an antipolitical prejudice is inscribed in democratic society and so is a constant that cannot be fully explained by variable circumstances and contingent events. This is not to suggest that circumstances and events are irrelevant, of course. Rather, fluctuations in the daily degree of our contempt for politics—fluctuations caused by the latest scandals, elections, wars, and so forth—take shape within a more general climate of political cynicism. At the same time, polling data clearly demonstrates that cynicism has increased significantly over the past half century. In what follows, particularly in Chapter 3, I develop a "punctuated equilibrium" analysis of this change. In its early confrontations with aristocracy, democracy was allied with liberalism in defense of political equality and self-government. In its later confrontations with slavery, democracy was allied with capitalism in defense of competition and the right of contract (radicalizing liberal democracy's antipathy toward paternalism). In its more recent confrontation with fascism and totalitarianism, democracy came to stand for the freedom of openness (an early formulation of the new order/openness dichotomy being Karl Popper's *Open Society*). In each phase the contempt for politics and government increases in degree and shifts in type, to the point where today's contempt is reflexive and rooted in the experience of politics as absurd.

46. See any of the wildly popular writings of Thomas L. Friedman for examples. A flat world is one sense of an open world.

47. Barber, *Con$umed*, 27.

48. Aristotle, *The Politics,* book 1, sect. 14 (1253a), trans. Ernest Barker (Oxford: Oxford University Press, 1962).

49. Sanford Levinson offers one striking formulation of the intertwined collapse of hierarchy and conventionality: "The 'death of constitutionalism' may be the central event of our time, just as the 'death of God' was for the past century (and for much the same reason)." Sanford Levinson, *Constitutional Faith* (Princeton, N.J.: Princeton University Press, 1988), 52.

50. For a representative expression of this sort of contempt, see Joe Klein's tellingly titled *Politics Lost: How American Democracy Was Trivialized by People Who Think You're Stupid* (New York: Doubleday, 2006). Klein (author of *Primary Colors* and *Time* magazine columnist) regrets the loss of a politics that was fun—spontaneous and authentic—in the rise of "political handlers" and the "pollster-consultant industrial complex" which churns out choreographed campaigns and prefabricated candidates.

51. See, for example, Ackerman, *We the People: Foundations*; and *Robert A. Dahl, How Democratic Is the American Constitution?* (New Haven: Yale University Press, 2002).

52. In his penetrating study of the postmodern sources of cynicism, Timothy Bewes identifies the "abnegation of politics on the basis of its inauthenticity," along with a more general "refusal to engage with the world" and the "flight into . . . interiority," as a central modality of modern cynicism. Analogous to my argument regarding the relationship between democratic openness and conventionality, Bewes writes that authenticity, an "extremely abstract value," "cannot by its very nature appear in the public realm, since by doing so it loses what is specific to it. Authenticity and its derivatives—honesty, sincerity, moral scrupulousness, 'good intentions'—may only be maintained intact in absolute privacy, or in personal communion with the divine." The rhetoric of authenticity, with its elevation of the values of "depth and energy" (intimacy and informality, respectively, in my terms) thus frames "the privatization or the depoliticization of politics." Bewes, *Cynicism and Postmodernity* (London: Verso, 1997), 1–2, 10.

53. The article recounting Edwards's comments, which came during a Seattle convention on Internet technologies in 2006, continues: "Several in the audience stressed the importance of authenticity in politics, and the potential for blogs and other technology to give Americans a more accurate view of campaigns and the legislative process by getting closer to what's really going on. . . . But one . . . attendee pointed out that the human voice so fundamental to blogs contrasts with the practiced messages delivered by many politicians." Todd Bishop, "John Edwards Courts Tech Crowd in Seattle," *Seattlepi.com,* July 1, 2006, http://seattlepi.com.

54. For his most recent detailed formulation of this idea, see Wolin, *PV,* 601–606.

55. Wolin, NF, 29, 53–54.

56. The historical playing out of this logic is described by James Miller in his classic account of how the participatory democracy of the New Left evolved into the antipolitics of the counterculture. See Miller, *Democracy Is in the Streets: From Port Huron to the Siege of Chicago* (New York: Simon and Schuster, 1987).

57. Tocqueville, *DA*, 272.

58. Wendy Brown, "American Nightmare: Neoliberalism, Neoconservatism, and De-Democratization," *Political Theory* 34, no. 6 (2006): 692.

59. Ibid.

60. Lefort, *DPT*, 19.

61. In his fascinating study of the radical striving—particularly evident in the writings of Rousseau, Marx, and Lenin (and to some extent, Hegel and Arendt)—to achieve a postpolitical society free of pluralism, conflict, and the need for political mediation, Joseph M. Schwartz writes, "The radical vision's desire to transcend the messy business of democratic disagreement through the instantiation of a solidaristic society embodying true universal human interests not only is profoundly antipolitical; it also violates the very democratic impulses that inspired the radical critique of . . . authoritarian regimes." Schwartz, *The Permanence of the Political: A Democratic Critique of the Radical Impulse to Transcend Politics* (Princeton, N.J.: Princeton University Press, 1995), 10. The radicalism Schwartz analyzes is born of the principle of democratic equality, and in envisioning a world beyond politics, it reflects its genealogy.

## 1. "More than Kings yet Less than Men"

1. Tocqueville, *DA*, 3–14.

2. Sheldon S. Wolin "Why democracy?" *democracy* 1, no. 1 (January 1981): 3–4. "Today it is difficult," Wolin writes, "to imagine that any political scientist or political sociologist in good repute would write a book about the irresistible tide of democracy or its incarnation in America." Wolin, PP, 78.

3. Wolin writes, "Thus democracy is poised to become for our time what aristocracy was for Tocqueville's, the archaic remains of a superseded past. Unlike Tocqueville's aristocracy, however, the passing of democracy, if that is what is happening, is not being experienced as loss, . . . but as freedom from an impossible obligation." Wolin, TBTW, 567.

4. Jean Bethke Elshtain, *Democracy on Trial* (New York: Basic Books, 1995), 1.

5. Axel Hadenius, "Victory and Crisis: Introduction," in *Democracy's Victory and Crisis*, ed. Axel Hadenius (Cambridge: Cambridge University Press, 1997), 7, 2–3.

6. Fareed Zakaria, *The Future of Freedom: Illiberal Democracy at Home and Abroad* (New York: W.W. Norton, 2003), 13, 162.

7. Wolin, "Why democracy?" 3; Wolin, NF, 39.

8. In 1970, Carol Pateman wrote that this minimalist "theory of democracy has gained almost universal support among present-day political theorists": "By the middle of the century . . . even the ideal [of democracy] seemed to many to have been called into question." Pateman, *Participation and Democratic Theory* (Cambridge: Cambridge University Press, 1970), 14, 2. How far have we come from this questioning of the ideal of democracy, where today it is difficult to even imagine a legitimate alternative to democracy?

9. Wolin, "What Revolutionary Action Means Today," *democracy* 2, no. 4 (Fall 1982): 23.

10. For all that Wolin's *Tocqueville between Two Worlds* contributes to our understanding of the life and works of Tocqueville, of his theorization of political life in democracy and of democracy against political life, and of his place in modern political thought's attempts to conserve the human in a world made of, by, and for power, perhaps Wolin's greatest contribution is to our appreciation of Tocqueville's approach to the practice of theory—to his "method," if that word is not too misleading. With Wolin's help we are able to see beyond the thicket of Tocqueville's apparent contradictions. Wolin writes, "The ascent of Tocqueville's *theoros* is an escape from details in order to achieve a panoramic vision. Unlike his contemporaries whose theoretical structures were methodically built on premises and hypothesis while professing deference to facts, the structure of Tocqueville's theory was shaped to organize impressions, developing what he called 'tableaux' and 'spectacles.' The model he followed was not that of the scientist but of the painter. The theory he created might be called 'political impressionism.' . . . [It] employs and evokes images, abounds in sweeping generalizations, is richly allusive, dwells on the quality and style of political performance, and persuades by exhibiting rather than demonstrating." Such a theory will, Wolin suggests, "often seem confusing, on the verge of collapse, forced, and artificial." He continues, "It may also compensate with dazzling insights and unsuspected truths produced by a refusal to constrict a particular idea by one invariant meaning." Thus, for instance, precisely in Tocqueville's "contradictions, evasions, and ambiguities" do we see democracy in its actual "multivalent" form and "variety of expressions." Wolin, TBTW, 138–143, 96–97.

11. Tocqueville most explicitly highlights the latter in a definition of democracy from a draft fragment for *Democracy II*: "A democratic people, society, time do not mean a people, a society, a time when all men are equal, but a people, a society, a time when there are no more castes, fixed classes, privileges, special and exclusive rights, permanent riches, properties fixed in the hands of certain families, when all men can continuously climb and descend and mix together in all ways." Quoted in James T. Schleifer,

*The Making of Tocqueville's Democracy in America,* 2nd ed. (Indianapolis: Liberty Fund, 2000), 336. Here, Tocqueville describes a type of freedom as being coconstitutive with equality of the democratic social state.

12. Tocqueville, *DA,* 551.

13. Ibid., 821.

14. Aristotle, *The Politics,* book 1, sect. 14 (1253a), trans. Ernest Barker (Oxford: Oxford University Press, 1962).

15. Patrick Deneen touches upon something similar: "The democratic citizen is simultaneously overconfident and overwhelmed. . . . Tocqueville, quite startlingly, sees these conditions as compatible, not contradictory, and, moreover, as extremes which democratic humanity is likely to simultaneously and perpetually manifest. . . . From the dynamics of democratic equality Tocqueville perceives a resulting democratic man who exists simultaneously at a version of both Aristotelian extremes, . . . [exhibiting] both an excess and a deficiency of felt personal significance." In his otherwise illuminating study of Tocqueville, Deneen badly underemphasizes the significance of political life for Tocqueville. We hear, for instance, that the institutions that Tocqueville envisions as moderating democracy's excesses include "the family, civic association, and, above all, religion." It is doubtful that Tocqueville would include the family in this list without qualification, and he most assuredly would include political liberty and political activity, beyond what plausibly might be lumped in with "civic association." Deneen, *Democratic Faith* (Princeton, N.J.: Princeton University Press, 2005) 223–225.

16. Claude Lefort offers a similar notion when he writes that democracy is properly understood as a regime or *politeia,* as "a 'style of existence' or 'mode of life,' " characterized by "those mores and beliefs that testify to the existence of a set of implicit norms determining notions of just and unjust, good and evil, desirable and undesirable, noble and ignoble." Lefort, *DPT,* 3.

17. As Pierre Manent describes it, democracy in Tocqueville's sense is "something that happens to us, that transforms us, that changes the depths as well as the surface of our lives, something that we do not desire because we do not take cognizance of it when it is most at work, when it has transformed us the most." Manent, *Tocqueville and the Nature of Democracy,* trans. John Waggoner (Rowman and Littlefield Publishers, 1996), xii.

18. At times Tocqueville seems to suggest that the advent of Christianity was the true turning point of history and the necessary precursor of the democratic revolution, with the Protestant Reformation and the French Revolution being successive extensions of this original movement.

19. Tocqueville, *DA,* 583, 432, 796 (emphasis added).

20. Tocqueville writes, "I have no doubt that the social and political constitution of a people fosters certain beliefs and certain tastes, which then easily

become second nature to it, while these same causes eliminate certain opinions and certain penchants without any active effort by the people in question and in a sense without their knowledge." Ibid., 634.

21. Ibid., 459–460, 92.

22. Ibid., 582, 290.

23. Claude Ake, "Dangerous Liaisons: The Interface of Globalization and Democracy," in *Democracy's Victory and Crisis,* ed. Axel Hadenius (Cambridge: Cambridge University Press, 1997), 287.

24. Wolin, *PP,* 41–42, 143.

25. Ibid., 155, 42, 147–148. Economy offers, Wolin notes, subverted "equivalents for democracy's values of participation (mass consumption), inclusion (work force), and mass empowerment ('consumer society,' 'shareholder democracy')." Economic production, Wolin concludes, is what political citizenship was to Aristotle. Ibid., 60.

26. Wolin himself seems to recognize this point when he writes of "the transmutation of democratic values into a democratized economy of opportunity" that is "opened to all" and defined by a sense of "unlimited possibilities." The question, it seems, is this: are we better off thinking in terms of an economic democracy (democracy's colonization by economy) or a democratic economy (economy's colonization by democracy)? Are opportunity, openness to all, and unlimited possibility originally democratic ideas, issuing from the collapse of hierarchy, or originally economic values, issuing from more material aspirations and imperatives? Similarly, Wolin writes that for "democracy to be exploited a semblance of popular sovereignty has to be preserved" in notions like consumer sovereignty and purchasing power. Why, though, should we think of this relationship between democracy and economy as democracy being "exploited" rather than being reiterated as the legitimizing principle of another sphere of activity—a sphere that has become predominant, overshadowing by far the political, precisely because it seems the venue for a more democratic (more open) democracy? Does this signify the "sovereignty of economy," which is "where real power is to be had," or the sovereignty of democracy, where it would seem real authority is to be had? Wolin, *TBTW,* 268, 274, 570–571.

27. As Lefort describes it, the art of Tocqueville's writing lies precisely in its dimensionality—in that looking upon society, he permits the ambiguities and contradictory properties of social existence into his analysis. Insisting always upon "reversals of perspective," Tocqueville is the most general and least reductive of theorists: "Tocqueville lets himself be guided by the exigency of his investigation. . . . Certainly he attempts to bring the democratic experience to the pure expression of its proper meaning; . . . however, he discovers that experience has more than one meaning and works at grasping the opposite aspects of the same phenom-

enon and at understanding how the oppositions refer from one phenomenon to the other." Our "contemporaries," Lefort continues, "often lose
the sense of ambiguity. Everything that happens in their eyes happens as
if society had no depth, as if they could see it in one fell swoop, as if they
could be satisfied with the celebration of the market or the critique of the
state-providence or the condemnation of individualism or the condemnation of mass culture or the glorification of social movements." In my own
analysis of Tocqueville and of democratic society, I attempt to do justice to
the capaciousness of this method. Claude Lefort, "Tocqueville: A Phenomenology of the Social," in *Liberty, Equality, Democracy*, ed. Eduardo Nolla
(New York: New York University Press, 1992), 110–111.

28. Quoted in Darren Rovell, "Baseball Scales Back Movie Promotion," ESPN,
    May 7, 2004, http://sports.espn.go.com; quoted in Darren Rovell, "The
    Tangled Web of Sports and Advertising," ESPN, May 6, 2004, http://
    sports.espn.go.com.

29. *Titanic*, one of the top grossing movies of all time, is only the most obvious
    example.

30. "Pornography Statistics," Family Safe Media, accessed February 13, 2011,
    www.familysafemedia.com/pornography_statistics.html.

31. "While marriage is losing much of its broad public and institutional char-
    acter, it is gaining popularity as a SuperRelationship, an intensely private
    spiritualized union," write sociologists David Popenoe and Barbara Dafoe
    Whitehead of Rutgers's National Marriage Project. Popenoe and White-
    head, *The State of Our Unions: The Social Health of Marriage in America*
    (New Brunswick, N.J.: National Marriage Project at Rutgers University,
    2003), 11.

32. Scott Stanley, "Myths about Soul Mates," *Boundless Webzine*, 2005, www
    .boundless.org/2005/articles/a0001123.cfm.

33. Tocqueville, *DA*, 832, 673.

34. Ibid, 821. I take up Tocqueville's notion of democratic elevation and gran-
    deur—of how we in democratic society take ourselves to rise above the
    level of humanity—in Part III of this chapter.

35. While Plato speaks of democracy as appearing at first sight like "a many-
    colored cloak decorated in all hues," Tocqueville sees only that democracy
    might take "the color out of the whole soul." Plato, *The Republic*, trans.
    Allan Bloom (New York: Basic Books, 1968), 235; Tocqueville, *OR I*, 377.

36. Tocqueville, *DA*, 743.

37. Tocqueville, *OR I*, 173.

38. Tocqueville, *Letters*, 155. "The further away I am from youth," Tocqueville
    writes in an 1841 letter to Jean-Jacques Ampère, "the more regardful . . . I
    am of passions. I like them when they are good, and I am not even very
    certain of detesting them when they are bad. That is strength, and
    strength, everywhere it is met, appears at its best in the midst of the uni-

versal weakness that surrounds us. . . . What we meet least in our day are passions, true and solid passions that bind up and lead life. We no longer know how to want, or love, or hate . . . as we flutter heavily around a multitude of small objects, none of which either attracts us, or strongly repels us, or holds us." Tocqueville, *Letters, 152–153.*

39. Tocqueville, *DA,* 743.
40. Tocqueville, *Letters,* 376.
41. Tocqueville, *DA,* 743.
42. Ibid., 759–760.
43. Tocqueville, *Letters,* 143.
44. Tocqueville, *DA,* 759, 881, 743. This characterization would seem to capture France's present for Tocqueville but only one possible future for America.
45. Alexis de Tocqueville, *Recollections: The French Revolution of 1848,* ed. J.P. Mayer and A.P. Kerr, trans. George Lawrence (New Brunswick: Transaction Publishers, 2005), 4.
46. Tocqueville, *DA,* 881, 617.
47. Ibid., 621.
48. Tocqueville, *Letters,* 287.
49. Tocqueville, *OR I,* 78.
50. Ibid., 178, 376.
51. Thus, in Tocqueville's view, "anarchy is not the principle evil that democratic centuries must dread, but rather the least of those evils." Tocqueville, *DA,* 622, 787.
52. Ibid., 6–7.
53. Ibid., 759.
54. Tocqueville writes that society even in his own time was "tranquil not because it [was] conscious of its strength and well-being but, on the contrary, because it believe[d] itself to be weak and infirm." Ibid., 11.
55. Ibid., 759.
56. Tocqueville, *OR I,* 451.
57. Tocqueville, *OR II,* 68. Tocqueville also noted that "everywhere it communicated the clarity, the intensity, the freshness of the emotions of youth," even as it displayed the reckless inexperience that is the "chief flaw . . . of youth." Tocqueville, *OR I,* 208, 244.
58. Tocqueville, *Letters,* 303.
59. Tocqueville, *OR I,* 208.
60. Tocqueville, *Letters,* 303. In a letter to J.S. Mill, Tocqueville offers some advice he himself does not always follow: "One cannot let a nation that is democratically constituted like ours . . . take up easily the habit of sacrificing what it believes to be its grandeur to its repose, great matters to petty ones; it is not healthy to allow such a nation to believe that its place in the

world is smaller, that it is fallen from the level on which its ancestors put it." Ibid., 151.

61. Tocqueville, *DA*, 9.

62. Tocqueville, *OR I*, 377 (emphasis added).

63. Tocqueville, *DA*, 819.

64. Ibid., 818.

65. For an insightful analysis of the theme of pride as a bulwark against democratic despotism, particularly as it arises in his discussion of the three races in America, see Harvey C. Mansfield and Delba Winthrop, "Editor's Introduction," in Alexis de Tocqueville, *Democracy in America*, trans. Mansfield and Winthrop (Chicago: University of Chicago Press, 2000), lvii–lxiii.

66. Tocqueville, *DA*, 744

67. Seymour Drescher, *Tocqueville and England* (Cambridge, Mass.: Harvard University Press, 1964), 126. Still the finest analysis of Tocqueville's critique of bourgeois politics and society is Roger Boesche's *The Strange Liberalism of Alexis de Tocqueville* (Ithaca, N.Y.: Cornell University Press, 1987). Perhaps the central reason Tocqueville continues to persuade, fascinate, and confuse, as Boesche explains, is the mix of conservative, Romantic, republican, and democratic elements of Tocqueville's critique of middle-class politics and society even as he remains firmly within the liberal tradition, defending liberal principles of representation and "negative" rights and liberties. See also Boesche, "The Strange Liberalism of Alexis de Tocqueville" and "Hedonism and Nihilism: The Predictions of Tocqueville and Nietzsche," in *Tocqueville's Road Map: Methodology, Liberalism, Revolution, and Despotism* (Lanham, Md.: Lexington Books, 2006).

68. Tocqueville, *Letters*, 118, 153; Tocqueville, *Recollections*, 4.

69. Over the past decade, perhaps the finest popular representation of the dread surrounding the decline into an emasculated softness and smallness (the seeking of childish pleasures, the infirmity of old age, feminine weakness and dependence) has been the television show *The Sopranos*.

70. Of course, this was no different in Tocqueville's time, when the inveterately bourgeois reign of Guizot was assaulted in similar terms by Right and Left alike.

71. Tocqueville, *DA*, 818.

72. As we shall see when we take up Lefort's critique of Tocqueville, there are elements of Tocqueville's own theory that suggest tutelary power would have to take an even more abstract and "disembodied" form than that of a centralized state (or even "public opinion," which can be represented via polling). Only something as impersonal as "market forces" would be sufficiently in accord with the outward signs of democratic freedom and equality to be embraced.

73. When I have had occasion to teach Tocqueville, it is quite evident that his critique of democratic softness and smallness is immediately familiar and utterly compelling to most students.

74. Tocqueville, *DA*, 830.

75. François Furet and Françoise Mélonio, "Introduction," in *OR I*, 37.

76. Tocqueville, *DA*, 525, 515.

77. The following characterization of what Tocqueville here terms "commercial society" and elsewhere terms "literary society" is typical of his thought: "In the very heart of the commercial city par excellence, Hamburg, among the very people who participated in commerce, . . . intellectual activity and [the] taste for high subjects of conversation, [and the] passion for ideas reigned." Tocqueville, *OR II*, 170.

78. Many interpreters of Tocqueville emphasize the distinctions he draws between democracy in America and democracy in France to distinguish between the two key concepts he associates with democracy: equality and revolution. Embodied in these disparate nations, it comes to seem as if Tocqueville is talking about two different social states, even as he calls both democratic. Jean-Claude Lamberti, for instance, writes that Tocqueville formulates "a revolutionary social state" between those of aristocracy and democracy, that America is the model of democratic equality and France of democratic revolution, and that "Tocqueville's mind was always occupied by one thought [the defense of political liberty against administrative centralization] whose development we can follow through his constant need to contrast democracy with revolution, democratic culture with revolutionary culture." Lamberti, *Tocqueville and the Two Democracies*, trans. Arthur Goldhammer (Cambridge, Mass.: Harvard University Press, 1989), 51, 196, 232. See also Cheryl Welch, *De Tocqueville* (Oxford: Oxford University Press, 2001), 106–112. My interpretation emphasizes the continuity of equality and revolution—of the absence of hierarchy and the destruction of hierarchy—in Tocqueville's thought as the original end of the democratic social state. While there are surely distinctions to be drawn, they are most often ones of degree rather than of type; within the egalitarian imaginary, the revolutionary spirit takes shape as restless energy and agitation, as the revolutionary disease of chronic rebelliousness, as the totalizing assault upon regime form, and all points in between. And while the historical paths to democratization diverged for America and France—departing to the new versus confronting the old, leaving behind versus tearing down—the ideas the nations pursued were analogous. In this interpretation, we can comprehend Tocqueville's multifaceted view, wherein equality and revolution alike promise and imperil political liberty. Tocqueville envisions not two democracies but the dualism of democracy.

79. Tocqueville, *DA*, 4–5, 34, 54, 748.

80. Ibid., 294.

81. Ibid., 37 (emphasis in original).

82. Ibid.

83. Ibid., 39.

84. Tocqueville, *OR I*, 101.

85. Ibid., 99 (emphasis added).

86. Ibid. Tocqueville describes the product of the Constitution of the United States in similar terms: "The Union is an ideal nation that exists only in the mind, as it were, and whose extent and limits can be discovered only through an effort of intelligence." Tocqueville, *DA*, 186.

87. Tocqueville, *OR I*, 208.

88. In a wonderful note, Tocqueville writes of how Plymouth Rock "has become an object of veneration in the United States": "I have seen fragments of it preserved in any number of cities of the Union. Does this not clearly prove that man's power and grandeur lie entirely within his soul? A rock is touched momentarily by the feet of a few wretched individuals, and that rock becomes famous. It draws the attention of a great people. Pieces of it are venerated, and its dust is distributed far and wide. What has become of the doorstep of many a palace? Does anyone care?" Tocqueville, *DA*, 38–39.

89. Ibid., 199 (emphasis added).

90. Ibid., 520.

91. Ibid., 561 (emphasis added).

92. Tocqueville, *OR II*, 162.

93. Tocqueville, *OR I*, 100.

94. Ibid., 196, 200–201. The revolutionary pilgrimage Tocqueville describes in the French context of 1789 seems to be reoccurring in the so-called Arab Spring popular uprisings of 2011, as recounted by *New York Times* op-ed columnist Roger Cohen: "J. Scott Carpenter, 46, who once held a senior Middle East job at the State Department . . . (notes that) 'In the Middle East you've had all these young people living free online and then coming to their stupid realities and seeing that the politics were not compatible with their online lives. And the two can only merge in one direction.'" Roger Cohen, "Positive Disruption," *The New York Times.com*, June 23, 2011, www.nytimes.com. Between worlds that see themselves as in revolution there are striking continuities.

95. Tocqueville, *OR I*, 195–200; Tocqueville, *OR II*, 30.

96. Tocqueville, *OR I*, 198.

97. Ibid., 195, 201–202. Tocqueville writes of how around the time of the Revolution the "administration of Roads and Bridges was . . . taken with the geometrical attractions of the straight line . . . ; it took great care to avoid following existing roads, because they seemed a bit curved, and rather than make a slight detour, they cut across a thousand inheritances." Ibid., 231.

98. Tocqueville, *OR II*, 213.
99. Ibid., 373.
100. Wolin writes that "ambitions were aroused because modern revolutions appeared to have transcended the received categories of political thinking about revolutions." Where once "the conception was of a closed cycle" in which "the system would return to its starting point and begin again," modern revolutions "seemed to have a greater potential for totally transforming society as well as political institutions and hence of permanently breaking the cycle" with "no predetermined end." The modern "revolution that was in the making, and that would soon spread to other domains of thought and activity," was in the "concept of revolution itself." Wolin, *TBTW*, 46–47.
101. Tocqueville, *OR II*, 213.
102. Tocqueville, *OR I*, 242.
103. Tocqueville, *DA*, 702.
104. Ibid., 495–499, 329. Tocqueville writes, "The Americans carry to excess a tendency that can, I think, be found in all democratic peoples." Ibid., 522–523.
105. Ibid., 463, 470, 466–467.
106. Moreover, administrative centralization in France proved a violent teacher, depriving the French of any chastening practical experience and habituating them to the thought of changing everything uniformly from the top down.
107. In the next chapter I argue that the schism of society and nature—or, better, of conventional society and natural society—comes to replace that of this world and the next.
108. Tocqueville, *DA*, 557, 554.
109. Ibid., 555.
110. Ibid., 556–558 (emphasis added).
111. Ibid., 558–560 (emphasis added).
112. Ibid., 559–560.
113. Ibid., 562.
114. This, of course, is one reason why Tocqueville suggests that religion not get involved in politics.
115. Tocqueville, *DA*, 702, 562, 522, 551–552.
116. Ibid., 536.
117. Tocqueville's most famous critique along these lines takes up the democratic receptiveness to pantheism: "As conditions become more equal and each man in particular becomes more similar to all others, weaker and smaller, . . . one forgets individuals and thinks only of the species. . . . In such times, the human mind . . . invariably aspires to associate a multitude of consequences with a single cause. The mind becomes obsessed with unity and looks for it everywhere. . . . Upon discovering in the world

but one creation and one Creator, it finds even that primary division of things troubling and deliberately seeks to enlarge and simplify its thought by subsuming God and the universe in a single whole. [It] . . . holds that everything in the world, material and immaterial, visible or invisible, is merely part of one immense being." Such a system "destroys human individuality. . . . All who are still enamored of man's true greatness should join forces to combat it." Ibid., 512–513.

118. Tocqueville writes, "The idea of an unrivaled central power that leads all citizens by itself is one that [democratic peoples] conceive as it were without thinking. In politics, moreover, as in philosophy and religion, the intelligence of democratic peoples delights in simple and general ideas. It finds complicated systems repellent and likes to imagine a great nation whose citizens all conform to a single model and are directed by a single power . . . [and] uniform legislation." Thus, even while "Americans believe that the social power in each state should emanate directly from the people, . . . once that power is constituted, they do not, as it were, imagine it as having limits." Tocqueville concludes that "they are prepared to grant that it has the right to do anything" and that "the rights of the individual" amount to "nothing." Ibid., 789–790.

119. Ibid., 499–500.

120. Ibid., 552.

121. Tocqueville writes, "An abstract word is like a box with a false bottom: you can put in any ideas you please and take them out again without anyone being the wiser." Along these lines, Tocqueville explains the passion for generalization as a practical response to the disorienting flux and bustle of life in democracy, as well as to the impracticality of the Cartesian attempt to independently judge everything for oneself. Too busy to stop and think and wracked by doubt, democratic peoples corner-cut their way out of complications and confusion by use of general ideas and terms. Ibid., 497–498.

122. Ibid., 569.

123. Ibid., 569–570.

124. Ibid., 571–572.

125. Ibid., 570–571.

126. For the history of and reflection upon the implications of this finding, see Jonathan Marks, *What it Means to be 98% Chimpanzee: Apes, People, and their Genes* (Berkeley: University of California Press, 2002). The cultural fallout from this factoid, both decrying it and celebrating it (to the point of T-shirts and coffee mugs being made in its honor), deserves a study of its own.

127. Tocqueville, *DA*, 571–572.

128. Ibid., 834.

129. Ibid., 570–572, 528, 552.

130. Ibid., 496.
131. Tocqueville notes that even the "most profound geniuses of Greece and Rome . . . never hit upon the very general yet at the same time very simple idea that all men are alike and that each is born with an equal right to liberty." Ibid., 496.
132. Ibid.
133. Ibid. On Tocqueville's association of the democratic and Christian abstractions, see Furet and Mélonio, "Introduction," 12–13.
134. Tocqueville, *DA*, 627, 759.
135. Michael J. Sandel, *The Case Against Perfection: Ethics in the Age of Genetic Engineering* (Cambridge, Mass.: Harvard University Press, 2007), 99.
136. Quoted in Sandel, *The Case Against Perfection*, 100.
137. Julian Savulescu, "New Breeds of Humans: The Moral Obligation to Enhance," *Ethics, Law and Moral Philosophy of Reproductive Biomedicine* 1, no. 1 (2005): 37.
138. Ibid.
139. Savulescu writes that "impulse control," "shyness," "memory," "patience, empathy, a sense of humor, optimism and just having a sunny temperament can profoundly affect our lives." He continues, "All of these characteristics will have some biological and psychological basis capable of manipulation with technology." Savulescu, "New Breeds of Humans," 37–39.
140. Sandel, *The Case Against Perfection*, 87.
141. For example, in debates surrounding the moral basis of our legal constructs, the question has arisen whether, if the physical processes of the brain determine our "behavior," we can be considered responsible for our actions at all. See Michael S. Gazzaniga and Megan S. Steven, "Neuroscience and the Law," *Scientific American Mind*, April 15, 2005: 43–49.
142. This pattern has played itself out in a remarkable number of conversations I have had with my students. Many seem no less than enchanted by the concept of evolution as a catchall explanatory determinant of (and norm for) most worldly phenomena. And many of these very same students readily suggest that modern technologies (the Internet, in particular) allow them to live increasingly in a literary society of their own invention, as the artists and architects of reality.
143. For example, the extent to which Barack Obama and Hillary Clinton embodied these extreme types in the 2008 Democratic presidential primaries is striking.
144. As I shall argue regarding Sheldon Wolin's theory of "fugitive democracy," today it seems that the marriage of principle and practice can be consummated only in the necessarily fleeting moment of revolution (thus the passion—evident everywhere from our commercials to our political commentary—to exaggerate even the most trivial changes as no less than epochal innovations).

145. Tocqueville, *OR I*, 222.
146. Tocqueville, *Letters*, 296.

## 2. Civilization without the Discontents

1. C. Fred Alford, *Rethinking Freedom: Why Freedom Has Lost Its Meaning and What Can Be Done to Save It* (New York: Palgrave Macmillan, 2005), 1–2, 16, 50.
2. Ibid., 7, 4, 31 (emphasis added).
3. Ibid., 19–20.
4. Ibid., 20.
5. Ibid., 4, 50, 14. Recall the emphasis on not having to compromise in the definitional statements of what it means to be soul mates.
6. Ibid., 16, 29, 12.
7. Ibid., 25, 34, 9, 27.
8. Tocqueville, *DA*, 584.
9. This is, in effect, Seymour Drescher's argument in his classic *Dilemmas of Democracy: Tocqueville and Modernization* (Pittsburgh: University of Pittsburgh Press, 1968). For Drescher, industrialization rather than democratization is the defining phenomenon of modernity. In turn, Tocqueville's vision of the egalitarian eradication of socioeconomic classes is "engulfed in a sea of social differentiation" that is produced largely by the division of labor and that results in a "functional elite" and a "functional hierarchy"—"a new aristocratic system." He writes, "Under the impact of industrialization, wealth was not radically redistributed, and social positions as defined by birth, religion, or occupation seemed a more empirically significant fact than the rhetoric of equality and of social mobility." Drescher, *Dilemmas of Democracy*, 255–279. One wonders, though, what we are to make of the empirical fact that, regardless of one's birth, religion, or occupation, most everyone today proudly declares their membership in the middle class, whether upper middle, lower middle, or some variation thereof. Perhaps this does suggest a certain democratization of class differences.
10. Alford, *Rethinking Freedom*, 1.
11. Like Drescher, Mark Reinhardt conflates inequality and hierarchy in an often-heard critique of Tocqueville: "While he worried about despotism born of equality, the despotisms of the present day are fundamentally inegalitarian. We work, play, go to school, and carry out the business of living amidst complex hierarchies of prestige, privilege, and power." Reinhardt, *The Art of Being Free: Taking Liberties with Tocqueville, Marx, and Arendt* (Ithaca, N.Y.: Cornell University Press, 1997), 51. Françoise Mélonio, conversely, captures Tocqueville's position well: "That in democracies there is inherited money and intelligence, Tocqueville did not doubt.

What is astonishing is the indignation their existence incites in us. . . . As a result, the economy is only a limited structure compared with the decisive importance of social representations. What held Tocqueville's interest was not so much equality in action as equality as a norm of social existence." Mélonio, *Tocqueville and the French,* trans. Beth G. Raps (Charlottesville: University Press of Virginia, 1998), 72. To illustrate this point to my students, I ask them to consider their likely response if the richest or most powerful person in the world (Bill Gates, say, or the president) came into the room and gave them an order (say, to shine his shoes).

12. The exception to the rule of equality in America was, of course, the utterly hierarchical relationship between master and slave. Tocqueville writes, "No amount of money can buy the Negro the right to sit next to his former master in a theater." Tocqueville, *DA,* 396.

13. "Most people," Alford writes, "are would-be stoics, desperate to preserve an inner realm of freedom from the intrusions of the world. At the same time, most people believe they are too weak to be true stoics, and so must pursue power and money, lest they end up with no freedom at all." Alford, *Rethinking Freedom,* 14.

14. Along these lines, Alford argues that there is not only a borderline and narcissistic quality to freedom today but also an element of paranoia. Ibid., 6–7.

15. Daniel Plainview, of Paul Thomas Anderson's 2007 film *There Will Be Blood,* is a spectacular representation of this way of being in society. Represented in the dual meaning of the title, a few are let in as family while everyone outside is encountered as a competitor.

16. Tocqueville, *DA,* 369–370.

17. Ibid., 367–368.

18. Ibid.

19. Alford comments that "perhaps the best analog in political theory to what most people practice" in terms of freedom "is what . . . [Tocqueville] called 'individualism.' " Alford, *Rethinking Freedom,* 45.

20. Tocqueville, *DA,* 586, 589.

21. Ibid., 72, 458, 63, 522, 585–586, 484. As Pierre Manent writes, "What tradition thought was the result of a rigorous exercise of civic and moral virtues—with the aid of Fortune or the grace of God—namely, to live free, democracy holds as the minimal requisite of humanity." Manent, *Tocqueville and the Nature of Democracy,* trans. John Waggoner (Rowman and Littlefield Publishers, 1996), 125.

22. Tocqueville, *DA,* 574.

23. Ibid., 667, 793.

24. Ibid., 574, 362.

25. Ibid., 819, 590–596 (emphasis added). In a contrasting point of view, Tocqueville writes, "Men in aristocratic societies . . . do not need to join together in order to act, because they are firmly bound to one another.

Each wealthy and powerful citizen is like the head of a permanent, com-
pulsory association comprising all who are dependent on him and whose
cooperation he enjoins in furtherance of his designs." Ibid., 595.

26. Ibid., 750–751, 731, 532, 326.

27. Ibid., 646, 410 (emphasis added). Tocqueville writes, "The American
    navigator sets sail from Boston to buy tea in China. . . . During a crossing
    of eight to ten months, he has drunk brackish water and lived on salted
    meat. He has battled constantly with the sea, with disease, and with bore-
    dom. But upon his return, he can sell his tea for a penny a pound less
    than the English merchant: his goal has been achieved." Ibid. 464–465.

28. Ibid., 681, 241, 548.

29. Interestingly, everything from bookstores to videogames goes by the
    name of "Pandemonium" today.

30. Tocqueville, DA, 466.

31. Tocqueville, Letters, 40; Tocqueville, DA, 548.

32. Tocqueville, DA, 432.

33. Of the conflict over the Second Bank of the United States, Tocqueville
    writes that people did not understand the complex issues at stake but
    opposed the institution on the grounds of its permanence: "In a society
    where everything is in flux, this immovable object is offensive to their
    eyes, and they want to see if they can oblige it to change along with ev-
    erything else." Ibid., 203.

34. Tocqueville, OR I, 323–324.

35. Tocqueville, DA, 740, 717, 736, 794, 523 (emphasis added).

36. At times, Tocqueville attributes this grabbing expansiveness to democratic
    man's self-conscious finitude: "The man who has given his heart entirely
    to the quest for the goods of this world is always in a hurry, for he has but
    a limited time to find, possess, and enjoy them. The memory of life's brev-
    ity constantly spurs him on. . . . This thought . . . keeps his soul in a state
    of constant trepidation that impels him again and again to change plans
    and places." Ibid., 625–626. In this account, democratic man's restlessness
    is less an expression of his freedom (as I argue) than of the conjunction of
    his materialism and mortality.

37. Ibid., 278.

38. Ibid., 640, 627.

39. Ibid., 623–624.

40. Ibid., 324–326.

41. Ibid., 58, 623, 229, 435, 356, 384 (emphasis added). Here again, compari-
    son to Tocqueville's representation of the savage's "habits of the wandering
    life" and the "solitude in which [the savage] lived free" proves illuminat-
    ing. Tocqueville writes that "in order to civilize a people, one must first
    persuade them to settle in one place" and cultivate the soil, but men "who
    have tasted the idle and adventurous life of the hunter feel an almost
    insurmountable distaste for the constant, disciplined labor required by

agriculture." Tocqueville continues, "The Indians of North America view labor as not only an evil but also a disgrace, and their *pride* combats civilization almost as obstinately as their indolence. . . . He likens the farmer to the ox hitched to its plow and in our arts sees nothing but the labors of slaves." Ibid., 378.

42. In Hobbes's Western, security is brought about only by the intervention of the vigilante lawman, who seems less a human than a sovereign force of nature. In Rousseau's Western, isolation is ended without inequality and unfreedom only in the unmediated union of the general will.

43. Tocqueville, *DA*, 277–281, 466–467, 103.

44. Ibid., 524, 751–752.

45. Ibid., 601, 830. We will revisit the idea that democratic peoples love the power but hate the power holder when we turn to the democratic theory of Claude Lefort.

46. Ibid., 736.

47. One of the decisive blows against the Old Regime came when the Catholic clergy was deprived of its land. Above all, Tocqueville notes, "what contributed to giving the clergy the idea, needs, feelings, often the passions of the citizen, was landownership." Cut that link, and the clergyman "no longer belongs to any place in particular." Tocqueville continues, "In the place where chance has dictated his birth, he lives as a stranger in the midst of a civil society almost none of whose interests can directly concern him." Tocqueville, *OR I*, 174.

48. Ibid., 176

49. Tocqueville, *OR II*, 425.

50. Tocqueville, *OR I*, 176–178. Tocqueville writes that without a "place in society where they could be seen" or a "voice capable of making itself heard," the "lower classes alone . . . found themselves almost powerless to resist oppression other than by violence." Ibid., 178.

51. Ibid., 179.

52. Tocqueville, *DA*, 600.

53. A Google search of the phrase on January 3, 2011, raised the prospect that health-care reform had been crammed down our throats, and that the "Dream Act" immigration reform bill is next. Apparently, political power has forced upon us everything from the Iraq War, tax cuts, Wall Street reform, socialism, and religion to a health-conscious diet, energy efficient light bulbs, and even cheese (by the FDA, to prop up the struggling dairy industry).

54. Tocqueville, *DA*, 586.

55. Ibid., 710, 558.

56. Ibid., 474–475, 805. "Accordingly," Tocqueville continues, "one finds less difference between Europeans and their descendants in the New World today, despite the ocean that divides them, than between certain thirteenth-century towns separated by nothing more than a river." Ibid., 475.

57. Ibid., 660–661, 658.
58. Ibid., 549, 558.
59. Ibid., 556.
60. Ibid., 832, 475, 818.
61. Ibid., 585 (emphasis added).
62. Ibid., 685–687. In his description of the Internet, Thomas Friedman describes the fatherless family: "Everyone is connected but no one is in control." Quoted in Fareed Zakaria, *The Future of Freedom: Illiberal Democracy at Home and Abroad* (New York: W.W. Norton, 2003), 15.
63. Tocqueville, *DA*, 688, 690.
64. Ibid., 688–689 (emphasis added).
65. Ibid., 688.
66. Tocqueville hardly develops the very interesting idea of collective individualism, and when he does mention it, he describes it as a transient phenomenon limited to the caste-bound Old Regime—a stepping stone between aristocratic solidarity and democratic individualism: "Our ancestors lacked the word 'individualism,' which we have created for our own use, because in their era there were, in fact, no individuals who did not belong to a group and who could consider themselves absolutely alone; but each one of the thousand little groups of which French society was composed thought only of itself. This was, if one can use the word thus, a kind of collective individualism, which prepared people for the real individualism with which we are familiar." Tocqueville, *OR I*, 162–163.
67. In explaining why the relatively new American government framed by the Constitution will have difficulty enduring, Tocqueville argues that the states convey a sense of collective individualism that can do without politics, while the federal government is merely conventional: "[The] sovereignty of the Union is a work of art. The sovereignty of the states is natural; it exists by itself, without effort." In the former, "everything is conventional and artificial" and a matter of "legal fictions"; the latter is "like . . . a family." Tocqueville, *DA*, 187–189.
68. For a wonderful exploration of the place of politeness in modern times, see André Comte-Sponville, *A Small Treatise on the Great Virtues: The Uses of Philosophy in Everyday Life*, trans. Catherine Temerson (New York: Metropolitan Books, 2001), chap. 1.
69. Tocqueville, *DA*, 691.
70. Tocqueville, *OR II*, 29.
71. George Kateb describes this devaluation of the conventional well as it relates to the possibility of moments of self-reliance: "These are occasions of independent thinking, newly innocent perception, self-expressive activity, unexpected creativity—occurrences possible in any individual's life. Release from convention is the key: all the conventions of democracy exist for such release: they sponsor their own abandonment, fleeting and

incomplete as such abandonment must (and should) be." Kateb goes on to explain how the aspiration to be released from convention leads to "a general disparagement and depreciation of the whole realm of politics" in the thought of Emerson, Thoreau, and to a degree Whitman. Kateb, *The Inner Ocean: Individualism and Democratic Culture* (Ithaca, N.Y.: Cornell University Press, 1992), 33, 100.

72. Tocqueville, *DA*, 690. Democracy, as Pierre Manent writes, "never ceases establishing the state of nature in order to continually abandon it." Manent continues, "Incessantly, human relations, which in a previous phase of the democratic process appeared given and obvious, now reveal themselves as founded on a principle other than the free association of equal individuals. It is thus necessary to dissolve those relations in order to reconstitute them on a new basis. So it goes indefinitely. Moreover, free associations themselves, with time, tend to be unfaithful to their democratic foundation. It will thus be necessary to dissolve them also, then reconstitute them." Manent, *Tocqueville and the Nature of Democracy*, 27. Here we have the whole of democracy's revolution movement, indeterminate yet circular, wherein the present world is perennially debased.

73. Tocqueville, *DA*, 661–664, 712–714. "Could it be," Harvey C. Mansfield Jr., asks us to consider, that even in democratic times "the formal is, if not the whole of reality, a part—even the greatest part?" Could it be "that a form can be a cause of behavior, not always a mask behind which the real action takes place"? When "people 'dress up' or otherwise behave formally they conceal certain things" and in so doing reveal other things, things they judge worth being seen. He writes, "They cover over defects they are normally content to let appear; they try to look their best." Mansfield, *America's Constitutional Soul* (Baltimore: Johns Hopkins University Press, 1991), 3, 9.

74. Tocqueville, *DA*, 725–733, 737.

75. It is primarily along these lines that Tocqueville famously argues for the value of lawyers and lawyerly ways to democracy: "Men who make a special study of the law take from their work certain habits of order, a taste for forms, and a sort of instinctive love of regular sequences in ideas that naturally foster in them a strong opposition to the revolutionary spirit and the unthinking passions of democracy." Ibid., 506, 826, 303.

76. Ibid., 483–484, 522, 497, 551, 542.

77. Ibid., 506.

78. Joshua Mitchell reveals precisely this connection in Tocqueville's thought between democracy and fundamentalism. While "the 'fable of liberalism' suggests that religion will be an archaism in the democratic age," Tocqueville's analysis of "the democratic modes of religious experience" demonstrates "the emergence of an impulse toward fundamentalism, which [Mitchell suggests] is a necessary development in the democratic age; the

increasing claims of unmediated personal religious experience and the decreased importance of religious formalities." Mitchell, "Tocqueville on Democratic Religious Experience," in *The Cambridge Companion to Tocqueville,* ed. Cheryl B. Welch (Cambridge: Cambridge University Press, 2006), 276–277.

79. We see a similar duality in America's civil religion, where the Constitution is either venerated as the quasi-sacred work of quasi-divine founders—the documentation of eternal rights and truths—or dismissed as the artifact of a particular time and place, foisted upon a docile people by the wealthy, white, dead hand of the past.

80. Tocqueville notes, "The French Revolution is founded on general ideas like a religion, which is what made it possible for it to spread like one." In comparison, the English Revolution did not have the same import or effect because, "even though it ended up in the same dogmas, [it] surrounded them with a particular form." Tocqueville, *OR I,* 325–327.

81. Tocqueville, *DA,* 342–343.

82. Tocqueville, *Letters,* 81–82.

83. Ibid., 181–182.

84. Tocqueville, *DA,* 598–599, 824. Tocqueville writes, "Nowhere are associations more necessary to prevent either the despotism of the parties or the arbitrariness of the prince than in countries whose social state is democratic. In aristocratic nations, secondary bodies constitute natural associations that halt the abuse of power. In countries where such associations do not exist, unless private individuals can artificially and temporarily create something that resembles them, I see no impediment to any form of tyranny." Ibid., 219.

85. Dana Villa analyzes this well in his outstanding contribution to *The Cambridge Companion to Tocqueville.* As opposed to "the currently popular view that 'civil' associations are the seed-bed of, or a substitute for, political association and engaged citizenship," and to the "longstanding tendency of liberals and conservatives alike to view commercial associations and the markets as the real counter-balance to the state, and religious association as the most important counter-weight to individualism," Tocqueville is interested, "first and foremost, in the political uses and effects of associational life." Villa continues, "Associations serve not only to decentralize administrative and political power, they also enable ordinary citizens to attain a degree of positive political freedom it would otherwise be hard to imagine." Fostering "the habit of joint action amongst the equal, isolated, and privatized individuals of modern democratic societies," political associations are the "primary means by which modern fragmentation and powerlessness are overcome." Villa, "Tocqueville and Civil Society," in *The Cambridge Companion to Tocqueville,* ed. Cheryl B. Welch (Cambridge: Cambridge University Press, 2006), 225, 231–232.

86. It is not sufficient to say that Tocqueville "construed the Ancients' liberty as guaranteeing that of the Moderns." Mélonio, *Tocqueville and the French,* 137. Rather, the political liberty he proselytized was very much an end in itself, as well as a means.
87. Tocqueville, *DA,* 608.
88. Ibid., 597.
89. Tocqueville writes, "The same aristocratic institutions that had made creatures of the same species so different nevertheless bound them together with a very tight political bond." This bond was born not of "natural interest" and "natural right" and "genuine sympathy" but of "duty and honor," "mutual obligation" and "political right." Ibid., 656.
90. Ibid., 604, 590. "The abiding concern of Tocqueville's thinking," Wolin writes, "was the revival of the political." As in his own writings, Wolin's theorization of Tocqueville's account of the political is elusive: What is the proper role of material interests in substantiating the political, and in what proportion to nobler ideas and ends? What is the relationship within the political between mundane participation and revolutionary action? What compromises are to be made between equality and particularity, the conservation of political culture and the exercise of progressive power, localism, and rights? At times it seems as if Wolin proceeds to either assimilate Tocqueville to current standards of the democratic political or to chastise Tocqueville according to those standards, despite Tocqueville's purported significance as a figure between past and present who exposes modern momentums to a rhetoric of the lost and forgotten. Yet, perhaps beyond any other interpreter of Tocqueville, Wolin perfectly captures the continuing centrality for Tocqueville of the place of politics in a fully human life. Against the prioritization of the liberty of the moderns, Tocqueville celebrates the American cultivation of "a politics that was not restricted to a narrow, bounded domain, but was a way of life": "Politics vitalized the whole society, transmitting its energies to civil society rather than reflecting the impulses coursing through civil society." Regarding the New England township, for instance, Tocqueville "seizes the possibility that within modernity itself, and despite the powerful attractions toward private concerns and pleasures, politics might nonetheless be restored as the defining center of social life and as essential to the development of human capacities." Wolin, *TBTW,* 5, 208, 277.
91. Tocqueville, *DA,* 593.
92. Tocqueville, *OR I,* 88. In America, for instance, "the electoral system permanently brings together a multitude of citizens who would otherwise remain strangers." In this way, "Americans have used liberty to combat the individualism born of equality, and they have defeated it." Tocqueville, *DA,* 591.
93. Tocqueville, *OR I,* 155.
94. Ibid., 163.

95. Tocqueville, *DA*, 604. In a fascinating study, Seymour Drescher demonstrates that over time Tocqueville came to see England rather than America as the land from which to draw lessons to educate democracy because quasi-aristocratic England was better able to sustain decentralization, political liberty, and political activity. Drescher, *Tocqueville and England* (Cambridge, Mass.: Harvard University Press, 1964).

96. If America was born into equality without having to become so, modern France was born depoliticized without having to become so. As François Furet writes, for Tocqueville (particularly by the writing of the *Old Regime*) "civil society is less a cause than a result of the political and moral environment," and absent the sustained and generalized practice of politics, French civil society was "split up into increasingly rival groups composed of increasingly similar individuals." Furet, *Interpreting the French Revolution* (Cambridge: Cambridge University Press, 1981), 148–149.

97. For a perfect example of the rhetoric of core beliefs and conviction, visit www.teaparty.org/about.php, which includes a long list of the Tea Party's "non-negotiable core beliefs." Tea Party "founder" Dale Robertson— described as "a man of courage and conviction, a rare commodity in today's topsy-turvy world"—was "frustrated by 'Politics As Usual' " and driven to risk all and leave home (literally) to "create a new voice, a voice that echoed from the pages of history." This "movement, born from obscurity, without funding, without planning, a spontaneous force," has united like-minded "patriots" from around the country and risen to shake the pillars of the party establishment, spawning a "new hope" that the American people might take their nation back.

## 3. The Regime of Revolution

1. Eric Foner, *The Story of American Freedom* (New York: W.W. Norton, 1998), 127, 157.

2. Ibid., 120–122 (emphasis added).

3. William Graham Sumner, quoted in James P. Young, *Reconsidering American Liberalism* (Boulder, Colo.: Westview Press, 1996), 131.

4. John M. Blum, quoted in Robert A. Dahl, *A Preface to Economic Democracy* (Berkeley: University of California Press, 1985), 72.

5. Bruce Ackerman, *We the People: Foundations* (Cambridge, Mass.: Belknap Press at Harvard University Press, 1991), 63.

6. Ibid., 401 (emphasis in original).

7. Foner, *The Story of American Freedom*, 122.

8. Cass R. Sunstein, *The Partial Constitution* (Cambridge, Mass.: Harvard University Press, 1993), 61.

9. James P. Young, *Reconsidering American Liberalism* (Boulder, Colo.: Westview Press, 1996), 134.

10. Louis Menand, *The Metaphysical Club* (New York: Farrar, Straus, and Giroux, 2001), 194.
11. We can extend this analogy and say that self-expression, with its concomitants of privacy and recognition, has come to replace liberty of contract in our social-symbolic order. Specifically, expression serves the role of social integrator against the otherwise potentially disintegrating effect of openness, just as contract held together what competition threatened to tear apart.
12. One of the most influential twentieth-century French political philosophers, Lefort is frequently cited as being among the central contemporary theorists of democratic openness. See, for example, Alan Keenan, *Democracy in Question: Democratic Openness in a Time of Political Closure* (Stanford, Calif.: Stanford University Press, 2003), 5–7; Patchen Markell, "The Rule of the People: Arendt, Arche, and Democracy," *American Political Science Review* 100, no. 1 (2006): 3, 5; and Seyla Benhabib, *Democracy and Difference: Contesting the Boundaries of the Political* (Princeton, N.J.: Princeton University Press, 1996), 8. Nevertheless, he is seldom discussed in the English-speaking world. The only book-length study of Lefort to appear in English is Bernard Flynn, *The Philosophy of Claude Lefort: Interpreting the Political* (Evanston, Ill.: Northwestern University Press, 2005). A student of the phenomenologist Maurice Merleau-Ponty, one of Sartre's strongest critics, and among the first intellectuals to break with Marxism in France, Lefort is perhaps best known for his work on Machiavelli. He situates his own study of the democratic regime and the democratic revolution in relation to Leo Strauss and Hannah Arendt and is one of those rare contemporary writers taken seriously by both so-called Straussians and postmodernists/post-structuralists. See Lefort, *DPT*, 2–6.
13. Lefort, *DPT*, 19.
14. My analysis of Lefort thus diverges from the perhaps more conventional view, wherein, as Martin Plot argues, democratic indeterminacy—born of the democratic division between otherworldly and political authority—represents an opening of society onto itself in a higher stage of its self-reflexivity. Plot, "The Democratico-Political Social Flesh and Political Forms in Lefort and Merleau-Ponty," *Theory and Event* 12, no. 4 (2009).
15. Thomas Frank, "A Distant Mirror," *New York Times*, Aug. 15, 2006. Frank continues, "Again Americans thrill to the exploits of the great tycoons."
16. For explanations of this synthesis of neoliberal "globalization" and neoconservative "fundamentalism," see, for example, Wendy Brown, "American Nightmare: Neoliberalism, Neoconservatism, and De-Democratization," *Political Theory* 34, no. 6 (2006): 690–714; William E. Connolly, "The Evangelical-Capitalist Resonance Machine," *Political Theory* 33, no. 6 (2005): 869–886; and Linda Kintz, *Between Jesus and the*

*Market: The Emotions That Matter in Right-Wing America* (Durham, N.C.: Duke University Press, 1997).

17. *The Corporation*, directed by March Achbar and Jennifer Abbott (Vancouver: Big Picture Media Corporation), 2004.

18. Claude Ake, "Dangerous Liaisons: The Interface of Globalization and Democracy," in *Democracy's Victory and Crisis*, ed. Axel Hadenius (Cambridge: Cambridge University Press, 1997), 287.

19. Gordon Bigelow, "Let There Be Markets: The Evangelical Roots of Economics," *Harper's Magazine* 310, no. 1860 (2005): 33.

20. Roger Rosenblatt, "Essay Explores the Origin of 'The Bottom Line,' " *The Newshour*, Public Broadcasting Service, July 10, 2006, transcript available at www.pbs.org/newshour/bb/entertainment/july-dec06/rosenblatt_07–10.html.

21. Wolin, *PP*, 41. Taken as "the 'real' constitution of society," this notion of economy functions as the "first principle of a comprehensive scheme of social hermeneutics" and "an interpretive category of virtually universal application." Wolin writes, "It is used to understand personal life and public life, to make judgments about them, and to define the nature of their problems. It supplies categories of analysis and decision by which public policies are formulated, and it is applied to cultural domains such as education, the arts, and scientific research." Ibid., 41–42, 143, 147.

22. Perhaps nothing illuminates a culture more so than the lessons it teaches its children. In programs and movies from *A Charlie Brown Christmas* and *How the Grinch Stole Christmas* to *Wall-E*, what lesson is more prevalent than that consumerism is dangerous and degrading (even as that lesson pauses for commercial breaks)?

23. George W. Bush, political speech at O'Hare Airport, September 27, 2001, www.washingtonpost.com/wp-srv/nation/specials/attacked/transcripts/bush_092701.html.

24. *Pleasantville*, directed by Gary Ross (Los Angeles: New Line Cinema), 1998.

25. In a single twenty-minute bus ride through Cambridge, Massachusetts, I was told to "Be Authentic" by a cigarette billboard ad and to "Choose Authenticity" by a beer ad, while a coffee proclaimed itself simply "Authentic." How can we make sense of such strangeness—that cigarettes, beer, and coffee offer something desirable that people recognize in terms of authenticity?

26. Thomas L. Friedman, *The Lexus and the Olive Tree: Understanding Globalization* (New York: Anchor Books, 2000), 72–73.

27. Participatory Culture Foundation, http://participatoryculture.org.

28. Markell, "The Rule of the People," 2–3.

29. Friedman, *The Lexus and the Olive Tree*, 45–46.

30. Keenan, *Democracy in Question*, 9–11.

31. Ibid., 9–14, 17.

32. Ibid., 10.
33. Ibid., 10, 19.
34. Stephen K. White offers what Keenan refers to as "democratic openness" as one (or depending on how you look at it, two) of White's four "weak ontological" universals: natality and mortality, along with language and "the articulation of 'sources of the self.' " White, *Sustaining Affirmation: The Strengths of Weak Ontology in Political Theory* (Princeton, N.J.: Princeton University Press, 2000), 9.
35. George Kateb, *The Inner Ocean: Individualism and Democratic Culture* (Ithaca, N.Y.: Cornell University Press, 1992), 156–157. Kateb writes, "If democratic equality owes much (though not everything) to Christian equality, it is probably the case that a break with Christianity was necessary to release the full social power of the ideal of equality." Ibid., 171.
36. William E. Connolly, *The Ethos of Pluralization* (Minneapolis: University of Minnesota Press, 1995), 153–155. As we shall see, Connolly adapts this notion of the "problematization of final markers" from Lefort's description of "the dissolution of the markers of certainty."
37. Wendy Brown, *Politics out of History* (Princeton, N.J.: Princeton University Press, 2001), 93. Here, Brown follows Arendt's notion of "thinking without banisters."
38. Bonnie Honig, "Difference, Dilemmas, and the Politics of Home," in *Democracy and Difference: Contesting the Boundaries of the Political* (Princeton, N.J.: Princeton University Press, 1996), 258. Chantal Mouffe confirms that only with "the critique of essentialism" and the "rationalistic and universalistic perspective" is it "possible to formulate the aims of a radical democratic politics." Only when we resist "the desire to reach a *final destination*" can we "guarantee that the dynamic of the democratic process will be kept *alive*." Mouffe, "Democracy, Power, and the 'Political,' " in *Democracy and Difference*, 245, 255 (emphasis added).
39. Connolly, *The Ethos of Pluralization*, 153–155.
40. Ibid., 153–154.
41. J. Peter Euben, "The Polis, Globalization, and the Politics of Place," in *Democracy and Vision: Sheldon Wolin and the Vicissitudes of the Political*, ed. Aryeh Botwinick and William E. Connolly (Princeton, N.J.: Princeton University Press, 2001), 259.
42. Gregg Easterbrook, "Messing Up Your Daggone Top 10," *Page 2*, May 2, 2006 (emphasis added).
43. Tellingly, in most every work of democratic theory, the tension, paradox, or opposition identified and wrestled with lies within democracy itself (as an inner tension, like that between liberty and equality) rather than between external and irreducible goods (like, for example, the opposition that Aristotle and Tocqueville present between the goods of different regimes or social states, unequal though those goods ultimately might be).

Democracy comes to seem the most "unmixed" regime history has ever witnessed, with no value or good left outside its limits. This gives democracy the quality of seeming at once infinitely capacious and complex, as well as infinitely simple and singular.

44. Lefort, *DPT,* 2–3, 216–217 (emphasis in original).

45. Lefort specifies that "giving form *(mise en forme)*" to the "dimensions of social space . . . implies both giving them meaning *(mise en sens)* and staging them *(mise en scène)*." Ibid., 11–12.

46. Ibid., 223, 216.

47. Ibid., 218, 223–225. Lefort writes, "Some readers will no doubt suspect that my reflections are nourished by psychoanalysis. That is indeed the case. But this connection is meaningful only if one asks oneself at which hearth Freud's thought was lit." Lefort, *PFMS,* 306.

48. Lefort, *DPT,* 225.

49. Thus, for example, in explaining the rise of the totalitarian state in the USSR, Lefort argues that it is certainly necessary to examine the "political events" that surround the formation of this state and the "strategy" of the Bolshevik Party in "taking" power: "But these phenomena . . . do not convey the full meaning of the situation. What we must understand is that [the Bolshevik Party's] force of attraction bore little relation to its real force. What . . . explains its success was its ability to identify with the Revolution as an irreversible movement . . . ; its ability to conceive of itself and to appear as the depository of socialist legitimacy and truth." Lefort, *PFMS,* 281–283.

50. Lefort, *PFMS,* 282. Lefort associates this approach with the one employed by François Furet in his history of the French Revolution. Lefort writes, "If power seems to [Furet] to be the central object of any reflection on politics, it is not because he regards as decisive the relations established between actors whose aim it is to win or keep power. . . . It is because the position and representation of power, and the figuration of its locus are, in his view, constitutive of the social space, of its form and of its stage. In other words, he recognizes that, quite apart from its real functions . . . power has a symbolic status." Thus "socio-economic oppositions are not fully significant at their own level. Social actors do not see their behavior as being strictly determined . . . by material conditions. . . . They decipher their condition and relationships in the context of the common situation imposed upon them by the fact of belonging to the same society, and that situation itself cannot be disassociated from a general system of representation." Lefort, *DPT,* 91.

51. Ibid., 11.

52. Ibid. (emphasis added). This description of the political applies in its entirety only to society after the democratic revolution. In prerevolutionary society, as we shall see, there is no concealment of the principle that gen-

erates the overall configuration of society. Before the revolution there is
visibility, not obscurity.

53. Lefort, *DPT,* 217. As Fred Dallmayr puts its, the distinction here is between
    "polity" and "policy." Dallmayr, *The Other Heidegger* (Ithaca, N.Y.: Cornell
    University Press, 1993), 78.
54. Lefort, *DPT,* 221–222 (emphasis added).
55. Ibid., 213–256.
56. Thus did Job not rebel against God.
57. Lefort continues, "When, therefore, it becomes generalized, opposition
    to power is not directed solely against those who control the decision-
    making and coercive apparatus, who are an obstacle to the destruction of
    certain hierarchies and who defend the interests of dominant groups. It is
    directed against the *reality principle* and the *legitimacy principle* which sup-
    port the established order. It is not political authority which is shaken; it is
    the validity of conditions of existence, and the modes of behavior, beliefs
    and norms which affect every detail of social life." Lefort, *DPT,* 92 (em-
    phasis added).
58. Ibid., 19.
59. Ibid., 251.
60. Ibid., 16–17.
61. Ibid. Lefort writes, "The image of the king's body as a double body, both
    mortal and immortal, individual and collective, was initially underpinned
    by the body of Christ." Lefort, *PFMS,* 302.
62. Lefort, *PFMS,* 303; Lefort, *DPT,* 253. While Lefort himself has apparently
    never written of it, Hobbes's own frontispiece image of the Leviathan
    captures this prerevolutionary mode of the social, wherein the societal
    multitude has an image of itself, united and ordered as one body, under
    the head of the king.
63. Lefort, *PFMS,* 303 (emphasis added).
64. Ibid., 304.
65. Lefort, *DPT,* 178.
66. Lefort, *PFMS,* 306 (emphasis added).
67. Lefort, *DPT,* 17 (emphasis in original).
68. Lefort writes that the democratic idea that "power belongs to no one" is
    not to be confused with the *modern* democratic idea that power "desig-
    nates an empty place. . . . The first formulation in fact implies that actors'
    self-representation, as they deny one another the right to take power. The
    old Greek formula to the effect that power is in the middle . . . still indi-
    cates the presence of a group which has an image of itself, of its space and
    of its bounds. The reference to an empty place, by contrast, *eludes speech*
    insofar as it does not presuppose the existence of a community whose
    members discover themselves to be subjects by the very fact of their being
    members. The formula 'power belongs to no one' can also be translated

into the formula 'power belongs to none of us.' . . . The reference to an empty place, on the other hand, implies a reference to a society without any positive determination, which cannot be represented by the figure of a community." In this crucial sense, then, ancient democracy is closer to Christianity than to modern democracy. Ibid., 225–226 (emphasis added).

69. Lefort, *PFMS*, 304 (emphasis added). Whenever "the people are embodied in power, and whenever an organ is created and claims to have been entrusted with the will of the people, or even simply to be exercising it, it becomes obvious that there is a discrepancy . . . between the institution and the institutor." By the very act of speaking in the name of the people, the "visible shape of the organ" of the people "is threatened with having to reveal that it is particular and not universal." Lefort, *DPT*, 108.

70. Lefort, *PFMS*, 303–305 (emphasis in original).

71. Lefort, *PFMS*, 279 (emphasis added). "Nothing," Lefort writes, "makes the paradox of democracy more palpable than the institution of universal suffrage. It is at the very moment when popular sovereignty is assumed to manifest itself . . . [that a citizen] becomes a mere statistic. Number replaces substance." Lefort, *DPT*, 18–19.

72. Lefort, *DPT*, 41.

73. Ibid.

74. Dallmayr calls this the "absent presence" of the people. Dallmayr, *The Other Heidegger*, 91.

75. Lefort, *DPT*, 41.

76. Ibid., 39, 19 (emphasis in original).

77. Ibid., 168–169, 24, 168.

78. Lefort, *PFMS*, 302.

79. Lefort, *DPT*, 14–16.

80. Ibid.

81. Lefort, *DPT*, 176 (emphasis added).

82. Lefort, *PFMS*, 305.

83. Lefort, *DPT*, 16. Even if democracy cannot be understood as the secularization of Christianity, Lefort argues that it can to some extent be understood as the radicalization of the "historical dimension of the divine," a dimension manifest, for example, in that "the event of [Christ's] birth took place at a specific time and in a specific place." Ibid., 236.

84. Lefort, *PFMS*, 185 (emphasis in original).

85. Lefort, *DPT*, 179 (emphasis added).

86. Ibid., 27.

87. Ibid., 28.

88. Ibid., 43. "Reason of state," Lefort writes, with its "characteristic impersonality," as the guarantor of rights and the public space "threatens to subdue all social activities and relations to its interests, and even to foster the illusion that it is a great individual, and that everyone has to recognize

its will as its own. . . . But it is equally certain that this tendency is held in check because the political competition and social conflict mobilized by the democratic process of contesting the exercise of power led to an indefinite transformation of right . . . and the public space." Ibid., 231.

89. Lefort, *PFMS*, 258. Lefort writes, "The fact that there is no master means that there is a gap, which is deemed to be intangible, between administrative power and political authority." Lefort, *DPT*, 29.

90. Lefort, *DPT*, 15–16. Lefort writes, "Opinion is a substitute for the people, for the current reality of the people is never what it should be. This is not to say that it provides a fully determined representation of the people; in order to exercise its function, it must, like the people, escape all given definitions, for if it were to be defined, it would cease to appear to be a source of meaning and value." Ibid., 110–111.

91. Ibid., 181.

92. Ibid., 18, 179.

93. Ibid., 39.

94. Lefort, *PFMS*, 256–258 (emphasis added).

95. Ibid., 259–260 (emphasis in original).

96. Lefort, *DPT*, 37. Lefort gives as an example of this right to declare rights the militants of Polish Solidarity, who, in not settling for the various concessions offered by the communist government, "expect not only those measures which would satisfy their demands": "They are also giving themselves an unlimited capacity to take initiatives. Their demand is not only for a specific object, but also for the right to make demands." Lefort, *PFMS*, 310.

97. Lefort, *PFMS*, 260, 257 (emphasis added).

98. Ibid., 258.

99. Lefort, *DPT*, 38.

100. Lefort, *PFMS*, 258.

101. Lefort, *DPT*, 32–33 (emphasis added).

102. Ibid., 37–38 (emphasis added).

103. Lefort, *PFMS*, 257.

104. Lefort, *DPT*, 170 (emphasis added).

105. Conversely, the classical notion of time as cyclical can be thought of as circumscribing the flow of history in the order of nature.

106. Tocqueville, *DA*, 676. As Pierre Manent writes, "The human mind left to its own resources only has two possible referents or standards, those of nature and history." Manent, *Modern Liberty and Its Discontents*, ed. and trans. Daniel J. Mahoney and Paul Senton (New York: Rowman and Littlefield, 1998), 61.

107. William E. Connolly, *Pluralism* (Durham, N.C.: Duke University Press, 2005), 83–84.

108. William E. Connolly, "Politics and Vision," in *Democracy and Vision: Sheldon Wolin and the Vicissitudes of the Political*, ed. Aryeh Botwinick and William E. Connolly (Princeton, N.J.: Princeton University Press, 2001), 4.

109. Wolin writes, "That is how modernity incorporates nature: as democratized infinity wherein nothing is privileged." Wolin, *TBTW*, 273.

110. Connolly, *Pluralism*, 83–84.

111. Matt Slick, "What is Open Theism?" Christian Apologetics and Research Ministry, http://carm.org/what-is-open-theism; John Sanders, "What is Openness Theology?" Open Theism Information Site, http://opentheism. info. For a popularization of this movement, see John Sanders, *The God Who Risks: A Theology of Providence* (InterVarsity Press, 1998).

112. Lefort, *PFMS*, 124 (emphasis added).

113. Ibid, 222.

114. Lefort, *DPT*, 16 (emphasis in original).

115. Lefort, *PFMS*, 304.

116. Lefort, *DPT*, 179–180.

117. Ibid., 234, 20.

118. Ibid., 233. Here the experience truly is of the death of God, of a society that recognizes no primal division and so is without any primal unity.

119. Ibid.

120. Ibid., 19–20.

121. Ibid., 233.

122. Ibid., 234 (emphasis in original).

123. This differentiates totalitarianism from previous notions of tyranny, despotism, and absolutism and from the notion of a general accumulation of power (regardless of extent) in the state, a majority, a class, and so forth.

124. Lefort, *PFMS*, 305–306.

125. In this sense, even though totalitarianism and democracy are both born of the revolution, Lefort writes that the notion of "totalitarian democracy" is *"a palpable absurdity"*; totalitarianism "inverts [democracy's] meaning." Lefort, *DPT*, 28 (emphasis in original).

126. Lefort, *PFMS*, 301–302.

127. Ibid., 305.

128. Lefort, *DPT*, 20; *PFMS*, 285.

129. Lefort, *PFMS*, 288.

130. Ibid.

131. Ibid., 211.

132. Lefort, *DPT*, 72 (emphasis added).

133. Lefort, *PFMS*, 291.

134. Ibid., 316 (emphasis added).

135. Lefort, *DPT*, 234–235 (emphasis added).

136. Lefort, *PFMS*, 316.

137. Lefort, *DPT*, 234–235.

138. Lefort, *PFMS*, 242.

139. Pierre Manent, *Tocqueville and the Nature of Democracy*, trans. John Waggoner (Rowman and Littlefield Publishers, 1996), 120.

140. Indeed, what we consume is sold to us in these terms. Most every television show is advertised as the "can't-miss event of the season," while we must see each new movie to "experience the event."

141. The *New Republic*, for instance, carries the story "Game Changer: Why Wikileaks Will Be the Death of Big Business and Big Government," while back in 2010 it made sense to write *Game Change: Obama and the Clintons, McCain and Palin, and the Race of a Lifetime*. The former is from December 27, 2010, by Noam Scheiber, and can be accessed at www.tnr.com/article/politics/80481/game-changer; the latter is by John Heilemann and Mark Halperin (New York: HarperCollins, 2010).

142. Steven Levy, "The Power of iPod," *Newsweek*, October 23, 2006, 72 (emphasis added).

143. A *Newsweek* piece about the "depth and dimensions of pleasure" reads, "For many Americans, sex is not just . . . physical or emotional—it's spiritual." For many, "sexuality is emerging from the realm of guilt and sin and becoming instead a divine blessing and a way to reach new, transcendent heights." Holly Lebowitz Rossi, "Periscope," *Newsweek*, October 2, 2006, 9.

144. Power migrates "from the fixed, determinate but occult place it occupied under the monarchy to a place" that is "unstable and indeterminate." Lefort, *DPT*, 110. But we do not arrive at an "unlimited transparency," an "all-visible, all-manipulable, all-explorable world." Lefort, *PFMS*, 235.

145. Roger Finke and Rodney Stark, *The Churching of America, 1776–2005: Winners and Losers in Our Religious Economy* (New Brunswick, N.J.: Rutgers University Press, 2005), 236. See in particular chaps. 3 and 7. Interestingly, adopting a method that belies their findings, Stark and Finke use a self-consciously provocative "market terminology" of "religious firms" competing for their "market share" of members under conditions of cost-benefit analysis.

146. Tocqueville, *DA*, 489.

## 4. Political Phoenix

1. Tocqueville, *DA*, 342–345 (emphasis added).

2. Thomas Hobbes, *Leviathan*, ed. Richard Tuck (Cambridge: Cambridge University Press, 1991), 70.

3. Wolin, *PV*, 601–602.

4. Wolin, *PP*, 31.

5. Wolin, NF, 39.

6. Wolin, *PV,* 601.

7. Wolin, *TBTW,* 182.

8. Wolin, *PP,* 41–42, 143.

9. Wolin, *PV,* 566, 578.

10. Wolin, *PP,* 42.

11. Ibid., 147.

12. Ibid., 109, 118.

13. Sheldon S. Wolin, "From Progress to Modernization: The Conservative Turn," *democracy* 3, no. 3 (1983): 16–17.

14. Wolin, *PV,* 559–563, 566–567. Wolin writes that the postmodern celebration of play in a reality rendered virtual only reinforces capitalism's hold: "The ideology of the market, with its idealized picture of an intricate dispersed system in which countless independent actors respond to 'laws' of supply and demand that no external authority decrees, complements postmodernist antipathies to 'centered discourse' and centered power. . . . A system that cannot conceive of stopping and dreads slowdown has developed its cultural complement in a postmodern sensibility that adores novelty, dreads boredom, and far from operating as a 'fetter' on capitalism, encourages its rhythms." Ibid., 588.

15. Wolin, *PP,* 155. Postmodern power "envisions endless expansion but its imperialism tends to be nonterritorial, degrounded, projecting its influence throughout the world, while militarizing the emptiness of space." Ibid.

16. Wolin, *PV,* 594–595, xvi–xvii.

17. In a suggestive metaphor, Wolin writes, "Superpower might be described in Freudian terms as ego driven by id (basic power drive) with only mild remonstrances from a weak superego (norms or conscience)." Ibid., 591.

18. Wolin, *PP,* 182.

19. Wolin, *PV,* xxi; Wolin, *PP,* 27.

20. Wolin, *PP,* 178–179.

21. Sheldon S. Wolin, "Higher Education and the Politics of Knowledge," *democracy* 2, no. 2 (1981): 50.

22. Wolin, *PV,* 394.

23. While postmodern in its fully realized form, Superpower's logic of limitlessness, according to Wolin, goes as far back as the Old Testament story of the Tower of Babel: "Precisely because the men of Shinar have one language and a highly unified social organization and thus have suppressed their differences . . . they are able to mobilize the power necessary to erect a tower whose rising pinnacle signifies a challenge to the heavens. Yahweh dissolves the threat by the simple device of introducing a multiplicity of languages. Disunion and scattered power result." Superpower learned well the lessons of monotheism: "oneness" is above all a "metaphor for power." Wolin, *PP,* 122.

24. Wolin, *PV*, 400.
25. Ibid., 397.
26. Wolin, *DI*, 46, x, 64, 198.
27. Ibid., 60, xvi.
28. Sheldon S. Wolin, "Transgression, Equality, and Voice," in *Demokratia: A Conversation on Democracies, Ancient and Modern*, ed. Josiah Ober and Charles Hedrick (Princeton, N.J.: Princeton University Press, 1996), 86.
29. Wolin, *PV*, 585.
30. Sheldon S. Wolin, "Fugitive Democracy," in *Democracy and Difference: Contesting the Boundaries of the Political* (Princeton, N.J.: Princeton University Press, 1996), 42.
31. Stephen Holmes, *Passions and Constraint: On the Theory of Liberal Democracy* (Chicago: University of Chicago Press, 1995), xi.
32. Wolin, *PP*, 8.
33. Holmes, *Passions and Constraint*, xi.
34. Wolin, *NF*, 35.
35. Wolin, "Fugitive Democracy," 39 (emphasis added).
36. Wolin, *PV*, 602.
37. Wolin, *PP*, 190. "Its politics" as Wolin puts it, "is based not, as its defenders allege, upon 'representative democracy' but on various representations of democracy." Wolin, "Fugitive Democracy," 34.
38. Wolin, *PV*, 602; Wolin, "Transgression, Equality, and Voice," 63 (emphasis added).
39. Wolin, "Fugitive Democracy," 31 (emphasis added).
40. Ibid., 31 (emphasis added). As we shall see, this is one of two formulations of the political, the fugitive democratic formulation that stresses the temporal confines of commonality to the momentary. The second formulation, the archaic democratic formulation, opts for a more traditional notion of community: "the democratic political" is the "ideal of a civic spirited community in which citizens [are] earnestly engaged in defining the common good and their responsibilities toward it." Wolin, *TBTW*, 195.
41. Wolin, *PP*, 139.
42. Wolin, *PP*, 149; *NF*, 54.
43. Wolin, *PV*, 602.
44. Sheldon S. Wolin, "The Liberal/Democratic Divide: On Rawls's *Political Liberalism*," *Political Theory* 24, no. 1 (1996): 98–102, 115. Wolin writes that Rawls perpetuates the antipolitical orientation of political theory that long predates liberal contract theory. From Plato onward, this depoliticization has taken the form of altering "the question of who should rule and how they should rule by inventing the question of *what* should rule." According to Wolin, "the essence of the contrast, which became, as well, the essence of constitutionalism, was between depersonalized principles and partisan politics"—between stable justice and reason and the people's unpredictable and disorderly passions, between the authority of law and

the power of actual people. The "objective status" of these principles is "contrasted with the flux, uncertainty, and subjectivism attributed to politics," leaving democracy more moral than political. The closest that citizens are allowed to power is through an abstract and constitutionally constructed notion of the voice of the people. Wolin, NF, 46–47.

45. Wolin, "The Liberal/Democratic Divide," 110–111.

46. Sheldon S. Wolin, "What Revolutionary Action Means Today," *democracy* 2, no. 4 (1982): 18–19. Wolin argues that a "political being" cannot be merely "an abstract, disconnected bearer of rights, privileges, and immunities" but is instead "a person whose existence is located in a particular place and draws its sustenance from circumscribed relationships: family, friends, church, neighborhood, workplace, community, town, city." For Wolin, "These relationships are the sources from which political beings draw power . . . and [the sources] that enable them to act together." Ibid., 27.

47. Wolin, "Transgression, Equality, and Voice," 87.

48. Wolin, *PP*, 31.

49. Wolin, *PP*, 190; Wolin, "Transgression, Equality, and Voice," 87.

50. Wolin, *PV*, 590; Sheldon S. Wolin, "The People's Two Bodies," *democracy* 1, no. 1 (1980): 19.

51. Wolin, *PP*, 149–150.

52. Recently, Wolin has argued that, at least conceptually, Superpower, which strives to be without limits, "represents the antithesis of constitutional power." He writes that "on the face of it" the "power imaginary" and the "constitutional imaginary" seem "mutually exclusive." Nonetheless, even if a constitution isn't inherently undemocratic—or at least is, against Superpower, the strange bedfellow of democracy—it is still an ineffective strategy for limiting Superpower. The constitutional imaginary is made either to serve a legitimating function and to manage and constrain democratic power or it is dismissed, undermined, and overridden by the imperatives of power. Wolin, *DI*, xiii, 19.

53. Wolin, *PP*, 83, 107, 77, 81.

54. For a fine discussion of the conservative elements of Wolin's theorization of democracy, see Joshua Miller, "Conservative Democracy in the expanded *Politics and Vision*," *Theory and Event* 10, no. 1 (2007).

55. Wolin, *PV*, 606 (emphasis added).

56. Sheldon S. Wolin, "Why democracy?" *democracy* 1, no. 1 (1981): 4–5.

57. Wolin, *PP*, 102–107, 73.

58. Ibid., 38–39, 142, 75.

59. Ibid., 119.

60. Ibid., 84, 92–95, 110–112, 124–128 (emphasis added). Hamiltonian political science, premised on the "biblical belief that order was a function of power," would "lend an aura of authority" and even "necessity" to a strong state. *The Federalist*, starting from a rhetoric of deliberation, of "establishing good government from reflection and choice," ended up repre-

senting the debate over the Constitution as a conflict between unity, power, and order on one hand and difference, weakness, and anarchy on the other. Ibid., 135.

61. Ibid., 86–87.
62. Ibid., 126–127.
63. Sheldon S. Wolin, "Democracy, Difference, and Re-cognition," *Political Theory* 21, no. 3 (1993): 464–465, 470.
64. Wolin, *PP,* 10, 88.
65. Ibid., 75, 88–90, 130–131.
66. Ibid., 130–131. Wolin writes, "Montesquieu adopted the idea that inherited rights and aristocratic institutions formed a natural barrier to absolutism, but he expanded it to include a complex array of local institutions and local bodies of law and custom. . . . In his hands feudalism became a term to designate an alternative to the centralized state . . . [and the] royal absolutism [of Louis XIV]." Ibid., 88–89.
67. Ibid., 129.
68. Wolin writes that despite its considerable benefits, the welfare state breeds dependence and empowers the state and so is "not a complement to democracy but a threat." Ibid., 80.
69. Wolin, "From Progress to Modernization," 18–19.
70. Wolin, *PV,* 604.
71. Wolin, *PP,* 80.
72. Wolin, *PV,* 604.
73. Sheldon S. Wolin, "America's Civil Religion," *democracy* 2, no. 2 (1981): 15.
74. Wolin, "What Revolutionary Action Means Today," 23.
75. Wolin, "Fugitive Democracy," 44.
76. Wolin, *DI,* 23.
77. The tensions between Wolin's two democracies is perhaps the central topic of Wolin scholarship. As Nicholas Xenos formulates it, "While democracy was to be partly concerned with recovering and transmitting traditions, the suggestion is that democracy has a protean quality that transcends tradition and leaves the future open. Thus the commitment simultaneously to renewal and radical change contains a tension that is a tension within the conceptualization of democracy itself. We might capture that tension by formulating it as the problem of democracy and form." Xenos, "Momentary Democracy," in *Democracy and Vision: Sheldon Wolin and the Vicissitudes of the Political,* ed. Aryeh Botwinick and William E. Connolly (Princeton, N.J.: Princeton University Press, 2001), 26–27.
78. Wolin, *DI,* 186.
79. This seems to be Wolin's view in his most explicit and recent attempt to reconcile the two democracies: "Democratic political interventions are, at the national level, necessarily episodic or fugitive. . . . The demos will never dominate politically. In an age where identities are potentially

plural and changing, a unified demos is no longer possible, or even desirable. . . . Democratic political consciousness, while it may emerge anywhere at any time, is most likely to be nurtured in local, small-scale
settings. . . . There is a genuinely valuable contribution which democracy
can make to national politics, but it is dependent upon a politics that is
rooted locally, experienced daily, and practiced regularly, not just mobilized spasmodically." Ibid., 290–291. As we shall see, this is a significant
scaling back in what we might expect from fugitive democracy and a
turning back to the priority of the archaic.

80. Wolin, NF, 29, 37.
81. Wolin, "Transgression, Equality, and Voice," 64.
82. Ibid.; Wolin, NF, 48.
83. Wolin, "Fugitive Democracy," 39.
84. Wolin, NF, 48.
85. Sheldon S. Wolin, "Democracy: Electoral and Athenian," *PS: Political
    Science and Politics* 26, no. 3 (1993): 476. Along these lines, Wolin writes
    that Rawls "seems to look forward to the elimination of the passions gen-
    erated by oppression and neglect . . . [without pausing] over the possibility
    that 'strong feelings' and 'zealous aspirations' might be directly related to
    frustration on the part of those social classes and groups for whom the
    rhetoric and processes of 'reasonable pluralism' have been least respon-
    sive." Wolin, "The Liberal/Democratic Divide," 107.
86. Wolin, "The Liberal/Democratic Divide," 107.
87. Wolin, "Fugitive Democracy," 37.
88. Wolin, "The People's Two Bodies," 12.
89. Wolin, PP, 2.
90. Wolin, NF, 30. Wolin's other modern example of democratic revolt is the
    radicalism of the 1960s and early 1970s: "This resistance originated and
    remained outside the conventional political institutions. For the most part
    its forms were local, spontaneous, and improvised. It had started with the
    civil rights demonstrations of the early '60s, gathered momentum in the
    campus rebellions of the mid-'60s, and become ominous in the revolts
    that occurred in the urban ghettos of major cities." Ultimately, the move-
    ment was rejected by "the overwhelming majority of middle-and lower-
    middle-class Americans," those leading advocates of materialism and
    conventionalism. Wolin, "The People's Two Bodies," 20.
91. Wolin, PV, 402.
92. Wolin, "Fugitive Democracy," 31.
93. Ibid., 38.
94. Wolin, NF, 54 (emphasis added).
95. Wolin, PV, 603.
96. As we shall see, perhaps the clearest indication that democracy for Wolin
    is fugitive by nature (rather than being a by-product of Superpower's

dominance) is his argument that ancient Athenian democracy was the exemplary occurrence of the fugitive phenomenon.

97. Wolin, "Fugitive Democracy," 41.
98. Ibid., 44; Wolin, NF, 58.
99. Wolin, "Democracy, Difference, and Re-cognition," 477.
100. Wolin, NF, 54; Wolin, PV, 603 (emphasis added).
101. Wolin, PV, 602–603.
102. Ibid., 603.
103. Wolin, "Democracy, Difference, and Re-cognition," 472 (emphasis added).
104. Wolin, PP, 140; Wolin, PV, 602.
105. Wolin, "Transgression, Equality, and Voice," 76, 74.
106. Wolin, "Democracy, Difference, and Re-cognition," 476 (emphasis added).
107. Wolin, "Transgression, Equality, and Voice," 64.
108. As Stephen White writes, commonality for Wolin is "radically contingent, . . . open and variable." It is born of the "rage and righteous indignation that in turn give birth to sentiments of solidarity against a common enemy." White, "Three Conceptions of the Political: The Real World of Late Modern Democracy," in *Democracy and Vision: Sheldon Wolin and the Vicissitudes of the Political,* ed. Aryeh Botwinick and William E. Connolly (Princeton, N.J.: Princeton University Press, 2001), 175, 177.
109. Wolin, PV, 603–604.
110. Ibid., 602.
111. Wolin, NF, 50.
112. Wolin, "The Liberal/Democratic Divide," 111.
113. Wolin, NF, 56.
114. We might interpret the Athenian "wall as defining a political space and symbolizing the scope and limitations of demotic rule." Wolin writes, "The enclosed space was commensurate with the everyday commonsense capability of a demos for exercising power while preserving democratic egalitarianism." Wolin, DI, 244.
115. Wolin, "Transgression, Equality, and Voice," 77.
116. Ibid., 67, 73–74, 85.
117. Wolin, "Transgression, Equality, and Voice," 74–75.
118. Ibid., 74.
119. Wolin, PV, 603.
120. Wolin, "Transgression, Equality, and Voice," 64.
121. Ibid., 86.
122. Wolin, "Fugitive Democracy," 39.
123. Ibid., 41.
124. Wolin, NF, 57.
125. Ibid., 42–43.
126. Ibid.
127. Wolin, "Transgression, Equality, and Voice," 76, 74.

128. Ibid., 77.
129. Ibid., 77–78. To portray an Athenian demos striving for empire—driven by an "extraordinary release of energy that was sublimated into the political"—Wolin quotes Thucydides: " 'The Athenians are addicted to innovation. . . . They are adventurous beyond their power, and daring beyond their judgment, and in danger they are sanguine. . . . They are never at home . . . for they hope by their absence to extend their acquisitions.' " Ibid., 82.
130. Wolin, "Fugitive Democracy," 43; Wolin, *PV*, 603.
131. Wolin, "The People's Two Bodies," 24; Wolin, "What Revolutionary Action Means Today," 25.
132. Wolin, "What Revolutionary Action Means Today," 25.
133. Tocqueville, *DA*, 623.
134. Wolin, "Transgression, Equality, and Voice," 75, 64.
135. Wolin writes that to "examine both the fugitive character of the modern demos and its form of rationality, consider how a citizenry materialized in response to the Hurricane Katrina disaster." Wolin, *DI*, 288. But what sort of citizenry is this that is unified and energized (materialized) in response to pressing necessity? Is it one that is likely to function along legislative lines of argument and persuasion, or one unlikely to require or see the use of words?
136. Wolin, *PV*, 596, 598.
137. Wolin, "What Revolutionary Action Means Today," 25.
138. We might read James Miller's great historical work *Democracy Is in the Streets* as charting precisely this self-radicalizing and self-subverting course of participatory democracy in America: from the archaic radicalism that framed the 1962 Port Huron Statement to the late-1960s embrace of revolutionary transgression of middle-class conventionality as such to the disengagement and quietism that took hold in the 1970s. Miller, *Democracy Is in the Streets: From Port Huron to the Siege of Chicago* (New York: Simon and Schuster, 1987).

## Conclusion

1. Neil Postman, *Amusing Ourselves to Death: Public Discourse in the Age of Show Business* (New York: Penguin Books, 2006), xix–xx.
2. Ibid., 3.
3. Andrew Postman, "Introduction to the Twentieth Anniversary Edition," in *Amusing Ourselves to Death*, vii.
4. Postman, *Amusing Ourselves to Death*, 156–157.
5. In the introduction to the twentieth-anniversary edition, Andrew Postman writes of how readers of the book describe it as "one of those I-didn't-realize-it-was-dark-until-someone-flipped-the-switch encounters with an

illuminating intellect." Tellingly, he recounts how most of these readers embraced their newly illuminated condition. Postman, "Introduction," vii.

6. Postman, *Amusing Ourselves to Death*, 6. Again with an uncanny accuracy, Postman writes, "In the Huxleyan prophecy, Big Brother does not watch us, by his choice. We watch him, by ours." Ibid., 157.

7. After a football game between the Philadelphia Eagles and the Minnesota Vikings was canceled in 2010 because of a blizzard, Pennsylvania Governor Ed Rendell made the news of the day by declaring, "We've become a nation of wusses. The Chinese are kicking our butt in everything. If this was in China do you think the Chinese would have called off the game? People would have been marching down to the stadium . . . and they would have been doing calculus on the way down." Rendell, interview by Mike Missanelli, 97.5 FM radio, Philadelphia, December 27, 2010. Senator Phil Gramm, an economic advisor to Senator John McCain in the 2008 presidential election, similarly made headlines when he dubbed America a "nation of whiners," regarding attitudes toward the Great Recession. Gramm, in "McCain Adviser Talks of 'Mental Recession,' " interview by Patrice Hill, July 9, 2008, WashingtonTimes.com, www.washingtontimes .com.

8. We can also think of John McCain's efforts to have the nation dismiss Barack Obama as a mere celebrity during the 2008 presidential election. McCain 2008 campaign television advertisement, released July 30, 2008.

9. For an example of just this argument, see James Cullen, *The American Dream: A Short History of an Idea That Shaped a Nation* (Oxford: Oxford University Press, 2004).

10. Postman writes, "An Orwellian world is much easier to recognize, and to oppose, than a Huxleyan. . . . We take arms against [an Orwellian] sea of troubles, buttressed by the spirit of Milton, Bacon, Voltaire, Goethe and Jefferson. . . . Who is prepared to take arms against a sea of amusements? . . . I fear that our philosophers have given us no guidance in this matter." Postman, *Amusing Ourselves to Death*, 156–157. Yet this tradition in philosophy seems at least as prominent and includes Plato, Augustine, Rousseau, Kant, Mill, Marx, Nietzsche, and the social theorists of the Frankfurt School, not to mention Tocqueville, Wolin, and many others.

11. Ibid., 155–156.

12. Ibid., 155. *Sesame Street* was conceived of as a show that would "master the addictive qualities of television and do something good with them." Michael Davis, *Street Gang: The Complete History of Sesame Street* (New York: Penguin Books, 2008), 8.

13. Postman, *Amusing Ourselves to Death*, 156.

14. Postman writes, "Whenever language is the principal medium of communication—especially language controlled by the rigors of print—an idea, a fact, a claim is the inevitable result. The idea may be banal, the fact irrel-

evant, the claim false, but there is no escape from meaning when language is the instrument guiding one's thought. . . . [It] is very hard to say nothing when employing a written English sentence. What else is exposition good for? Words have very little to recommend them except as carriers of meaning." Ibid., 50.

15. Ibid., 49–51, 147–148.

16. In contrast, Postman argues that in previous centuries the spoken word took on the character of print. He recounts the "seven hours of oratory" of one of the Lincoln-Douglas debates, during which at one point "Douglas responded to lengthy applause with a remarkable and revealing statement. 'My friends, . . . silence will be more acceptable to me in the discussion of these questions than applause. I desire to address myself to your judgment, your understanding, and your consciences, and not to your passions or your enthusiasms.' " Ibid., 45.

17. Ibid., 128.

18. Ibid., 155–156.

19. Ibid., 157.

20. The ideal of "Jeffersonian democracy" similarly captures the complex aspiration to pastoral independence and community, as well as to the fugitive moment of revolutionary transcendence, whether articulated as the return to pristine past or the leap into untouched future. Historian Joseph Ellis describes this well. Jefferson's "essential obsessions and core convictions," Ellis writes, take shape in the "the vision of each generation starting from scratch, liberated from the accumulated legacies of past debts, laws, institutionalized obligations and regulations." In his "utopian radicalism," Jefferson longed for a world where "innocence had not yet been corrupted": "This was the world of . . . the prepolitical Indian tribes, the world of the independent yeoman farmer on the edge of the frontier, the world after a rightful rebellion has cleared the air. It was a world . . . where coercion was unknown and government unnecessary. Though transient—history would begin to make its inevitable inroads almost immediately—the idyllic harmonies sustained themselves for that one brief, shining moment." Jefferson's utopia was "a society devoid of contaminating institutions and laws; an effort to routinize their removal so that the deadening hand of history was regularly slapped away in order to make room for a pristine encounter with what he believed to be the natural order." Joseph J. Ellis, *American Sphinx: The Character of Thomas Jefferson* (New York: Vintage Books, 1998), 133, 136.

21. Ayn Rand captures the logic of democratic openness perfectly: "When I say 'capitalism,' I mean a full, pure, uncontrolled, unregulated laissez-faire capitalism—with a separation of state and economics, in the same way and for the same reasons as the separation of state and church." Ayn Rand, *The Virtue of Selfishness* (New York: Signet Books, 1964), 33.

22. Discussing the America he discovered, Tocqueville claims, "If . . . an American were reduced to minding only his own business, half of his life would be stolen from him. He would feel as though an immense void had hollowed out his days, and he would become incredibly unhappy." Tocqueville, *DA*, 279.

23. This insecurity finds one of its earliest seminal modern statements in Kant's "An Answer to the Question: What Is Enlightenment" (1784): "Immaturity is the inability to use one's understanding without guidance from another. . . . Laziness and cowardice are the reasons why so great a proportion of men . . . gladly remain in lifelong immaturity. . . . It is so easy to be immature. If I have a book to serve as my understanding, a pastor to serve as my conscience, a physician to determine my diet for me, and so on, I need not exert myself at all. I need not think, if only I can pay." In the "immaturity that has all but become his nature," man sinks to the level of "dumb" and "docile" "domestic livestock." Two hundred years before Postman warned of the power of television to undermine the typographic mind, Kant warned of the power of the book to undermine autonomy; in both cases, the door opens to man's domestication.

24. Tocqueville, *DA*, 15.

25. Ibid., 818.

26. Richard Sennett, *The Fall of Public Man* (New York: W.W. Norton, 1974), 338, 29–30, 8.

27. Ibid., 27.

28. Ibid., 16–24.

29. Along these lines, the civil society that Robert Putnam, for instance, advocates actually demonstrates rather than works against Sennett's fall of public man. The bowling alley is a venue for private man in public space, where trust allows the participants to do away with mediating formalities.

30. Marshall McLuhan (whose famous dictum "the medium is the message" is central to Postman's analysis of television culture) perfectly states the aspiration for a social—indeed global—intimacy beyond words: "Our new electric technology that extends ours senses and nerves in a global embrace has large implications for the future of language. . . . Electricity points the way to an extension of the process of consciousness itself, on a world scale, and without any verbalization whatsoever. . . . The computer, in short, promises by technology a Pentecostal condition of universal understanding and unity. . . . The condition of 'weightlessness,' that biologists say promises a physical immortality, may be paralleled by the condition of speechlessness that could confer a perpetuity of collective harmony and peace." Marshall McLuhan, *Understanding Media: The Extension of Man* (New York: McGraw-Hill, 1964), 80.

31. Sennett, *The Fall of Public Man*, 5.

32. Ibid., 338.

33. Pierre Manent formulates the modern imperative of intimacy in terms of the passion for immediacy and informality: "Modern humanity is impatient with regard to all mediations. In earlier, predemocratic centuries, mutual recognition was conditioned, and therefore, limited by a multitude of forms. Politeness and ceremonies played an eminent role. . . . Democracy seeks in all domains [the] common human expression that signifies that one belongs to the same humanity as others." As people are compelled by this sublime idea of an intimate humanity, the "desire, the demand for immediacy, tends to dominate all aspects of modern democratic life." The democratic order in turn disbars politics as an external and oppressive hindrance to immediate and authentic experience—unnecessary *and* inadequate for allowing diverse experiences to communicate with one another. Thus the "democratic political order itself contains something antipolitical, since it claims to reduce the place of politics as much as possible." Manent, *A World beyond Politics?: A Defense of the Nation State,* trans. Marc LePain (Princeton, N.J.: Princeton University Press, 2006), 168–169.

34. Tocqueville describes something like the intimate society in the passage immediately preceding his introduction of tutelary power. Each member of that society, "withdrawn into himself, is virtually a stranger to the fate of all others": "For him, his children and personal friends comprise the entire human race. As for the remainder of his fellow citizens, he lives alongside them but does not see them. He touches them but does not feel them. He exists only in himself and for himself, and if he still has a family, he no longer has a country." Tocqueville, *DA,* 818.

35. Wolin argues that "Rousseau's citizen looks like a political animal," but he is "forbidden to discuss political matters outside of formal assemblies or to form 'partial associations' ": "Rousseau's democracy without politics was prefigured by the innovations he effected in the social contract. While retaining contractualist language, its meaning was radically transformed from a negotiation into a political sacrament, from an agreement among signatories into a rite among communicants, from the founding of a political society to transubstantiation into a *corpus mysticum.*" Wolin, *TBTW,* 178.

36. Wolin describes a major element of this impersonal informality well, contrasting it to previous despotic regime-forms: "There is a sense in which democratic despotism is not a 'form' at all. Save for an omnipresent bureaucracy, it has little in common with the highly personalized tyrannies of the twentieth century and their charismatic leaders. Tocqueville's despot appears as faceless and nameless, a shadowy presence, enveloping rather than domineering." It seems "as though he might easily disappear into the system, as though despotism is the archetype of the impersonal,

which overcomes even the despot." In the representations of contemporary American culture, this is very nearly the oppression of *The Matrix*
(or Postman's television society) rather than of earlier iterations like
*Star Wars.* Wolin, *TBTW,* 569–570.

37. Manent, *A World beyond Politics,* 168–169 (emphasis in original).
38. Tocqueville, *DA,* 834.
39. Ibid. Thus, Françoise Mélonio concludes that, for Tocqueville, "denounc-
ing the state was less important than restoring the political vocation of
citizens." Mélonio, *Tocqueville and the French,* trans. Beth G. Raps (Charlottesville: University Press of Virginia, 1998), 207.
40. François Furet and Françoise Mélonio, "Introduction," in Tocqueville,
*OR I,* 53.

# Acknowledgments

This book has been written over several years and at a number of institutions, from the University of Texas at Austin, to Harvard University, the University of Pittsburgh, and most recently Yale University. I am grateful for my many wonderful teachers, colleagues, and friends at all of these institutions. I am particularly grateful for all of the students I have gotten to know over the years. More than anything else, time spent in conversation with them has shaped this book and sustained me during its writing. I would like to thank those who have read and commented on different portions and versions of this manuscript, including Stefan Dolgert, Blake Emerson, James Fishkin, Michael Goodhart, Benjamin Gregg, Sanford Levinson, Thomas Pangle, and Steven Smith. I would also like to thank the Jack Miller Center for its generous support, as well as Michael Aronson and all those at Harvard University Press who helped to see the manuscript into print. And I owe a special debt of gratitude to Bryan Garsten, Russell Muirhead, and especially Jeffrey Tulis. Their support and guidance throughout the process of writing this book have been truly invaluable.

# Index

176, 182–183, 185, 188, 189, 192, 194, 200, 205, 206, 210–211, 214; and liberal democracy, 177–179, 185–188, 191, 192, 203, 205, 210, 217–218; and cultural and historical place, 177–178, 181, 183, 184–185, 189–190, 191, 193, 194–197, 199, 202–203, 205, 208, 209, 211, 213, 218; and democracy as archaic, 177–178, 185, 192–195, 198–203, 205, 211, 213, 217; and the co-opted rhetoric of democracy, 177, 179, 185, 192, 207; and domestication, 177, 179, 187, 188, 191, 192, 194, 206, 211–213; and constitutionalism, 177, 186–189, 191, 192, 196–198, 202, 204–205, 209, 212, 213; and participatory democracy, 177, 188, 200, 213; and the Anti-Federalists, 177, 198, 200; and conventional form, 178, 179, 181, 192, 193, 203, 204–205, 213–215; and Jefferson, 178, 211; and equality, 179–180, 184, 190, 191, 207, 216; and Weber, 180; and modern power, 180–183; and postmodern power, 180–182, 185, 193, 194, 196, 200, 202, 206, 213, 234; and capitalism, 180–181, 183, 185–186, 192, 194, 209, 213, 214; and the state, 180–181, 183, 188–189, 192, 196, 200; and science, 180–181, 183, 196; and the disincorporation of power, 181–182, 186; and Hobbes, 181, 195–196, 211; and pluralism, 183, 184, 194, 196–203,

207, 212–213, 217; and the political, 188–189, 209; and Rawls, 189–190; and liberal theory, 189–191, 213–214, 216; and rights, 190–191; and collective action, 193, 201–204, 207–210, 212–213, 215–218; and civic education, 193, 203, 209, 211, 213, 218; and democracy as natural, 193, 203, 211–214, 215, 218; and Montesquieu, 194–195; and conservatism, 194–196, 199, 201, 202; and feudalism as democratic, 194, 198–200, 203; and fundamentalism as democratic, 194, 198, 200–201, 203; and radicalism, 194, 198, 202, 217; and the social contract, 195–196; and Descartes, 195, 196; and the American founding, 196–199; and the Federalist, 197, 198; and Madison, 198, 207; and localism, 201–202, 208, 218; and empire, 203, 211, 213, 214; and the rule of the people, 204–208, 210, 212; and freedom, 207, 215; and Schmitt, 209; and Machiavelli, 210; and Athenian democracy 211, 213; and conatus (Spinoza), 211, 213; and Locke, 212–213, 217; and Aristotle, 213; and Nietzsche, 215; and two-tiered citizenship, 216–217; dualism of idealism and cynicism, 216–218

Xenos, Nicholas, 286n77

YouTube, 221

Harvard University Press is a member of Green Press Initiative (greenpressinitiative.org), a nonprofit organization working to help publishers and printers increase their use of recycled paper and decrease their use of fiber derived from endangered forests. This book was printed on recycled paper containing 30% post-consumer waste and processed chlorine free.